BREAK THE CHAINS
of poverty pay, casual labour and exploitation

Richie Venton

Richie Venton grew up in Northern Ireland, before emigrating to Liverpool, then Scotland. A trade unionist and socialist with decades of dedicated experience, he is widely respected for building support for workers and communities in struggle. Richie was the central organiser of the Merseyside socialists who led a victorious mass movement against Thatcher's government in the '80s, which won big reforms for the people of Liverpool. He was expelled from the Labour Party by Neil Kinnock's leadership for being an effective socialist. Richie was a founding organiser of the Scottish Socialist Party in 1998. He is the SSP's national workplace organiser, and west of Scotland regional organiser, and an elected Usdaw union convener in retail. Richie is a regular writer in the *Scottish Socialist Voice*, and has a blog at richieventon.blogspot.co.uk

D1381850

For Kathy, Jemmy, Ciaran, Rory, my mother,
and to the memory of my father -
the man they hired but could not buy

First published in December 2015 by the Scottish Socialist Party
Suite 370, Central Chambers, 93 Hope Street, Glasgow G2 6LD
www.scottishsocialistparty.org

ISBN 978-0-9571986-6-1

The right of Richie Venton to be identified as the author of this work has been
asserted by him in accordance with the Copyright, Designs and Patents Act 1988

A CIP catalogue record for this book is available from the British Library

Typeset and cover design by Simon Whittle • @revolbiscuit

Printed and bound by Forward Graphics
100 Elderpark Street, Glasgow G51 3TR • www.forwardgraphics.co.uk

CONTENTS

Acknowledgements

A big warm thanks to all who've helped this book to be born. My friend and comrade Colin Turbett for reading and correcting a draft, making very helpful suggestions, and simply encouraging me to keep going. My son Ciaran for his insightful comments, impressions and suggestions on the draft. Simon Whittle, who worked long days and longer nights on the design and typography, with his usual calm, friendly diligence and dedication. Christine and Jim McVicar for arranging the printing and finances to produce the book, and the team at Forward Graphics for their professional helpfulness. And thanks to the thousands of workers over the years whose struggles I've learnt from, having my socialist commitment reinforced by their courageous resistance to capitalist exploitation.

Introduction

Back in August 1981, 13,000 air traffic control staff in the United States went on strike, demanding a substantial pay rise and a 30-hour, four-day week. In response, President Ronald Reagan and his administration unleashed class war on the workers and their union, PATCO. They gave the strikers 48 hours to return to work. They seized PATCO's funds, and sent in military personnel alongside hired scabs and a minority of strikebreaking staff to undermine the impact of the workers' withdrawal of their labour. They arrested and jailed strike leaders. Reagan issued a life-time ban on the strikers being re-hired in their jobs.

In an iconic image of the times, they hired the services of the broadcast media to parade imprisoned strikers on the TV screens of millions, clamped in irons, manacles, the instruments of the era of black slavery in America.

Across the wide Atlantic, but joined at the hip with Reagan in a right-wing capitalist crusade against workers, presided his friend and mentor, the British Prime Minister, Margaret Thatcher. She matched and outstripped Reagan with her own trumpeted assault on trade unionism and socialism, in their trans-Atlantic symphony of brutal class warfare on workers' rights and living standards.

Thatcher's ruthless mission on behalf of the rich culminated in the deliberately provoked showdown with the miners, their communities and trade union, in 1984-5. Thatcher led the full forces of the capitalist class and their state, fangs bared, in crushing the heroic resistance of the National Union of Mineworkers and their allies.

In a mission to destroy the industry and its powerful trade union, and thereby teach all workers a harsh lesson, no cash was spared. The police were bought off with massive pay rises; a nationally coordinated campaign of police violence against picket lines injured thousands; miners were beaten up, arrested, jailed and sacked from the industry; secret service agents were planted in the NUM; the media conducted a relentless year's campaign of venomous attacks, smears and lies against the strikers and their leaders; and government benefits were slashed and withdrawn to starve the miners' families (children included) into submission.

Ultimately, Thatcher and her class defeated the miners. But it could have been a different outcome altogether, but for the treacherous role of the Labour Party leadership of the time, and a big proportion of the wider union leadership, who left the miners isolated, instead of building a broader struggle in tandem with them, which could have toppled Thatcher's elective dictatorship of the rich, and thereby altered the subsequent course of history.

These two events were decisive turning points in the modern struggles of working class people. Here in Scotland and Britain, millions are still suffering the consequences. The events of the '80s altered the balance of power and wealth between workers and employers, labour and capital, the rich and the rest of us – radically.

We've just suffered the most prolonged period of declining wages since 1856. In the past 30 years, the Great Wage Robbery by capitalist employers and governments has robbed workers of a cumulative total of £1.3trillion – by coincidence the same sum, from workers' taxes, that was handed to the profligate bankers to shore up their profits and bonuses from collapse.

Under the new Tory regime of, by and for the rich, we suffer the spreading plague of casual, insecure labour and the most repressive anti-union laws in the western world.

The chains of exploitation fashioned by Thatcher (and Reagan) are being toughened and galvanised in a mission to achieve an even bigger wealth transfusion to the rich from the rest of us.

This book is written as a contribution to the ongoing struggles to reverse the defeats workers have faced at the hands of capitalism and its hired governments.

It aims to equip workers, trade unionists and socialists with explanations for 'the state we're in', so we're all the readier to resist and defeat the new Tory rule by the rich, as they take a claw hammer to workers' rights, swing a wrecking ball at public services and jobs, and blitz the benefits of people in and out of work. Explanations based on fundamental socialist theories, but in plain language, rooted in real events, with workers' own voices and experiences used to clarify the theory.

It seeks to be a handbook of facts that can be used as weapons in the hands of those principled people fighting for a decent standard of living for the working class majority population.

It exposes the crushing poverty and inequality that blights us in this fabulously rich country.

It cuts through the fog of lies from the Tories about their misnamed 'National Living Wage'.

It offers an armoury of arguments for an immediate £10-an-hour minimum wage for all aged 16 and over, with equal pay for women.

It answers the many objections to this policy that trade unionists and socialists face, in their workplaces, communities and on the streets, from friends as well as foes. Will it shed jobs? Can small businesses afford it? Can the economy afford it? Is immigration the problem?

It outlines some of the history of struggles for a decent living wage over the past century; the origins, advantages and limitations of the semi-official Living Wage; inspirational struggles by working people at home and abroad.

But the battles we face go far beyond the boundaries of a decent living wage for all.

This book argues for a broader socialist alternative for the 21st century, presenting concrete fighting policies and strategies to transform the lives of millions, on the road to a democratic socialist future.

I make no pretence of being neutral. All the facts and figures are meticulously researched, undeniable, and enough to make anyone with half a heart feel passionate about the need to change this system for the benefit of people and planet. In the face of the facts, a pretend-neutrality only helps to protect the status quo from being challenged.

My appeal to readers of *Break the Chains* is to study it, discuss the arguments in it, and then join with other workers, trade unionists and socialists in active pursuit of the radical socialist transformation of the nation and world we live in.

Two centuries ago, a crowd of 80,000 assembled in a Manchester field, to demand an end to the corruption that infested parliamentary elections, so that working people could vote and demand change from a system that cursed them with famine and chronic unemployment.

The government ordered armed soldiers into action against this peaceful demonstration of workers. The ensuing cavalry charge, sabres drawn, injured 700 and killed 15, in what became known as the Peterloo Massacre of 1819.

In response, the revolutionary poet, Percy Bysshe Shelley wrote the passionate, stirring *Mask of Anarchy*, which included this verse:

"Rise, like lions after slumber
In unvanquishable number!
Shake your chains to earth like dew
Which in sleep had fallen on you:
Ye are many – they are few"

In a later line, Shelley made an appeal for action that I would make to all who, 200 years later, want to break the chains of capitalist exploitation and carve out a socialist future:

"Let a great assembly be, of the fearless, of the free."

Richie Venton, October 2015

SCARS ON SCOTLAND

Poverty and inequality scar the face of Scotland, like a pair of poisonous plooks.

The lives of a multitude of men, women and children are stunted, shattered and shortened; their dreams turned to dust; their talents tossed in the bin, because they are chained to poverty, insecurity and exploitation. Worst of all, there is absolutely no excuse nor justification for anyone going without in this rich nation.

Scotland is the 14th-richest nation on earth, based on national wealth output (GDP) per man, woman and child – as measured by the OECD in 2014. Furthermore, it's part of the fifth-richest economy on the planet – Britain – not some struggling 'basket-case' economy with at least a superficial excuse for deprivation amongst its people.

Yet a million people eke out an existence below the breadline in 21st century capitalist Scotland. In part, because the three richest families in Scotland possess more personal wealth than the poorest 1.1 million people sharing the same nationality with them. In part, because the richest tenth of the Scottish population possess 900 times as much combined wealth as that shared by the poorest tenth of people inhabiting the same country. For the first time since records began on such gruesome measures of poverty amidst plenty, the absolute majority of those struggling (and failing) to survive the mounting cost of living are in jobs; working to remain poor.

Poverty takes many forms, all of them economically inexcusable and morally reprehensible. Pensioners and the poorest families shivering their way through every winter, unable to heat their homes in energy-rich Scotland. Thousands of older people dying of cold-related illnesses in their poorly-heated and poorly-insulated homes each winter. Registered deaths in Scotland of 22,011 in the four winter months of 2014-15, the highest for fifteen years, meaning there were 4,060 'excess winter deaths' compared with the average for the rest of the year. A cruel cull of senior citizens who had devoted a lifetime to work, family and society. The ultimate condemnation of a system driven by profit rather than people.

Proud people – including many holding down a job – pleading for referrals to the burgeoning network of food banks for an emergency handout, staving off literal starvation, three days at a time, through the generosity of mostly working-class donors to the food collections held in shops, communities and workplaces.

All this in a Scotland which is a net exporter of food. The ultimate condemnation of a system with publicly-funded bailouts of £1.3trillion for the bankers, but food banks for those famished by cuts in benefits and wages in the wake of the 2008 bankers' crisis.

Children going to bed hungry, going to school hungry, their energy sapped, their ability to concentrate undermined, their future marked out by disadvantage from an early age compared to their high-income contemporaries. The ultimate condemnation of a system driven by cash and greed, not children's needs.

During the Scottish independence referendum, Labour leader Ed Miliband repeatedly spoke of "The value of pooling resources in something bigger, the UK." Like a well-rehearsed choirboy, Better Together's Labour front-man Alistair Darling chimed in: "The security of being part of something bigger, with a share of the larger resources."

The British capitalist edifice that we were relentlessly told – by Tory, Lib Dem and Labour politicians alike – makes us all 'better together', treats its retired citizens to the worst state pensions in Europe; its children to one of the worst levels of child poverty in Europe; those on benefits to insufferable incomes and a punitive regime of sanctions that has driven many to suicide.

At the very heart of all these forms of poverty lies poverty pay. The simple, stark, shattering fact that 52% of those officially classified as in poverty are in jobs, working to stay poor, tells its own story. That feature of modern society is further confirmed by the fact the unemployed only constitute 11% of Breadline Britain's poor; the sick and disabled a further 15%... with the 'working poor' the single largest group in poverty now for several years – and an absolute majority (52%) since 2012.

In trying to reverse this monstrous theft of lives and livelihoods from millions of workers and their families, another form of poverty needs to be confronted: a widespread poverty of expectations.

I'll never forget the headline, in 2014: "We can't afford the luxury of new school shoes." On the one hand that is the harsh reality for tens of thousands of working class families. Their kids wear the same flimsy trainers during the winter months that they kicked about in over the summer, because families on low pay or benefits simply can't afford the outrageously-priced footwear in the shops. Prices in flagrant contradiction to the sweated overseas labour usually used to produce them, or the pathetic wages of the retail staff selling them.

But what a sad commentary this is on the state of mind, the systematically lowered expectations in life, which the governments and media of the multi-millionaires have nurtured amongst millions of people... "the luxury of new school shoes." Numerous sociological studies have shown how every mother or father of a new-born baby shares fundamentally the same hopes and ambitions for their little one. As the Joseph Rowntree Foundation reported in November 2014:

"Whilst poverty is entrenched, there are shared expectations and aspirations across society. For example, 97% of all Mums say they want their new born child to attend university, and the desire to work and the belief that work should be the way to improve material circumstances is found across the population – including where two generations of the same family have never worked."

But the class-divided realities of daily life knock those hopes and dreams out of far too many parents. People struggling to cope and care for their child end up having little expectation of improvements in their situation because we are told day and night that this is as good as it gets. They begin to half-believe that big, impersonal, incomprehensible forces dictate that we have to 'tighten our belts'. Meantime families – including toddlers and teenagers targeted by specially designed, sophisticated media outpourings – are bombarded by messages of all the expensive goods and gadgetry we must have.

We live in a 'must have' society; a consumer-driven frenzy of getting people to buy things they don't actually need; people made to feel useless and inadequate if they can't keep up with their peers at school or their neighbours, let alone match the glamorous images entering our living rooms via TV, magazines and the internet. No wonder those arrested in the 2011 English urban riots for helping themselves to some of the goods constantly thrust in their faces were then hammered by savage jail sentences. This draconian punishment was designed to broadcast a message to not only the rioters, but the rest of us scraping by on low incomes: learn the lesson that whilst we (the state) want you to aspire to these things, you will never be able to have them, and don't get too rebellious in trying to get a share of the nation's wealth!

* * * *

Thankfully, one of the most positive outcomes of the mass engagement in debate that was the Scottish referendum campaign is the growing, mass rejection of the lies peddled by the rich and their political puppets. Foremost amongst the lie machine's relentless outpourings are the mantras that 'we are all in this together', that we must 'tighten our belts', accept growing poverty so as to 'balance the books', that 'this is as good as it gets'.

Perhaps most insidious of all the lies is the idea that poverty is the fault of the poor. The lie perpetrated that it's personal weaknesses; poor choices in life; indolence, 'benefit-dependency', and downright drunkenness which hurl millions into the dark pits of poverty. It's not a new notion, but it's been pumped out with growing volume in recent years in the media and by the political elite – by Westminster MPs, whose ranks are infested by millionaires, don't forget!

In fact this atrocity against the victims of poverty dates back to at least Victorian times, with their gospel of 'the deserving and the undeserving poor'. Charitable handouts to the former salved the consciences of a few rich philanthropists of the time; the latter were demonised and persecuted. Sound familiar? It should. We've been treated to a dose of divide-and-conquer propaganda by the likes of the Old Etonian razor gang of David Cameron, George Osborne and their ilk, designed to divide different sections of the working class from each other, scapegoating the sick, disabled and unemployed in order to justify their savagery against benefits.

For instance, these obnoxious Tory millionaires and tax-dodgers systematically smeared those not working with tales of 'their curtains closed as hard-working neighbours go to work in the morning', to soften up those in work for the Westminster Coalition's assault on benefits in early 2014. What they thereby tried to smother from sight, with a systematic fog of lies, was the fact 68% of those whose benefits were slashed were actually in work. Child Benefits and Working Tax Credits were high on the target lists of the Twin Tories, but they used the pliant media to conjure up an utter falsehood that they were trying to save workers' taxes from scroungers who just couldn't be bothered to find a job!

As the cuts to state expenditure hit working people, as well as those too sick or disabled to work, or those simply unable to find a job – particularly a job that means they are better off than by remaining unemployed – more and more are seeing through the Tory lies that poverty is the fault of the poor.

Most people are too proud to describe themselves as poor. But they recognise poverty pay in their monthly or weekly wages. They know how it is to wish it was pay day, tapping friends and family for the final week or more of the month; hunting for coins down the sofa or in an unworn jacket to put a meal on the table; or worse still, succumbing to the loan sharks, legalised or otherwise. So, increasingly, workers see through the propaganda about poverty being the fault of those with no money – lies always initiated by the most parasitical rich, but peddled by the media and the politicians they have bought to sustain the wealth of the obscenely wealthy.

One of the greatest gains from the Yes campaign in Scotland's referendum was the mass of people whose eyes were opened to the fabulous wealth of the nation, but also the excruciating levels of poverty and nauseating levels of inequality in Scotland. Fury erupted as people encountered the stunning statistic that whilst Scotland is one of the richest nations on earth, it is also the fourth-most unequal. As workers swim in a sea loch of poverty, struggling to keep their heads above water, they are surrounded by mountain peaks of wealth that make Ben Nevis look like a puny molehill. The task of socialists, trade unionists, community activists, anyone with a social conscience, is to help workers in poverty lift their chins, look up, raise their sights, and challenge the obscenely unfair distribution of wealth, the yawning chasms of inequality.

Lowered wages are a primary source of poverty in the Billionaires' Breadline Britain. The lowered share of national wealth going to wages is not an accident of nature; it's planned poverty, ruthlessly fought for by the employers and their kept governments since the Dark Ages of 1980s Thatcherism in particular.

Both are tied by mental chains to lowered expectations. Mental chains in large part forged by fear – the weapon of choice of the ruling capitalist class. Fear of losing your job if you dare ask for a pay rise. All too often succumbing to the mantra, 'You're lucky to have a job – any job'. As the band The Last Internationale sing, "We learned how to walk, but the spirit in us crawls."

Those of us who have lived through the mass political education of the referendum debate will have none of that. We refuse to lower our expectations. We demand a decent living wage as a human right. We know it's easily affordable in such a rich nation. We intend to show that poverty pay is not inevitable, but the product of economic systems and political decisions made by those in power. It's a choice made by the ruling elite, not an unavoidable necessity. And we seek to help organise those who create society's wealth to raise their sights, refuse to let 'the spirit in us crawl', and forge a campaign to banish poverty pay and inequality in our lifetime.

The purpose of this publication is to help that struggle over ownership of wealth, by providing facts for fighters, arguments for activists, solutions for socialists to pursue.

2

POVERTY DENIERS &
REPUGNANT REALITY

There are some who dispute the existence of poverty in Scotland or the UK. And no, not all of them are registered members of the Flat Earth Society!

Back in the Dark Ages of the 1980s, under the elective dictatorship of Maggie Thatcher, government and civil service officials were actually banned from using the word 'poverty'. The same attempt to erase reality by banning a word – a noun seen as far too inflammatory – was conducted by Thatcher's right-hand ally in the USA at the time, President Ronald Reagan. An American satirical cartoonist, Jules Feiffer, aptly replied with a picture of two homeless men philosophising in their rags:

> "We used to be poor, then disadvantaged, then deprived, then discriminated against, then socially excluded. We have not got any more money, but we do have a lot of labels."

The Tories spawned by Thatcher, the batch now in the saddle at Westminster, are carrying on her tradition as poverty deniers. Witness their moves to re-define child poverty, as opposed to recognising it and then eradicating it. Within weeks of crawling into power courtesy 24% of the registered electorate, David Cameron's Tory regime declared plans to effectively repeal the Child Poverty Act of 2010. They aim to scrap the four statutory measures of child poverty contained in the Act: relative poverty, absolute poverty, persistent poverty and material deprivation – along with removing the targets set by the Act to tackle this crime against kids, which binds the government to eliminate child poverty by 2020.

The Act – which the Tories find far too inconvenient for their plans to inflict even more pain on youngsters – sets out multiple strategies to tackle child poverty, including parental employment, skills, information, advice, physical and mental health, education, childcare, social services, housing, the built environment and social inclusion.

The relative poverty measure used up until now – 60% of median household incomes – is open to searing criticism for being set at far too low a level, but at least it recognises something that most human beings and every dictionary accepts as the core, primary definition of poverty: lack of money.

Those Tory politicians with plenty of money, representing the 1% with obscene mountains of money, want us all to believe that child poverty is caused by levels of worklessness and educational achievement in families, alongside family breakdown and drug and alcohol addictions. This is a pernicious attempt to make us think the roots of suffering lie in the symptoms rather than the real underlying causes – increasing and staggering levels of deprivation and inequality.

So the fact more than two-thirds of children currently in poverty live in working families will be rendered irrelevant at the stroke of a Tory Minister's pen. As the CPAG warned in July 2015:

> "The absurdity of this approach is best seen when we look at working poverty. Children are much more likely to be in poverty because they have a parent who is a security guard or a cleaner than one who is an alcohol or drug addict. Two-thirds of poor children live in working families."

Back in the real world, the number of children in poverty in Britain in 2015 has risen by a grotesque 500,000 since 2010. A shameful 222,000 children in Scotland are currently defined as in poverty.

Regardless of the statistical lies constructed by new Tory definitions, it's already a fact that two parents both working full-time, on the national minimum wage, fall 16% short of the real cost of rearing a child to a minimum standard of living.

Here in the real Scotland, the biggest teachers' union – EIS – is circulating members in schools and colleges with advice on how to spot if a child in their class is going hungry, as they found to be "moving from the exceptional to the more commonplace" in a comprehensive union survey of 300 schools and colleges. They discovered increasing cases of teachers having to help underfed kids out of their own pockets. The EIS gives practical advice to teacher-members on how to 'Poverty Proof' their classes, for the first time including hunger in the guidance booklet:

> "Pupils may appear pale, fatigued, irritable or lacking concentration, or complain of headaches or feeling unwell. While there may be underlying causes… for a growing number of children and young people the reason will be hunger."

They include in their advice, referrals to breakfast clubs and… food banks!

Back in this corner of Planet Earth, independent research has calculated that a family with two parents working full-time on next year's £7.20-an-hour – assuming they're both over 25 and thereby qualify for George Osborne's viciously misnamed 'National Living Wage' – will be £850-a-year worse off after the same Osborne's tax credit cuts have bitten.

Of course there is cynical, callously calculated method in the Tories' apparent madness. Removing lack of money in a child's family as the core measure and cause of child poverty coincides with their assault on Child Tax Credit and Working Tax Credit, which will add massively to the numbers of kids suffering deprivation in their formative years. The Tories are preparing the framework to blame and demonise parents who don't work, or suffer addictions, just as their wider attacks on incomes and public services increase the likelihood of some people suffering these conditions.

By abolishing the common-sense measures of poverty (lack of money), the Tories would remove people who work – and all those who lack enough money for a decent life for their kids – from counting as poor. They are not just moving the goalposts; they are banishing both football teams from the pitch, in order to bring on upper-class teams for a gentle game of croquet. They plan to abolish the concept of child poverty so they can add drastically to the reality of child poverty – but behind society's back.

Poverty consumes mental resources, leaving less for other tasks. Recent studies show that poverty directly impedes cognitive abilities, which can lead to poor decision-making. Poverty wastes human talent. It condemns children to under-achievement from infancy onwards. The first systematic study of the impact of persistent poverty on children's cognitive development in contemporary Britain was conducted in 2012 by Professor Andy Dickson and Dr Gurleen Poli of Sheffield University. They used the semi-official 'household incomes below 60% of the median household income' as their measure of poverty. After studying 8,000 children, and looking at those in poverty at the ages of 9 months, 3 years, 5 years and 7 years, they unearthed horrifying trends. They found persistent poverty had more impact on cognitive development than factors such as whether parents regularly read to their children, took them to the library, or helped them with reading, writing and maths – or their parenting style and skills. The researchers wrote:

"Much is made of the importance of parenting for children's cognitive development, and our study supports these claims. But, importantly, our analysis shows that low income has a two-fold effect on children's ability: it has an effect on children regardless of anything their parents do, but also has an impact on parenting itself."

They concluded:

"Seven-year-olds who have lived in poverty since infancy perform substantially worse in a range of ability tests than those who have never been poor – even when family circumstances and parenting skills are taken into consideration. On a scale of 0-100, a child who has been in persistent poverty will rank ten levels below an otherwise similar child who has no early experience of poverty."

So for all its merits – and the crying need to invest far more in it from infancy onwards – education in and of itself cannot achieve equality. It can't even achieve equal opportunity for cognitive or intellectual development, let alone equality of social or economic conditions. It's material conditions, material deprivation that needs to be tackled, if we're ever going to allow the innate abilities and talents of our children blossom – with free and equal access to a good education of course being a vital component of that.

There are many proud working class people who dislike being labelled 'poor'. Personal pride would sometimes lead them to deny being 'poor'. But they know what poverty pay and poverty benefits look like, from direct experience.

Anyone who doubts the existence of poverty in 21st century Scotland should get out more! Out to speak to people on the streets across the country, or in the workplaces, where low pay and insecure job contracts are spreading like a modern plague. They would have met some of the people I've spoken to in Scotland's workplaces, or at SSP street stalls on the fight for an immediate £10 minimum wage, or at public meetings.

"I'm 55. I've worked all my life. I've got five different part-time jobs as a cleaner, but I still can't cope. I can't meet the bills."

"I'm 23, and I'm going to have to give up my job as a hairdresser and go back to college. I can't afford to stay working at the big hairdressers' chain I'm in any more. We only get paid £4.50 an hour in actual wages. The rest of the £6.50 minimum wage is made up from commission, which is drying up as people can't afford to spend as much on hairdos, shampoos or hair products."

"I've been off sick but can't survive on the £80 a week Statutory Sick Pay. I want to go back to work because I can't afford to be off any longer. But my employer insists I need to first go to the Occupational Health Service. But if I pay the cost of petrol to travel there for an appointment, I won't have any money left for food this weekend."

"Ach no thanks, I don't want a Community Care Grant [a £40 emergency loan off the Council], I just wondered if I could get a food voucher to tide me over."

"I'm 71. I've come from Somalia to live here. The special food bank has been very good to me. They gave me some rice, an onion, two tomatoes and a bit of halal meat, so I should be alright for about five days."

These snippets of everyday life serve to confirm and illustrate the human agonies behind the Niagara of statistics on poverty and inequality that pour out daily from a host of academics, government departments, anti-poverty campaigns and social surveys. The picture is devastating, a searing condemnation of the type of society we live in; statistical reminders of the world we have to change.

* * * *

On a global scale, rule by the rich means literal starvation, disease and death for millions of people, little children included. The cold statistics merely hint at the heartbreaking slaughter of lives and livelihoods that is the inherent nature of capitalism and landlordism.

Half the globe's human population – over three billion people – eke out an existence on less than $2 a day (£1.30). A gobsmacking 1.3 billion humans have less than $1 (65p) a day to live on. In 2012, the ILO estimated that 21 million people globally live and work in conditions of 'quasi-slavery'. That includes debt bondage, forced labour, child labour, human trafficking, sex trafficking… all in what the exponents of capitalism would defend as 'modern civilisation', the 'best of all possible worlds'. All that in the 21st century, the age of the internet, space flight – and after a minuscule period in human history (1950-1968) during which more wealth was produced than in the entire preceding period of all recorded economic history!

The World Food Programme exposes the fact 66 million children attend school hungry across the developing world; 23 million in Africa alone. One out of every three kids in these countries is stunted in their physical growth, and 100 million are underweight. Poor nutrition causes 45% of all the deaths of children under the age of 5; a heartbreaking cull of 3.1 million kids' lives every single year through malnutrition, the product of poverty. Hunger kills more people every year than malaria, AIDS and TB combined. One human being dies of hunger on this rich, fertile planet every 3.6 seconds. Capitalism and landlordism mean the slaughter of the innocents.

Of course the people of Scotland do not suffer such Biblical scales of war and pestilence as billions do in those continents plundered by western imperialist powers for centuries. Continents invaded and plundered precisely because of their fabulous natural wealth. Continents and communities which continue to be ripped apart by multinational corporations, western governments, their agencies – the IMF, World Bank, World Trade Organisation, G8 – and ultimately conquered or quelled, if they dare revolt, by the use of the military might of western armed forces and nuclear war-machines like NATO.

But levels of poverty and deprivation in Scotland are all the more criminal, given (as the OECD accepts) we live in the 14th-richest country on the planet – ahead of Finland, Iceland, France, Japan, Italy, New Zealand... and indeed the rest of the UK!

When 117,689 people in Scotland – and over a million in the UK – relied on three-days' emergency food parcels from food banks to fight off their hunger pangs last year alone, to my mind that is poverty, absolute poverty. When thousands of people on benefits or low wages self-disconnect the gas or electricity in their homes for days on end because they have no money to feed the pre-payment meter, that to me is poverty, absolute poverty. When one in ten households now live in a damp home, the worst in 30 years, that is poverty, absolute poverty. When one in ten kids lacked either a warm winter coat or two pairs of shoes – in 2013 – that is poverty, absolute poverty. When 222,000 children in Scotland today live below the official breadline – including one in every three in Glasgow, and one in every ten in Shetland, the best area of the nation in that respect – that to me is poverty, rampant, repugnant poverty. But these facts and figures are merely a drop in the sea of poverty measurements conducted by various research projects.

Some of the many surveys conducted over the past 30 years are those by the Breadline Britain project. Their methods are profoundly illuminating. After decades of debate over what exact figure represents the poverty line (more on that in a later chapter), they devised what could be termed a social audit, a crowd-sourced measure of what represents poverty. A needs-based assessment of where to draw the poverty line.

The same method was deployed by the Poverty and Social Exclusion surveys of 1999 and 2012 – the largest ever research into poverty in the UK. From their very first survey in 1983, and in subsequent studies, they questioned thousands of people, from all ages, social classes, gender, and political affiliations, asking them to name what items of everyday life they thought essential to a decent minimum standard of living. Each time this social research was conducted – 1983, 1990, 1999, and 2012 – the representative sample of the population were offered 35 items of everyday life and asked to name those absolutely essential to a decent living standard, and those that are desirable but not essential.

The items and activities named as essential show a remarkable consistency across the population, but also allow for adjustments over time, as habits and trends of life change. For instance, phones and washing machines went from the preserve of the rich, to mass-produced, cheaper commodities with mass ownership, which changed the way people lived – and were more recently identified by the public as essential to modern life (by 77% and 82% respectively in 2012).

Likewise, in the 1983 survey, personal computers (PCs) didn't even register. In 1990 only 5% thought them essential; by 1999 they were still only named by 11% as a necessity for adults, though 38% thought them necessary for children to do their homework. As part of the IT and internet explosion of recent years, by 2012 a full 40% of the mass population sampled thought a PC essential to a minimum standard of living for adults, and 66% for kids. So the methodology of these mass surveys reflected both the consistent core of the things in life regarded as indispensable for a decent basic lifestyle, plus the shifts in social and cultural expectations.

These researchers then surveyed the population and classified anyone lacking three or more of the items – classed as essential by the wider population – as being below the breadline. The list of core items demonstrate how modest people's expectations are, and therefore how appalling an indictment of capitalism and ruling governments it is when large numbers can't even access these daily essentials.

For adults, they include adequate heating; a damp-free home; two meals a day; visiting friends or family in hospital or other institutions; fresh fruit and veg every day; a washing machine; dental treatment; celebration of special occasions; a warm, waterproof coat; a phone; meat, fish or vegetarian equivalent every other day.

For children, top of the modest expectations agreed by those surveyed include a warm winter coat; fresh fruit or veg daily; new, properly fitting shoes; three meals a day; a garden or outdoor space to play in; celebrations of special occasions; books at home suitable to their age; meat, fish or veggie equivalent every day, etc. Hardly asking for the moon and the stars!

* * * *

Given the wealth of the nation – wealth produced by 'workers by hand and by brain', let's not forget – it is almost unimaginable that anyone in the UK or Scotland should not have access to every single one of the items deemed, in a famous phrase, "the necessary minimum for decency" (JK Galbraith, *Affluent Society*, 1958).

But you don't need imagination; just a look at some of the horrendous facts from the 2013 Breadline Britain survey. A staggering 20 million people in the UK fall below this breadline. They are not meeting the modest Minimum Living Standard set by society as a whole, through the mass social audit of their contemporaries on life's daily essentials. That's 30% of the population of one of the richest states in the world; the fifth-biggest economy on Planet Earth. And the survey shows things are getting worse; drastically worse.

Back in the 1997 General Election campaign, New Labour adopted as their theme tune the D:Ream hit, *Things Can Only Get Better*. Aye, right! D:Ream on! Thirteen years of Labour government later, followed by five years of Tory/Lib Dem Coalition rule, the number of people in poverty is TWICE those below the breadline in 1983.

The number unable to heat their homes adequately has trebled since the 1990s, from 3% to 9%. The number skimping meals has more than doubled since 1983, from 13% to 28% of people. One in four kids in 2013 couldn't afford a holiday away from home. One in five children lives in a cold or damp home. One in 20 families couldn't afford to feed their kids adequately. 2.5 million parents went without meals so as to feed their children. As the 2013 Breadline Britain survey observed:

> "Increased numbers of families live a hand-to-mouth existence, missing out on a range of the most basic contemporary needs."

And don't believe for a minute that these shocking statistics reflect an economic collapse, a decline in national wealth, where we are 'all in it together', where we all have to 'tighten our belt' to drag the country through a period of economic famine, with promises of a feast the other side of the journey. Far from it.

We live in a society of abundance; superabundance. In a nutshell, as the Breadline Britain researchers conclude, in the 30 years since 1983, national income has doubled, but the numbers in poverty has also doubled! And no, that's not because the measure of poverty they used has changed. Virtually all the daily necessities of life they classified as essential to keep people above the breadline have remained exactly the same since 1983.

What has changed, drastically, devastatingly, is the distribution of wealth, the share that goes in the pockets of the working class majority of the population in the form of wages, benefits, and social wages – compared to the proportion of overall wealth plundered for profit. As the well-worn phrase goes, the rich are getting richer, the poor poorer. At an unprecedented rate of polarisation of wealth in the last 30-odd years. The size of the cake has doubled in 30 years. But the size of the slice consumed by the working class – the class of people who grew the ingredients, prepared, baked and designed the cake in the first place – has shrunken, drastically. How? And what should we do about it?

3

PAY & PROFIT

So what's the connection between pay and profit? We will go on to argue that this connection, this relationship, is at the very heart of inequality, and indeed poverty. So where does profit come from?

Let me indulge in a very personal story to illustrate the answer to this vital, unavoidable, indeed central question. Back in 1920s Ireland, my father left school at the age of 10, and stood in a village market square in County Cavan on Fair Day, alongside his siblings and other children of a similar age. This was the Hiring Fair. Landowners and other 'gentry' examined my father's teeth, muscles and limbs to see if he was fit to hire for work, just as they did with horses and cattle in the same place.

He was hired to work on the land, and his sister as a servant girl in the houses of bigger landowners, initially for £3 and 10 shillings (£3.50) – not per hour, nor per week, but in sum total for six months at a time. In that half-year, he had two Sundays off, during which he walked several miles home to visit his parents.

This was naked, undisguised sale of his labour-power, his ability to work, for which he was awarded £3.50 for six months. During that time he was at the beck and call of his landlord employer, to work whatever hours were demanded of him, however strenuously he was instructed to, but for a set amount of pay.

Whatever new value my Da's work produced for the landowner, he still only got the £3.50. So everything above that amount went straight to the big farmer's profit margin.

A clear, undisguised example of profit being the unpaid labour of the working class. A stark example of a worker only spending a percentage of his or her working day producing the equivalent of their wage for that day. But having sold their ability to work – their labour-power – on the labour market, they are then obliged, contracted, managed, even bullied, to produce the maximum added value for the remainder of the working day.

In this crude, almost primitive version of the undertakings between buyer and seller, employer and worker, my father's working day ended whenever his boss decided it should end. Its length was only restrained by the need to make sure he was rested sufficiently – and healthy enough – to work all the subsequent days he was hired at the marketplace to labour.

From the Hiring Fairs of the 1920s, and the well-named Labour Exchanges set up from 1909 onwards, we get a clear clue to the economic system, the source of profit under capitalism. Workers sell their labour-power on the marketplace like any other commodity, with competition for the price received (wages) not only between workers vying for the same job, but also competition between the employers and those seeking work – over the share of the value of the work done that goes back to workers' wages. Nowadays all this is more disguised, with language designed to hide the truth, including names like Jobcentreplus displacing the more explicit 'Labour Exchange'. But the method remains. Workers are hired for their ability to work for the lowest wage socially acceptable at any given time and place.

So whilst it's plain to see the wages of my sons today in no way resemble those my father earned in his childhood and youth, and likewise they are not tied day and night to their employers the way he was for six months at a time, the fundamentals remain.

Workers in the 21st century still encounter attempts to make them work harder within the hours they are hired for. More work is heaped on fewer and fewer staff in the wake of 'down-sizing' to make companies 'leaner and fitter'. And the working day is lengthened without any equivalent increase in workers' pay – through the likes of unpaid overtime, which has reached epidemic levels in 21st century Scotland. Profit is the unpaid labour of the working class. For every pound gained in profit for the owners of a privately-owned, capitalist enterprise, a pound thereby is lost to the wages of its workforce.

Class conflict is not the product of 'troublemakers', the favoured insult cast up at trade union activists and socialists by capitalists and their apologists. Class conflict at bottom is a battle over who gets what share of the total wealth produced by the collective efforts of workers 'by hand and by brain'. A battle between workers for a greater share to come to wages and conditions of work, and company owners for a bigger percentage to accrue to them to pay rent to landlords of the workplace site (if they don't directly own it), interest on loans taken out through the banks for investment, and direct profits for the handful of giant shareholders in ownership of the company. It's a battle between labour and capital, pay and profit, workers and capitalist employers.

But perhaps the last word on this should be handed over to one of the globe's richest men, Warren Buffet. With personal wealth of £43billion – yes, that's billions – Buffet spelled out the source of the opulence of his tiny minority class, when in 2006 he told the *New York Times*:

"There's class warfare alright, but it's my class, the rich class, that's making war, and we're winning!"

* * * *

In this age of spin, where corporations and capitalist political parties hire hordes of overpaid experts on systematic lying – to cover up the truth, put a positive gloss on downright lies, and smear opponents – it's sometimes hard to spot the sources of inequality. A whole industry consists of hiding the truth behind euphemisms for daylight robbery by a rich cabal; spinning webs of deceit about the crude theft of workers' wealth-production by handfuls of owners who hire their labour; burial from sight of the intimate, indissoluble links between pay, poverty and profit.

So it's refreshing when some shameless exploiter blurts out the true thinking of those whose source of wealth is the poverty of others; whose opulent lifestyle is built on the broken lives of hundreds, even thousands, systematically denied anything over and above bare subsistence, if that.

Twenty-first century Tories sing songs of praise to their own cuts to state welfare by claims that they are 'making work pay'. A more honest portrayal of the methods underpinning capitalist profits, and the consequences for millions of people whose only 'capital' is their ability to work, was blurted out by a Scotsman in 1806.

Patrick Colquhon was a merchant, magistrate and statistician. He owned cotton plantations in Virginia and sugar plantations in Jamaica. In deeds he left no doubt about what class he represented, what philosophy he lived by. As a magistrate he was to the fore in prosecuting textile workers in this country who tried to survive by recycling waste material in the mills for their own use. He ordered the hanging of those deemed guilty of 'money crimes'. He organised spies and informers against anti-slavery campaigners. As one historian described Colquhon:

"He was an agent of violent oppression in service of the industrialist and property-owning class in the early Atlantic economy – a class in need of a labouring class in thrall to subsistence wages to maximise profits."

But the same Colquhon didn't limit himself to such systematic repression in pursuit of profit for him and his ilk; he also put pen to paper to expound the thinking behind the system he helped pioneer, the thoughts behind his deeds. In 1806 he wrote what should be inscribed on the notice-board of every capitalist corporation, such is the brutal clarity of its account of capitalist society:

"Poverty is a most necessary and indispensable ingredient in society, without which nations and communities could not exist in a state of civilisation. It is the lot of man – it is the source of wealth, since without poverty there would be no labour, and without labour there could be no riches, no refinement, no comfort, and no benefit to those who may be possessed of wealth."

4

POVERTY IMPOVERISHES SOCIETY

Poverty pay impoverishes not only its direct victims – the growing horde of workers denied access to society on a par with their neighbours and contemporaries – but also impoverishes the whole of society. The lack of spending power that low wages curses affected families with, in turn depresses the wider economy. It's an indisputable fact that unlike 'the 1%' filthy rich, working class people spend almost every penny extra in their pay packet.

Those with mountains of cash already, tend to stick any additional wealth they acquire into savings, speculative financial dealings on the money markets, or luxury items that do precious little to fuel the growth of national income. They tend to invest in items such as luxury yachts; personal engorgement at ultra-exclusive restaurants with absurd prices; or works of art that they stash away in their private homes or bank vaults, never to be viewed or appreciated by the wider population. So those sitting on the giddy pinnacles of income distribution do little to grow either the output of goods and services, or the cultural development of the population.

And contrary to what historically was the capitalists' raison d'être, the rich elite of Britain and Scotland are notorious for not re-investing their wealth in new technology and modernisation of the units of wealth production. Investment by them in this country is lagging far behind that of most major international competitors, contributing to the current crisis of plunging productivity in the economy, compared with other nation states.

In stark, statistically proven contrast, working-class and middle-class people have a far higher 'Marginal Propensity to Spend', as the economists label the percentage of increased income that they spend. They do so in the local shops and supermarkets, boosting the profits of both. If they had a decent wage, they'd spend some of it on the occasional family outing or entertainment. That fuels the income of transport providers, coffee shops, pubs, clubs, restaurants, cinemas and football clubs. If they can afford a new coat or shoes or outfit for themselves or their kids, it boosts the retail sector.

One concrete example of the impact of higher wages – or to be more exact, higher disposable incomes for workers – was revealed in a document by the trade union UNISON in April 2014 – *Lifting the Cap*. After exposing the savage, sustained pay cuts in the public sector over the previous five years, the researchers used information from the government's own Living Costs & Food Survey of previous spending patterns, to examine where the additional spending would go if public sector workers were awarded a 3% pay rise over three years.

They concluded that – based on established patterns in the Survey – a full 19% of additional spending would be on transport; 16% on leisure and recreation; 13% on housing, water and electricity; 11% on food and non-alcoholic drink; 11% on restaurants and hotel; lesser proportions on furnishings, household goods, carpets, clothing and footwear. All of which would have a positive spin-off effect on jobs (and potentially wages) in those sectors, above and beyond the positive impact on the lifestyles of the public sector workers themselves. And in a clear rebuttal of the reactionary image of working people conveyed by many of those in power, and the tabloid media, far from spending any pay rise on 'booze and fags', a mere 2.6% of additional spending was found to head that direction!

The reverse of all this is equally true. Lack of spending power for the mass of the population has been a fundamental weakness in the capitalist economy throughout its history, one of its inherent crazy contradictions. As a system driven by the profit motive, only a percentage of the wealth produced by the collective effort and division of labour between workers goes back to them in the form of wages. The rest is creamed off as profit for the private, capitalist owners of the firms that hire them to work.

But that means, in overall terms, the working class cannot afford to buy back the aggregate total of goods and services they produce. So we've had the obnoxious lunacy of building workers unable to afford a house; car workers unable to buy a motor; retail workers too low-paid to afford many of the consumer goods they sell; and in 21st century Scotland, fast food workers on zero hours contracts, and low-paid supermarket workers, turning to food banks for an emergency supply of meals.

* * * *

In earlier decades, this periodically led to a very visible version of what socialists term 'a crisis of overproduction'. In physical form, this meant acres of newly-built cars parked outside the factory so as to keep market prices up (and therefore profits). It featured capitalist farmers being given government grants to destroy crops, and to literally chuck dairy milk down the sheugh or drain, to keep prices and profits high in a marketplace suffering a glut of production (if in doubt on this, ask any family farmer, or have a read of Joseph Heller's *Catch 22*). The inbuilt lunacy of capitalist production meant beef mountains, butter mountains and wine lakes in the European Union 20-30 years ago – stockpiles to keep market prices (and therefore profits) up, at the same time as families went hungry.

Modern technology – the manifold products of human genius – has helped avert literal stockpiles on most occasions in recent times. But the periodic 'crisis of overproduction' written of by Karl Marx in *Das Capital* 150 years ago still occurs; it's just more disguised now, not always as visible, and usually re-labelled 'overcapacity'. Instead of the literal stockpiles of just a couple of decades ago, when there's a glut of production on the market, with each private capitalist competing for the biggest possible share of that same, finite market, commonly the answers nowadays are factory shutdowns; short-time working and accompanying pay cuts; temporary lay-offs of workers; redundancies and outright closures.

For instance, at the time of writing, there is 30% overcapacity in the global motor industry. That means the likes of Fords, General Motors, Toyota, Fiat, Peugeot and all the rest of the multinationals in this sector could shut down 30% of their factories, make 30% of their workers redundant, and still struggle to sell the motors currently produced at a profit margin they deemed 'adequate'.

As we correct this publication for sending to the printers, a catastrophic crisis in the steel industry has erupted, with wholesale closures, including that of the last substantial steel plants in Scotland. An industry with a tradition spanning 150 years now faces extinction, because of a crisis that typifies all that is rotten to the core of capitalism as a system of political economy.

Tata Steel Ltd invested in its two Lanarkshire steelworks – Motherwell and Cambuslang – a few years ago to produce steel products that Chinese steel plants are now churning out on a gargantuan scale. World prices have collapsed by nearly 50%. Chinese capitalist producers are turning the screw tighter on their international competitors by dumping cheap steel imports on the market – often at below production costs – so as to seize greater control of the global steel market when demand (and prices) rise again. And there's nothing unusual in what the Chinese capitalists are doing; they are behaving exactly the same as all capitalist profiteers do, all the time, regardless of their nationality, in the jungle of the so-called free market.

Precisely because capitalist production is for private profit, what at first may be a niche market is identified, and then produced for by several competing capitalists, in competing capitalist nations, until inevitably the volume of production reaches a point where no more can be sold profitably. Right now, there's a vast glut of steel production on the world market. One claim is that the surplus steel production globally is 50 times bigger than the entire productive capacity of the whole remaining British steel industry. So working class families and communities are made to pay the terrible price of this crisis of overproduction.

Not – as the case of steel illustrates perfectly – because there's a lack of social need for the product, but only 'overproduction' in the sense that competing capitalists cannot carve out a thick enough profit margin for themselves by producing it. For instance, if the Scottish Government possessed the political ideology and willpower to nationalise the steel industry, and integrate it into a broader industrial strategy – embracing democratic public ownership of sectors such as transport, construction and energy – steelworkers could enjoy a secure future producing steel for the likes of social sector house-building;

the fleets and infrastructure for a vastly expanded, integrated public transport network; flood barriers; marine engineering equipment and wind turbines for a huge new green industry.

Always, it's the working class that pays the price for the inherent inability of the capitalist system to plan and produce for social need – because its entire raison d'être is private greed. Capitalism is a system of social production for private profit.

* * * *

Of course the system whose entire motor force is the accumulation of profit for a tiny minority at the expense of the living standards of the mass of the population – and its inbuilt inability to reward the working class with 'the full fruits of their labour', in turn limiting spending power – finds numerous mechanisms to avoid being in permanent recession, perpetual crisis.

In one of these multiple mechanisms, individual capitalists can gain temporary escape, and boost their short-term profits, by carving out a new niche product, or conquer a corner of the market at home, thereby also usually boosting overall national production. This includes new technologies, their development and mass production – as with mobile phones, iPhones, tablets, information technology and such-like recent gadgetry, which have amassed fabulous profits for an oligopoly of multinational firms like Vodafone, Microsoft, Apple, Facebook, etc.

Such new inventions, converted into new mass production, can for a spell turn a fall in national economic output (recession) into a boom period. And although no guarantee of a boost to the combined incomes of the mass of the population, let alone the directly-employed workforces, it certainly ensures a boom for the individual capitalist enterprise involved. For instance, Facebook recorded a leap in quarterly (not annual) profits by a third, to £462million in the last three months of 2014. In the first three months of 2014, Apple broke all previous records for quarterly profits, shooting up to £11.8billion. And in both cases, these ultra-profiteers registered their business in the South of Ireland to exploit the lucrative 'double Irish' tax-dodging deals.

The most extreme examples of these cyclical conversions from slump to boom include the aftermath of mass destruction through wars – after which the demand for reconstruction can lead to a phase of economic recovery. The classic case was the post-1945 prolonged upswing in the western economies. In that exceptional period, a combination of post-war reconstruction, new technologies and several government interventions, boosted the population's spending power. One of the major factors was the injection of billions of Euro-dollars into the economies of post-War Europe by the newly-dominant imperialist power, the USA, in what was called the Marshall Aid Plan. This was in large part state investment to avert revolutions in many of these western European states. This combination of political and economic factors ushered in an unprecedented phase of human history. In a time-span not even amounting to an eye-blink in human history – from 1950-1968 – twice as much economic wealth was produced as in all of previous recorded human history combined.

* * * *

Another escape route for a capitalist system that builds a wall round the potential buying power of its own population by its very essence – being a system hunting profit from 'the unpaid labour of the working class', and simultaneously a system rooted in that modern phenomenon, the nation state – is the conquest of markets outside the borders of the nation state. That is the essence of colonial conquests, the construction of empires, including the ruthless subjugation and enslavement of the peoples of the lands seized; the environmental destruction of their homelands for cheap raw materials; and mass impoverishment and starvation in rich and fertile lands, when capitalist conquerors dictate what these countries produce (such as cash crops for export) and impose brutal terms of trade on them.

The expansion of world trade is a further device for survival employed by the capitalist Masters of the Universe. Recently, the phenomenal development of markets and production in China, for instance, gave temporary reprieve to the capitalist producers of other nation states that invested there, or trade with them. But the system can never permanently overcome its own limitations. The explosion of world trade brings its own unwelcome consequences, from the point of view of the profiteers, such as chunks of the domestic markets of Britain or the US being conquered by Chinese competitors. Plus the same inherent problems of Chinese workers never getting the full value of their output back in wages, thereby limiting their spending power – and limiting the potential markets for multinationals from outwith the new giant of capitalist production.

Because the whole global capitalist system rests on ruthless competition between capitalist corporations for market shares and the highest possible rates of profit, it cannot create rational planning of the world's economy for the benefits of its people and the planet. For instance, phases of vastly expanded 'free trade' that ignore national boundaries as a bloody nuisance in the dash for trade and new world markets, are then habitually followed by panic at the penetration of their own domestic markets by foreign multinationals, with frequent outbursts of 'protectionism'. That new twist – with barriers erected to curtail imports, for example, to protect profit margins within each nation state – creates new problems, especially in firms that rely heavily on trade and exports for their loot. So neither free trade nor protectionism solves the problems suffered by working-class people of any country, because those in power still rob them of a decent standard of living by one means or another.

* * * *

To overcome this built-in contradiction – the pursuit of profit slashing the spending power of workers and therefore causing periodic slumps or recessions, in a system characterised by booms and slumps – to reverse and delay the crises, capitalists and their governments periodically extend credit to artificially boost spending power. We've all been there. The plastic money; succumbing to the bombardment from banks and other (legalised) moneylenders to stretch our spending power, to buy those few extras, family treats, new furniture, a holiday, a car, or even just to meet the urgent bills our wages are too miserly to match. Then, inevitably, it's crash, bang, wallop: credit turns into what it really is, debt.

The lenders start pounding you to repay what you owe. In far too many cases, people in desperate need – because of the inhumane level of benefits they live on, or the poverty pay they suffer – turn to the loan sharks to tide them over. And the loan sharks are not only the ones who stand on the street corner hassling people to pay up, with the threat of a visit with baseball bats or claw hammers. It also includes the legalised robbers, the Pay Day Loan sharks like Payday Pig or Wonga – with its 'representative' annual interest rates (APR) of 5,853%!

These legalised Pay Day Loan thieves preside over an industry worth £2billion. Loan sharks are a cancer at the heart of a low wage economy. Poverty pay, benefits cuts, and the refusal of the High Street banks to offer loans, let alone affordable loans, to ordinary people, create a pool for these predators to swim in search of the blood of the most impoverished. Over 1.75 million people in Britain are denied a bank account. Another nine million have bank accounts that deny them any credit. Those granted overdraft facilities are charged exorbitant daily rates for using them. So when the rent is due, or shopping for food unavoidable, but it's still a week or more to pay day, it's tempting to succumb to the deluge of seductive emails and adverts from an array of 'magic solutions'. That's how Wonga was named Europe's fastest-growing business in 2010. That's how these predatory capitalists stole £62.4million in profits out of workers' pay packets in 2012.

Surveys in 2013 found that a horrifying one in six workers aged 18-34 – precisely the lowest-paid – planned to incur the crucifying interests charges on Pay Day loans over the subsequent six months. Because wages didn't match daily needs. In January 2012, for instance, *Which?* Magazine found that over half the population had used credit cards, store cards and Pay Day Loans to pay for Christmas – borrowing on average over £300.

Another shark swimming round the districts awash with the worst poverty is the 'rent-to-own' company BrightHouse. Look at the most deprived towns and areas, with many of the most desperate people, and you'll see one of BrightHouse's 270 branches. One of their favourite advertising slogans is 'Making Christmas more affordable'. They are the biggest single company in this sector – a variation on hire purchase – which leases household furniture, electronics and domestic appliances on the basis of monthly payments, with exorbitant interest rates, and the 'option' of eventual outright ownership. By issuing prolonged leases to the poorest, they cash in vast amounts of interest charges. Typically, those seeking to furnish their homes – with beds, fridges, TVs, electronic goods – this way pay over twice the original price, due to BrightHouse's parasitic usury. Several of the victims of their 'cheap credit', of 'making Christmas more affordable', have testified to how BrightHouse send heavies round in a van to seize goods they were late paying for that month, or indeed just prior to them having completed the entire payments, allegedly on the brink of being entitled to then own the goods they'd 'rented-to-own' on a monthly lease.

They've been exposed for repossessing goods without even seeking a Court Order. One former BrightHouse employee told BBC *Newsbeat*, in 2009, how they bullied people into handing over goods they'd already paid a fortune for: "We would just lie our way around it. Tell them we had the legal right to be there, and refuse to leave until they gave us the stuff." And far from being cheap in the first place, these vultures charge base prices that are frequently higher than those in the retail outlet of the upper class – Harrods!

Whilst preying on people whose wages don't stretch as far as adequate home appliances or the 'must have' electronic gadgets they rent-to-own, BrightHouse piles up fabulous profits – and dodges paying Corporation Tax like the very worst of their class of robbers. In early 2015, *Private Eye* magazine exposed how this Watford-based outfit had revenues of £1.6billion and operating profits of £191million, but paid less than £6million in UK Corporation Tax over the entire seven years from 2007 to 2014 – with the aid of siphoning off profits to subsidiaries registered in tax havens like Luxembourg and Malta. Not holiday destinations the same BrightHouse are likely to 'make Christmas more affordable' in for their impoverished customers!

So the extension of various forms of credit fuelled a fireworks display of profits for the capitalist minority – but left millions of the poorest badly burnt.

The credit binge of the 1990s and 2000s led to a massive consumer boom, egged on by the 'must have' advertising, driving up the profit margins of an increasingly monopolised retail sector and property development companies. The criminal failure of governments and councils to build houses for affordable rent prolonged the housing shortage crisis, and the get-rich-quick merchants in the banks charged into the gap in the market, issued mortgages that people didn't have a snowball's chance in Hell of repaying, given the protracted decline in wages, which drove up house prices to the stratosphere.

As one illustration of this drunken binge of credit-fuelled over-spending, housing charity Shelter calculated that if retail inflation had ballooned at the same rate as house-price inflation between 1971 and 2011 (a 400-fold increase!), we'd have been paying £47 for a chicken and £20 for a jar of coffee. The hooligan abandon with which banks and other moneylenders issued credit in the 1990s and 2000s meant, for instance, that people spent more through credit in 2006 than the entire UK GDP that year – fuelling the housing bubble and consumerist frenzy for a few fat years, only to turn into the extended lean years since.

The massive extension of credit also played a part in dampening down the readiness of workers to take action, collectively, including industrial action, to demand and win higher actual wages; a higher share of wealth for the one productive class. Plastic money seemed an easier route to comfort (or even just survival) than the harsh road of strikes and struggles to wring a few extra quid out of the sweaty paws of profit-crazed employers or axe-wielding governments.

By 2008, the proverbial chickens came home to roost – and to do what chickens do when they roost, from a great height! The credit-fuelled, consumer-led boom in the western capitalist economy imploded, with subsequent bailouts for bankers from public funds, so as to avoid total economic collapse – followed by several years of savage attacks on public services, benefits, and wages... all of which are still ongoing.

So the low-wage economy of Scotland and Britain doesn't work. The crazy contradictions might have been partially covered up by the credit craze for a few years, but now it's back to the harsh realities of a shrinking slice of the cake going to wages, people struggling to cope with bills for gas, electricity, food, rent, mortgage, transport – with savings at a record low and no room for 'extras' for the low-paid, or even workers on middle incomes.

In fact, for a short phase following the 2008 financial meltdown, banks held onto the public funds given them to avert collapse, and refused loans to small businesses and individual 'consumers', displaying all the generosity of a corporate Ebenezer Scrooge with their – actually our – money.

That undoubtedly exacerbated the slow and shallow 'recovery' after the post-2008 deep recession, the worst in 80 years in its impact on the living standards of the 99%. Terrified, most people were reluctant to spend their modest savings, further slowing the recovery of the consumer-led economy. But as wages were suppressed, people began to eat into their savings, and the UK government started to push measures to boost spending – but only for a small minority. For instance, two of their schemes – Funding for Lending and Help to Buy – have driven more people onto the property ladder, despite stagnating incomes.

Secured loans have also risen in more recent years, although borrowing against the value of homes has not yet reached pre-2008 levels. But horrifying signs of a possible re-run of the pre-2008 housing bubble are visible, more particularly in London and the south east of England, with mortgagees left more vulnerable to income and interest rate shocks because of a steady rise in the size of new mortgages compared to borrowers' wages.

Household borrowing is on the rise again. Unsecured loans – such as credit card debts and Pay Day Loans – are rocketing at the rate of an extra £1billion a month. So with the devastating cuts to real wages – and the shrinkage of the slice of national pie that goes to wages – it is consumer debt that is helping to trigger and sustain the economic recovery.

Economist Robert Reich, of California University, Berkeley, recently calculated that in the US, 70% of the economy depends on consumer spending. The figures for this country are broadly similar. For instance, a BBC report stated that in 2012, UK consumer spending amounted to £927billion, compared to a total wealth production – Gross Domestic Product (GDP) – that year of £1,504billion.

Put another way, consumption was the single biggest component of demand for production, equivalent to 61% of GDP. But with household debt – as opposed to real actual wages – being the main prop for the feeble recovery, harsh times loom in the years ahead. The capitalist system is more akin to a house resting on spindly chicken legs than anything with a sound, secure foundation. Poverty pay doesn't even work from a capitalist standpoint.

* * * *

In February 2015, David Cameron addressed the assembled worthies of the British Chamber of Commerce and handed them the message: "Britain needs a pay rise." He was echoing the slogan of the British TUC over previous months.

There are several things you can deduce from such a bizarre outburst from this hateful Old Etonian Tory multimillionaire. The obvious one first: there was a General Election looming two months after his speech! Secondly, the same Tory butchers in office at Westminster who'd worked like Trojans at robbing ordinary people, to pay their pals at the tops of the banks and big business, are worried there's a growing revolt against poverty and inequality.

They are echoing the thoughts of one of their own kind in the US, Nick Hanauer. He's a billionaire, and describes himself as "one of the 0.1%ers." In 2014, he converted to support of the campaign for a $15 minimum wage in Seattle (twice the federal rate of $7.25 in the US) with some very telling comments:

> "Why, since the 1950s, has the pay ratio of a Chief Executive Officer compared to a worker risen by 1,000%? I see pitchforks... it is the masses that are the source of growth and prosperity, not us rich guys."

Cameron may fear 'the pitchforks' coming over the hill, despite the superficial lack of struggle for better pay in recent years.

More fundamentally though, this is in part recognition that without greater spending power for the mass of working-class people, the capitalists face a problem in harvesting their profits. But this is where the system cannot solve its own problems. The capitalist class as a whole would gain from greater consumer spending, and therefore a hike in wages would boost their economy. But for the individual capitalist it's less straightforward: they fear their precious profit margins would be cut by increased wages for their workforce.

So David Cameron telling a room of capitalist bosses that "Britain needs a pay rise" is like Dracula appealing to a conference of vampires for volunteers to donate blood. These bloodsuckers have moved mountains for the past 30-40 years to slash the real wages of workers, boosting their profits by driving down the share of wealth that goes to wages. As the British TUC calculated in 2012, since 1975 this consciously chosen path has robbed workers of a cumulative £1.3trillion, compared to what they'd have got in wages if they'd remained at the same share of GDP as they were in 1975. That's £1,300billion that working people could and would have spent, thereby boosting job security and other workers' wages – a virtuous circle.

It will take two fundamental things to win a significant boost to workers' wages. Recognition that the battle for better wages is a battle with capitalist employers whose short-term profits maximisation drives them to restrict wages to the lowest they can get away with. And readiness on the part of trade union leaders, trade unionists, and working class communities to wage a determined struggle. And 'Cut profits, not pay' could be one useful fighting slogan for such a crusade to win a decent living wage for all.

5

CRIMES & PUNISHMENTS

In December 2014, the Scottish Poverty Alliance's latest Report confirmed that the crime of poverty pay is becoming even more criminal. They identified 418,000 workers in Scotland earning below £7.65 an hour. That's one in five workers. 110,000 of the 222,000 Scottish children inexcusably suffering poverty have at least one parent working. Another 100,000 kids in Scotland – 700,000 in the UK – are expected to fall into this miserable existence by 2020 as a result of the planned cuts to benefits, including in-work benefits, issued by the previous Tory/Lib Dem Coalition

More recently still, in the summer of 2015, the Child Poverty Action Group condemned the new Westminster Tory regime's savage benefit cuts with forecasts of an additional 100,000 kids in Scotland tumbling down into the abyss of poverty. Several different social research bodies have concluded that since at least 2012, over half – 52-53% – of all the adults in poverty are in work, but still denied the bare necessities of life. Incredibly, the Joseph Rowntree Foundation's annual Report of November 2014 found that almost half of all the families living in poverty have not just one, but two people working. As confirmed by the Child Poverty Action Group, two-thirds of the children condemned to poverty have at least one, and often two, parents working.

Past generations were taught by their parents to work hard at school, get an education, get a good job, and thereby improve their standard of living compared with that of their parents. In the 1950s and 1960s the unprecedented growth of capitalist output in this and other western countries allowed social reforms that reduced both poverty and inequality. The growth in numbers and strength of the organised workers' trade unions in that post-war period won substantial pay improvements for many, plus advances in the 'social wage' in the form of the NHS, affordable public sector housing, comprehensive education, welfare benefits and other social provision.

But since the late-1970s this trend has been put into reverse gear, with society travelling backwards at breakneck, accelerating speed – long before the 2008 banking crisis and its horrendous consequences for the working class. We now have the brutally graphic illustration of this social and economic regression: for the first time since the 1930s, the expectation is that the next generation will be worse off than the current one. That is heartbreaking for any parent; demoralising for young people setting out on life's journey; a criminal waste of talent and hope.

* * * *

To further ram home this bleak trend, the 2010-15 Westminster Twin Tory Coalition was the first government since the 1920s where wages were lower at the end of their term (May 2015) than when they took office (May 2010). In fact since the Cameron-Clegg cabal of upper-class boot-boys seized power in what amounted to a bloodless parliamentary coup – because nobody ever voted for this Coalition, and back in 2010 many people were gullible enough to think by voting Lib Dem they were voting against the Tories – we have had an unprecedented collapse in workers' wages... and a simultaneous, stratospheric rise in wealth for a tiny handful.

Since 2010, the average worker's wage has plummeted by £40-£50 a week in real terms. Simultaneously, the richest 1,000 grotesquely bloated fat cats in the UK have seen their wealth more than double in the same five years, to a monumental £547billion. During 2010-13, workers in the UK suffered the 4th-worst drop in real wages in 27 EU countries, only outstripped by the declines in Greece, Portugal and Holland. Cheek-by-jowl with that decimation of workers' living standards, the minimum personal wealth required to join the Rich List of Britain's wealthiest 1,000 citizens rose from £85million each in 2014, to £100million in 2015. That's a rise of 18% in one short year for the ultra-wealthy – a trifle larger than the pay rises of zero to 2% endured by millions of workers, the actual wealth creators!

One further startling fact: we have just experienced the longest, deepest decline of wages in Britain since 1856 – 160 years ago!

There's only ever been seven consecutive years of decline in annual wages twice before: after the deep recession of the late-nineteenth century, and in the 1930s, after the Great Depression.

Whilst public sector workers suffered a prolonged government 'pay freeze' more akin to an Arctic Winter, the richest 1,000 individuals amassed wealth at a galloping pace every time the same Westminster Tory/Lib Dem Coalition announced a new round of bloodletting to jobs, wages, benefits and public services. In 2010, as the plans for savage cuts to the lives of millions were declared, driving women, men and children into destitution, the richest one-thousand's fortunes leapt by 30%. Another 20% rise followed in 2011; an additional £35billion piled onto their fortunes in 2013... and by 2014, this tiny group's wealth (£519billion) was eight times greater in relative terms than when the *Sunday Times* first published their Rich List in 1989.

To add insult to injury, just days before the knife-wielding Tories took office in May 2015, announcing a further £35billion in public spending cuts, the latest Rich List was published, with very little fanfare or publicity. It was as if it's of no great consequence that the richest 1,000 people in Britain now sit aloft combined fortunes of £547billion, in the same state where over a million people swallowed their pride and turned in desperation to food banks last year.

The rich are getting richer, the poor poorer... but at a rate that is mind-boggling by any historic comparisons. As Philip Beresford, the compiler since 1989 of every *Sunday Times* Rich List, said when they published the 2014 figures:

"I've never seen such a phenomenal rise in personal wealth as the growth in the fortunes of Britain's richest 1,000 people over the past year. The richest have had an astonishing year."

It's worth bearing in mind another incredible feature of this Rich List: these calculations of the enormous personal fortunes of Britain's wealthiest 1,000 take absolutely no account of what they have in their bank accounts! So it's a huge underestimate of just how stinking rich they are. Not that everyone was in the least disturbed by this disgusting accumulation of ill-gotten opulence. The same publishers' daily paper, the *Times*, shamelessly commented: "Britain needs to be seen as a place where success is applauded." Success at what? Making things? Inventing or manufacturing socially useful products? Bettering the lives of others? Educating children? Keeping transport networks, fuel supplies, food production, clean water supplies, and care for the sick, elderly or young going? No, that's what the working class do, day and daily, but don't exactly get 'applauded' for it by the likes of Rupert Murdoch's *Times*.

The wealthy elite are unimaginably successful at one thing: making themselves wealthy! As a columnist in the *Independent*, Terence Blacker, wrote in the wake of this year's Rich List revelations:

"The list is dominated by those with the words 'investment', 'finance', 'inherited' and 'property' beside their names... money-making is an end in itself for these people, rather than a by-product of what they happen to do."

The rich are getting richer, the poor poorer, but on a scale and at a pace that beggars belief.

* * * *

At the heart of this phenomenon is the devastating fact that wages as a share of national wealth (Gross Domestic Product, GDP) are at their lowest since records began in 1956. It is no accident that the share of GDP that went to wages peaked in this country in 1975 – with the total wages bill amounting to 64.5% of national output that year. Just glimpse at the background events, nationally and internationally.

1968 was the year of mass uprisings, civil rights struggles, general strikes and mass radicalisation across several continents – including the US, France, Ireland, Britain. Young people, students and workers challenged ruling powers. Workers occupied factories, offices, shops, even beauty parlours and the Moulin Rouge, in the momentous uprising of France 1968. They built street barricades to defend themselves from

assault by the riot police, sent into action by a terrified President de
Gaulle, who fled to shelter in Germany, declaring "The game's up!"

These heady events infected the mood of young people and workers
here too. 1968 was also the year of the historic strike of women
sewing machinists (who made the car seat covers) in Ford's Dagen-
ham and Halewood car plants – a mere month after the revolutionary
May days in France. The women were fighting for equal pay, through
job re-grading to match the skills of their work, instead of being paid
15% less than men using similar skills. After three weeks of action
they won an immediate rise to 8% below the men's rate of pay, with
promises of the full re-grading the next year (which actually required
a further six-week strike in 1984 to enforce!). Most significantly, the
Ford's women's strike transformed the confidence of women workers,
and ultimately triggered the 1970 Equal Pay Act at Westminster.

Without their strike there would have been no Equal Pay Act. Furthermore, despite that Act being passed, it took the second, more prolonged strike (in 1984) to win equal pay, because of the legal minefield
surrounding comparators for equal pay claims. This story is a graphic illustration of the central role of class struggle methods in the pursuit of
equality, rather than exclusively relying on benevolent legislation, important though the latter also is.

The early 1970s were marked in Britain by the biggest industrial unrest
since the 1926 General Strike. Literally millions marched and went on
strike to 'Kill the Bill' – the new laws aimed at crushing trade union rights.
Massive strikes by miners, building workers, postal workers, dockers, car
workers, civil servants and a host of others swept Britain – bringing down
the Tory government of Ted Heath in February 1974 in the wake of the
victorious miners' strike of that winter.

A highly organised, increasingly politicised trade union movement
– with a peak membership of over 13 million in the TUC – forced employers and the government to concede a bit more of the national cake
to the plates of workers. That concession was despite these convulsive
struggles being partly provoked by the early onset of international capitalist economic crises in the early 1970s. A clash of classes triggered
by a decline in the rate of profit for big business, and the attempts by

the political arm of capitalism to recover their profiteering spree by clawing back some of the hard-won gains for working people of the post-WW2 period of economic upswing in the 1950s-early 1970s.

With this background of militant struggle by workers and their unions, it's no accident that workers' wages peaked as a share of national wealth in the year 1975. Equally, it's hardly surprising that most mainstream politicians and historians have shamelessly doctored the history of that period, so as to bury the realities from the gaze of today's generation of working class people, in particular those too young to directly remember what happened. Unless you were there, you could be forgiven for thinking the 1970s (and indeed early 1980s) were 'the bad old days' when selfish, greedy trade unionists brought the country to its knees; wrecked the economy; always going on strike for the least thing; with 'the unions out of control'. That's how the bourgeois want us to view the recent past, in order to stop today's generation of workers emulating the struggles – including many successful ones – by their parents' generation.

In fact, the primary feature of that decade was a strong, emboldened, organised working class fighting what turned out to be rearguard action against a brutal class of capitalist exploiters and their hired politicians, who were intent on mugging workers' rights, workers' incomes and public services – in order to shore up profits for the rich. Widespread strikes and protests by the trade union movement and socialists succeeded in reducing inequalities for a time, winning workers a slightly fairer share of the wealth they collectively produced. That's the real story of the '70s which they never want told – because the rich dread its example would encourage workers in this day and age to stand up for greater equality; to unchain themselves from capitalist exploitation and its inevitable, inherent inequality.

* * * *

Compared with the slice of the cake allocated to wages in 1975, a catastrophic collapse in the 'wages-output ratio', also known as 'wage share', has robbed workers of £billions in the subsequent 30 years. A major study, published by the TUC in January 2012, charted how this 'wage share' plummeted from the early 1980s onwards, with the occasional weak and very partial recovery, until it fell from 64.5% in 1975 to 53.7% in 2011. So for every £100 wealth output by each UK worker, they got an average wage of £64.50 in 1975 – but only £53.70 in 2011.

The TUC study measured what it called 'The Wage Grab' each year, over the previous 30 years, as less of the national economic cake came back in wages and more went to profits. For instance, the average-paid worker lost £6,200 in 2006; a further £6,900 in 2007; £7,000 in 2008; another £6,200 in 2009; and an additional loss of £7,000 in wages in 2010.

In aggregate total, the TUC concluded, this 'Wage Grab' meant workers across Britain taking home £60billion less in their wages in 2012 than their equivalents did 30 years earlier (in 2012 money). That's £60billion that would have been spent, boosting the local and national economy, as well as the lifestyles of workers' families. To keep such mind-boggling figures in perspective, £60billion is the entire Scottish Government budget for two whole years.

Let's look at what this means in practice in more easily grasped facts about workers' wages. If the wage share of total national economic output (GDP) was the same in 2011 as it was in 1975, a worker in 2011 earning £12,000 would instead have been on £21,016! Somebody on £15,000 in 2011 would instead have got £26,270. A worker on £18,000 would have enjoyed a rise to £28,169. A wage of £20,000 would instead have been £31,299. And so the monstrous tale of robbery by the rich goes.

In one mind-blowing statistic, the TUC estimated that the cumulative loss of wages over the 30 years studied, due to the falling share of GDP going to wages, added up to £1.3trillion! By coincidence, that's also the amount of taxes invested in the bankers' bailout in 2008; taxes garnered from a working class that had been robbed of the same amount over the previous 30 years. Robbed of that sum twice over, in other words; first to bail out profits, then to bail out bankers.

In August 1963, there was a hue and cry about The Great Train Robbery, where Bruce Reynolds, Ronnie Biggs and their 13 pals meticulously planned and executed the theft of £2.6million on the Glasgow to London Royal Mail train. In today's money, the equivalent sum stolen – and never recovered! – would be £48million.

In the past 30-40 years we truly have witnessed the Great Wages Robbery, with sums involved that make Reynolds and Biggs look like petty pickpockets. What's £48million grabbed in The Great Train Robbery by comparison with the £1.3trillion Great Wages Robbery? And in both cases, the loot has never been recovered; in both cases the robbers got away with it – except that Ronnie Biggs and Co were jailed, whereas the capitalist thieves have been praised, fêted and given knighthoods for their 'entrepreneurship'!

* * * *

That trend – the reduction in size of the slice of the cake conceded in workers' wages – has been in full swing for the past 30-40 years. It's not been an accident of nature, nor the outcome of the alleged magical powers of 'supply and demand', but part of a concerted, politically planned and ruthlessly executed assault on workers' rights, workers' conditions and workers' wages.

After the bloody nose administered to the Ted Heath Tories and the British ruling class by the miners and their allies in 1974, the Tories sought revenge. A notorious strategy document circulated within the Tory high command in 1977 was leaked – the Ridley Plan. In it, right-wing founder-member of the Selsdon Group of extreme free-market Tories, Nicholas Ridley, mapped out a carefully planned attack on workers – and the strength of their unions – in one industry and sector at a time.

Ridley spelt out how the next Tory government should choose its battles; stockpile in preparation for a showdown; train and equip a large, mobile squad of police, ready to employ riot tactics against pickets; and, to quote verbatim, "cut off the money supply to strikers and make the union finance them." He made no bones about the underlying motivation behind this manual of monstrous assaults on workers and their unions; he wrote that the unions were too powerful, interfered with 'market forces', and therefore had to be tamed to "restore the profitability of the UK." His proposals were to culminate in the class war launched against the miners in 1984-85.

The subsequent Thatcher-led defeat of the NUM in a year-long 'civil war without bullets', as TV presenter Brian Walden called it, was a decisive watershed in the struggle between workers and employers over who gets the bigger slice of the cake; the battle between labour and capital, pay and profit, that constitutes the fundamental class conflict in any capitalist society. In the 1980s, Maggie Thatcher acted as an unflinching enemy of workers – and their first line of defence, the unions – and waged war on behalf of profit and privilege.

The infamous economic philosophy of Thatcher (and US President Ronald Reagan) derived from Milton Friedman and the Chicago school of economists, at the time labelled 'monetarism', more recently re-branded 'neo-liberalism'. It was an economic body of thought first applied by the fascistic dictatorship of General Pinochet in Chile, after he'd seized power in the bloodthirsty coup of 1973 – with the aid of the American CIA, and to the acclaim of the British Tories, who were the first government to officially recognise Pinochet's regime. The core thinking and aims behind this strand of capitalist thinking was scathingly, succinctly described by the eminent economist J.K. Galbraith in one sentence:

"The poor have too much money, and the rich do not have enough!"

Thatcher and her disciples of monetarism launched an unholy crusade to reverse what they and their class perceived as a wholly unacceptable state of affairs, wherein public welfare and workers' wages were modest and totally inadequate, but from a capitalist viewpoint had taken a few shavings off profit margins. The unions had to be smashed to restore profits at the expense of pay, and to slaughter manufacturing industry in favour of the spivs and speculators of the financial wing of capitalism.

Thatcher and her regime constructed the most vicious battery of anti-union laws of anywhere in Europe. One piece of legislation was piled on another, imposing well-nigh impossible pre-conditions on workers seeking to take action in self-defence from the marauding hordes of employers and the Tory government itself.

Unions had to give employers notice of their intention to hold ballots for any action; lawyers crawled all over the wording of ballots to find loopholes to halt them; lists of members had to be provided, with the risk of outdated home addresses making the ballot illegal; further seven-day notice had to be given before a vote to strike was enacted, enabling employers to prepare to defeat the action; solidarity strikes with fellow workers in the same industry or others were simply banned, as were all strikes deemed 'political', such as ones against privatisation; union funds and assets faced sequestration in a legal battering ram de-signed to smash the power of the unions; blacklisting of union activists was organised, encouraged and allowed to run rampant, whilst scabs were granted almost unlimited rights to sue their union for daring to discipline them for undermining democratically-agreed collective ac-tion. Benefits for the families of strikers were slashed, through changes in law, in order to starve workers into submission... to "cut off the money supply to strikers", as the late, unlamented Old Nick had cal-lously recommended in his secret strategy document years earlier.

The Tories had test runs at smashing the unions at the likes of the Stockport Messenger printers' strike, in late 1983, when they froze the funds of the National Graphical Association in aid of the owner and union-buster, 'the (Eddie) Shah of Warrington'. That dispute was also where I first witnessed the use of baton-wielding mounted police against solidarity mass pickets of the plant – with paramilitary shields and well-rehearsed snatch squads that grabbed peaceful pickets and beat seven colours out of them.

Next came the miners' Titanic year-long battle for survival in 1984-85, and the printers at Wapping, who staged strikes against Rupert Murdoch's News International group, from January 1986. Murdoch sacked the 6,000 printers who resisted his mission to de-recognise the powerful unions, who had won elements of control over hiring-and-firing, as well as winning excellent working conditions. Massive police deployments, over 1,000 arrests of workers, and a virtual curfew of local residents, were some of the methods used – with the back-up of Thatcher's anti-union laws. All to smash one of the most powerfully-organised union workforces in the land, in pursuit of their avowed aim, "to restore the profitability of the UK."

For the miners' strike, the Tory government beefed up police with pay rises, established a national police command centre, deployed para-military-style and mounted police, undercover army personnel and the secret services (planting an MI5 agent at the heart of the NUM leadership, as MI5's former Director General Stella Rimington sub-sequently confessed) – plus merciless media lies and propaganda de-signed to demonise and isolate those workers standing up for themselves, their families and their communities.

* * * *

The Tories in the 1980s consciously decimated whole swathes of manufacturing industry. In part because that was the sector with the most powerful and well-organised unions; but also as part of a short-termist turn towards the interests of the financial, most parasitical wing of capitalism – the bankers and service sectors – rather than in-dustrial capitalism. An entire flank of the capitalist class, their econ-omists, and a big section of the Tories openly advocated the 'virtues' of the French concept of 'a rentier economy'.

They initiated what economists and academics now commonly call the 'financialisation' of the economy. Dominance by the banking and financial services sector, with rampant profiteering through specula-tion, and enormous proportions of the huge and rising profits made by this sector going straight into the pockets of chief executives, di-rectors, financiers and hedge fund managers.

This process has led to the abominable situation where in 1948, manufacturing (including gas and oil extraction, and utilities) ac-counted for 41% of the UK economy, but by 2013 the numerals had reversed, with a pathetic 14% of the economy coming from that pro-ductive sector. That's the fastest decline in manufacturing of any ad-vanced capitalist economy. Over the same time-span (1948-2013), agriculture plummeted from 6% to 1% of the UK economy, whereas the service sector rocketed from 46% to 79% of the total wealth output. A fast buck for the profiteers – a small, particularly parasitic sub-sector of the richest 1% – rather than any concern for the longer-term interests of the national economy.

Britain isn't unique in this burgeoning of a particularly parasitic version of capitalism. In 1950, 2.8% of the US economy was in the financial sector; by 2011 that had rocketed to 8.7% of GDP.

And as an illustration of the fast-track fortunes this meant for the parasitic rich, the highest-income chief executive of any industrial company in the US, in 2013, was Larry Ellison, CEO of Oracle. His combined income from salary, bonuses and stocks that year was $78.4million… converted into sterling, £24,205 an hour! However, he was made to look a 'hobo' by comparison with the top hedge fund manager in the US, Ray Dalio of Bridgewater Associates. His annual income, two years earlier, in 2011, was $3.9billion – £2.5billion. But the parasitism of finance capital in the UK has reached even dizzier heights, accounting for 9.6% of GDP in 2011 – and making up 29% of all service sector exports from Britain – historically 'the workshop of the world'.

And far from being different, Scotland is if anything even more heavily colonised by the get-rich-quick wing of finance capital. One stark statistic captures the parasitism of capitalism in Scotland: prior to the financial meltdown of 2008, a succession of mergers and hostile takeovers meant the Royal Bank of Scotland had assets worth £1.9trillion – that's more than the entire annual national wealth production (GDP) of the whole of Britain at the time!

This is the sector of capitalism that more than any fails to add value or add to society's welfare. It simply finds ever-more perversely ingenious ways of siphoning off profits and wealth from other corners of the economy into the pockets of the financial oligarchy. To borrow the memorable image of Matt Taibbi of *Rolling Stone* magazine, in his condemnation of Wall Street in 2009:

"This is a great vampire squid wrapped around the face of humanity, relentlessly jamming its blood funnel into anything that smells like money"!

The failure of the previous generation of British capitalists to invest and modernise industry left them utterly incapable of competing with the likes of their German or Japanese competitors. Witness the shipyard industry, where by the 1970s, for every £1 invested in machinery per worker in the UK, Japanese shipyard workers had over £3.50 of capital investment at their elbow.

But on top of that, the political decision in the 1980s to deliberately wreck manufacturing industry left mass unemployment and social degradation in its wake in whole communities, which in turn were used to drive down the wages of those in the remaining jobs. The Tories whipped up fear and despair, to clear the path to ratchet up profits for the parasitic class they unashamedly represented.

Over the subsequent 30 years, the ruling elite in Britain have continued that baleful tradition of not ploughing profits back into investment in the real economy. Profits have risen through the roof; investment has fallen through the floor. As Stewart Lansley and Howard Reed explained in their research for the TUC in their publication *How to Boost the Wage Share*, the profits share of the national economy (GDP) has risen from about 25% in the 1950s and 1960s, to over 30% of GDP since 1980.

But in the same periods, capitalist investment from these profits – both in the form of Gross Fixed Capital Formation and Research and Development – has slumped from about 20% of GDP to 15% or less. The investment rate by the capitalist class in Britain currently, in 2015, is the lowest of any country in the rich G20 states. Amounting to the equivalent of 15% of the UK's GDP, the British capitalists act like billionaire misers, even by comparison with their kindred exploiters abroad: the French capitalists last year invested the equivalent of 25% of national GDP, and the Canadian 22%. And they're getting even stingier with old age: the amount of capital investment in 2013 was 16.2% less than in 2008.

Instead of reinvestment to modernise the economy, this ultra-parasitic wing of the capitalist class have poured their plentiful profits down the throats of company chief executives, hedge fund managers and corporate directors in financial packages, and in a modern mania of mergers and hostile company takeovers.

For instance, the Royal Bank of Scotland's $100billion takeover of Dutch bank ABM Amro in 2007; Glaxo Wellcome's takeover of pharmaceutical giant SmithKlineBeecham in 2000; and the £112billion squandered by Vodafone in seizing control of Mannesman in 2000. That's parasitism given dictionary definition in action: profiteers feeding off the body of other organisms, doing nothing productive for the benefit of society as a whole.

* * * *

Alongside their decimation of productive industry in favour of parasitic 'financialisation' of the economy, the rich, ruling elite has systematically fought to dismantle the one major force standing in their way, as they rob wages to engorge the profiteers: the trade unions. As academics Dr Lydia Hayes and Professor Tonia Novitz published in July 2014, it is no accident that inequality was at its lowest in the period when well over half the British workforce – 58%; 13 million workers – were members of unions, and 82% of them were covered by collective union bargaining on wages and conditions. Nor sheer coincidence that by 2012 Britain sported its worst levels of inequality ever, since records began, when union membership was down at 26% (including only 18% of private sector workers), with a mere 23% of UK workers covered by collective bargaining between employers and workers' unions.

Britain sits at a derisory 21st out of 27 EU countries in its level of union representation in workplaces. It is also the second-worst – only the USA is worse – of all the world's advanced economies for the percentage of workers earning below two-thirds of national median earnings. These two facts are conjoined twins, two parts of the same feature. For all their shortcomings, the collective organisation of workers through unions makes a huge difference in the share of wealth won back in wages.

The experience of the past 30 years' Great Wages Robbery proves beyond doubt the need to revive the size and fighting strength of workers' unions – including the right to collective bargaining – to help win decent wages in this fabulously rich economy. Intertwined with that is the dire need to overcome the terrible weakness and downright refusal of many trade union leaderships to fight back for workers and their share of the wealth they create. One of the pivotal tasks of this age is the urgent need to win socialist leaderships and members' democratic control of the unions, so their potential is unleashed in a war on poverty pay.

6

PROPAGANDA AGAINST THE POOR

In dredging up excuses for their attacks on working class people, the Tories are like a desperate crowd at a Jumble Sale, scavenging a pile of discarded rubbish in search of something 'new'. In their ruthless blitz on benefits, slaughter of public services and jobs, and wipe-out of workers' rights, they adorn the rubbish of the past 200 years or more.

There is nothing new about branding people 'skivers' or 'scroungers', as the marauding Old Etonians that infest the Westminster Cabinet unleash the cruellest cuts to benefits and public provision of the post-World War Two period. There is nothing original about trying to poison the working class majority with division and bitterness between themselves, to help the obnoxiously rich engorge themselves on the fat of the land. There is nothing 21st century about dressing up cuts to incomes that have driven some people to suicide as if it was a moral duty to humanity being benignly enacted by Cameron, Osborne or Business Secretary Sajid Javid. Previous generations of Tories, landowners, capitalists and their ideological apologists rehearsed all these pernicious excuses as far back as the 18th century, and throughout the Victorian era.

In more ancient times, Britain's Poor Laws of 1597 and 1601 were cruel enough, but they at least acknowledged poverty as a social condition; as the position of those who did not possess property. The Poor Law Guardians of that age at least seemed to recognise that unemployment was a feature intrinsic to the workings of the economy, rather than the fault of the unemployed.

Fast forward to the late 18th century and as economic crises threw more and more at the mercy of their parishes, some ideologues of the rich began to redefine poverty as if it was not only a moral, but even a biological condition that had to be stamped out by cruelty, not kindness. So, in 1786, a clergyman called Joseph Townsend wrote a notorious *Dissertation on the Poor Laws* in which he stated:

"The poor know little of the motives which stimulate the higher ranks to action. In general it is only hunger which can spur and goad them into labour. Yet our laws have said they shall never hunger."

Two decades later, in 1798, Thomas Malthus wrote *An Essay On The Principle of Population*, in which he argued that Poor Relief causes poverty, destroys the work ethic, reducing productivity. Further, he argued it "creates an incentive to reproduce", drawing his conclusions that "poverty should be tackled through shame and withdrawal of assistance" and more coldly cruel and reactionary still:

"Nature should take its course. If people were left to starve to death, the balance between population and food supply would be restored."

The crude barbarism of early capitalist development tossed hordes of people onto the dung-heap of 'surplus to requirement', and rising numbers therefore depended on Poor Relief to avert literal starvation – the Malthusian method of culling the plebs that many of the propertied class subscribed to. Those with property began to rear up in revolt at having to pay the Poor Rate, a mild tax levied to provide a pittance to those discarded like used rags by the manufacturing and agricultural system of capitalism. The propertied classes blamed rural poverty on immorality, imprudence and low productivity, all – they alleged – caused by Poor Relief, which they claimed "educated a new generation in idleness, ignorance and dishonesty."

These were the dishonest 'moral' arguments, of the idle rich, entirely ignorant of the realities facing the victims of the built-in lunacies of their economic system – which relies on a mass reserve 'surplus' population to fill in the gaps during boom years, callously tossing them back on the scrapheap during recessions.

By 1832, the Reform Act extended the franchise to wider numbers of those with property, which in turn obliged them to pay Poor Rates. They wielded their political monopoly over the right to vote – the propertyless masses didn't have a vote – to amend the Poor Laws in 1834, creating a regime of unimaginable cruelty. This centred round the Workhouses, a system where families were broken up and effectively imprisoned, used as forced labour, with brutal punishment beatings meted out. This abomination lived on in practice and then in folk memory for a major part of the 20th century: I remember in my childhood, in Ireland, older friends and relatives speak with a mixture of fear and loathing about 'the workhouse', with some of the buildings still standing in local villages.

* * * *

That was then, but what about now? What about the 'compassionate Conservatism' mouthed by Cameron's Tories in 2015; the 'party of working people' as they've recently dubbed the modern inheritors of this appalling history of cruelty, inhumanity and exploitation? Well, the Jumble Sale of ideological dirty rags from the 18th and 19th centuries has provided the oh-so-modern Tories with a whole wardrobe of ideas on how to scapegoat and demonise the poorest, how to batter them into even worse depths of deprivation, and how to whip up a frenzy of acceptance of their vicious cruelty amongst at least some of the less independent-thinking population.

Iain Duncan Smith, longstanding Tory Welfare boss, declared a Damascean conversion on the road to Easterhouse in 2002, forswearing a determination to tackle the appalling poverty he witnessed there, declaring a revival of 'compassionate Conservatism'. Back in the real world of Tory Britain, the same IDS since repeated one of the vicious, ill-informed nostrums of his predecessors 230 years ago when he declaimed against "the damaging culture of welfare dependency." This, and similar phrases, he trots out as he slashes the incomes of the sick, disabled, children and workers (in and out of work), as part of the Great Benefits Robbery of recent times.

In the July 2015 Emergency Budget – what emergency? – they keep telling us that Britain is booming; that it's 'the bounce-back kid'? – multi-millionaire George Osborne carved out plans of truly Malthusian stock. He restricted child benefits – including top-ups to low-paid workers' family incomes – to the first two children per family.

That's one way to halt the inconvenient growth of the working class; stop them breeding, leave procreation to the rich, implement Malthus' reactionary notions of population control through starvation. And as a throwback to the teachings of Townsend in 1786, the Tories have smuggled a battalion of 350 psychologists into Job Centres, presumably treating unemployment not as an inevitable by-product of the Tories' beloved capitalist system, but as a mental health disorder blighting people who subsequently become 'the unemployed'.

It's the centuries-old trick of blaming the poor for poverty, of blaming the brolly for the torrential rain. It's a consciously crafted ideological war on working class people and universal state provisions, designed to stop the working class majority population from identifying the real causes, and therefore the real solutions.

But there's hope for us yet. In contrast to earlier centuries, working class people in this country are vast in number, widely educated, in at least some cases organised into collective entities like the trade unions and community campaigns, and not so willing to swallow the poisonous propaganda of the Tories and the class of shameless parasites whose eager mouthpieces they are.

* * * *

In their mission to dismantle the welfare state, redistributing wealth away from the needy to the greedy – from the millions to the millionaires – the 2010-15 Westminster Tory/Lib Dem Coalition and their pliant media indulged in a sustained, dirty lie. They tried to portray those in poverty as the 'work-shy', 'scroungers', 'skivers'. On this demonisation of the poorest, the Cameron-Clegg government only extended and escalated the propaganda offensive of their New Labour predecessors, who spoke of 'strivers and skivers', 'workers and shirkers', with former Labour Shadow Chancellor Ed Ball blurting out the line, "Labour are not the party of those on benefits; the clue is in the name."

Thirteen years of Labour governments paved the road and sharpened the knives for the Old Etonian butchers. Blair (and Brown) acted as a latter-day John the Baptist preparing for the arrival of Christ, with the Biblical exhortation: "Prepare the way of the Lord; make his paths straight."

Labour initiated Workfare schemes and benefit sanctions, a regime of punishment beatings which is now driving 70,000 a month into destitution. They introduced the system of Working Capacity Assessments in 2007 – an inhumane crusade to drive the sick and disabled off marginally higher benefits which has meant nearly 90 people died every month after being declared fit to work: a total of 2,380 from December 2011 to February 2014.

More recently, in March 2015, Labour's Shadow Secretary of State for Work and Pensions, Rachel Reeves, made sure nobody was left in any doubt about her party's convergence with the Tories in their demonisation of sections of the working class. As Labour pledged to carry out at least 90% of the austerity cuts planned by the Tories, though perhaps a little more slowly, Reeves declared:

"We are not the party of people on benefits. We don't want to be seen, and we're not, the party to represent those who are out of work."

The recently-elected Tory government (well, elected by 24% of eligible UK voters, or a minuscule 10% of those in Scotland), is hellbent on an even shriller denunciation campaign, as they launched a 100-day blitzkrieg on benefits, aiming to carry through their three-year plan of attack on working class people in just two years. Cameron's emboldened Tories are out to blitz benefits, slaughter services and wipe out workers' rights. They clearly plan the social and economic equivalent of George W. Bush's infamous 'shock and awe' military onslaught in Iraq, designed to overwhelm any resistance, through the sheer scale and speed of their attacks.

This shrieking chorus of demonisation by the Etonian boot-boys is designed to divide and conquer working class people, to set the employed and unemployed at each other's throats, to divide the sick and disabled from those all the mainstream parties keep hypocritically banging on about: 'hard-working families'.

TV shows like *Benefits Street* are used to maliciously demonise the poorest, and whole working class communities, to soften up the wider population for assaults on benefits and public services. To blame the poor for poverty. They've rightly been dubbed 'poverty porn'. When will we see a TV series called Bankers' Boulevard, portraying the hooligan spending habits and gut-wrenching greed of the money-men who brought the economy to the brink of collapse in 2008? And got bailed out to the tune of £1.3trillion from the public purse, so they could go on seizing their bonuses from this state subsidy of the criminally rich. Or which channel will boldly broadcast something called Tax Dodgers' Drive, to give the viewing public an insight into the obscene opulence of a bunch of big business criminals who rob society of at least £120billion a year in tax dodges? That's £2,000 a year stolen from every man, woman and child in the UK by this tiny gang of capitalist thieves. Sad to say, the repeated waves of such divisive propaganda, under both the Coalition and previous Labour governments, have left an imprint on the thinking of many. As the Child Poverty Action Group reported in October 2014, back in 1993 a full 50% of people thought benefits were too low, but in 2011 a mere 19% of people thought so. Whenever they succeed in splitting one layer of the working class from others, the rich elite laugh all the way to the bank – including banks in offshore tax havens where they systematically dodge paying tax, on an industrial scale.

* * * *

It's a damned, dirty lie, to portray those out of work as scroungers who sit back in the lap of luxury. Their accusers should try living on £70-80 a week benefits, not for a gimmicky week, but for a sustained period, and see if they still think it's 'a lifestyle choice' to rely on state benefits! And it's a consciously crafted lie, even according to the government's own Department for Work and Pensions, which in 2014 reported that:

> "Eight out of nine of the people out of work are looking for a job, or feel prevented from doing so by their circumstances, such as mental health problems, disability or caring responsibilities."

You only need recall the queues of people applying for even the lowest-paid jobs to see this claim – that it's people too lazy to work that bring poverty on themselves – for the filthy lie it is. To take but one example, the GMB union 'awarded' retail giant Next a series of ASBOs at street protests in mid-2014, "for failing to make work pay." The GMB were highlighting Next's reliance on derisory pay, short-hours contracts (with 30% of the jobs being less than twelve hours a week) and zero hours contracts for their fabulous profits. In reply, these brazen profiteers boasted that "staff will get £6.70 an hour from June 2014." Yet when Next announced 1,200 vacancies, 45% of them for temporary jobs, they got 30 applicants for every single vacancy!

More fundamental still is the fact that 'the unemployed' are not some separate species; some kind of standing army forever removed from those of us in work, with entirely separate interests. The blunt fact is that people are constantly moving in and out of jobs, on and off unemployment benefits, living the spreading uncertainties and anxieties of life under 21st century capitalism. There are pockets of the most pauperised who have suffered long-term unemployment; in some cases for more than one generation in the same family. But they are a small minority, and certainly not to be envied for their life of luxury! However, as the Joseph Rowntree Foundation pointed out in November 2014, 51% of those on Job Seekers Allowance had been on it for less than six months – despite Scotland having just come through a recession, and despite the huge numbers of applicants for every job vacancy on offer.

Those who do get jobs then discover work is no longer a route out of poverty. They soon discover that the Tories' 'justifications' for savage, life-threatening benefits cuts and sanctions – their assertions that they are merely taking steps 'to make work pay' – is a filthy fiction, a low-down lie by the party of the idle rich. In recent years, Scotland and Britain has shifted from the plague of mass unemployment to the pestilence of mass poverty pay.

7

A MILLION MODERN SERFS

Jim is a McDonald's worker in Glasgow. He recently described to me the daily realities facing up to 120,000 Scottish workers hired on zero hours contracts (ZHCs).

"I'm on a zero hours contract at McDonald's, on the £6.50 minimum wage. The majority of people I work beside are on less because they're under 21. A big majority are young people, either still at school or at university. I've never worked a shift where my entire day's wages wasn't taken in sales in half-an-hour, and often literally in minutes. Yesterday the place was dead, but the first order was for £85, which covered the two kitchen staff's wages for the whole day. I've just done three shifts in a row that were from 4.30am until 2.30pm, then the next day from 1pm until 10pm, followed by a day off and then 4pm until 2am. And that's not unusual shifts for me. My body-clock is f***ed. I can't sleep."

Zero hours contracts perfectly encapsulate the disgustingly exploitative system we live under. These are the ultimate in casual labour, the pinnacle of job insecurity, the worst extremes of the 'race to the bottom' on workers' rights and conditions. They are increasingly at the very heart of the spreading pestilence of poverty pay. All in the name of profit maximisation.

Far from being on the obscure margins of the labour market, zero hours contracts are growing at an unprecedented rate, encouraged by the main employers' organisations. To use but one illustrative quote, in February 2015 the Institute of Directors described zero hours contracts as "an extremely attractive proposition." And they're allowed to flourish like noxious weeds by the mainstream pro-capitalist political parties.

Up until about three years ago the Office of National Statistics estimated around 250,000 workers in the UK suffered these contracts; condemnation enough of 21st-century capitalist Britain. But in 2013, a survey by the Chartered Institute of Personnel and Development (CIPD) put the estimate at over a million – 4% of the entire workforce – and growing astronomically in the last two or three years. The government's own ONS since reinforced and coloured in this miserable picture of rampant job insecurity, when they published figures for the number of actual contracts: 1.4 million in January 2013, rising to 1.8 million by August 2014. That takes account of the fact some individual workers are so desperate to survive that they have more than one zero hours contract.

In Scotland, the STUC showed in May 2014 there are nearly 120,000 workers – 118,720 – cursed with this modern form of serfdom. And far from any slowdown in the spread of this serfdom – Third Millennium-style – in just the first three months following the election of Cameron's Tory dictatorship in May 2015, the numbers relying on zero hours contracts in Scotland for some form of work rocketed by a full 20%.

One other thing that needs to be made crystal clear: zero hours contracts are not some passing phase, a temporary measure to fit into adjustments by companies – let alone a stop-gap arrangement of shifts that suit workers changing their career path. They are increasingly not just standard practice, but long-term forms of employment. Recent research demonstrates that 44% of zero hours contracts jobs have lasted more than two years with the same employer. An incredible 25% of them last over five years with the same employer. So what we have is not a temporary, mutually helpful flexibility of working patterns; it's permanent insecurity for workers, long-term uncertainty, permanent impermanence.

* * * *

Zero hours contracts (ZHCs) give all the flexibility to the employers and all the risk and insecurity to the workers on them. It means being contracted to work for a particular employer, but with absolutely no guarantee of how many hours of work you get – if any – and insistence that the worker is on call, unpaid, ready to work whenever asked to. It's fully flexible exploitation. Such workers are tied to a low-paying employer by chains of desperation and uncertainty. Capitalist apologists for this system claim it suits people who want flexibility on the hours they work. That may apply to a tiny handful. But their argument is utter baloney, a cover-up for a system of ruthless exploitation. One of the many High Street outfits using them – Subway – summarises the reality in the wording of their contracts:

> "The company has no duty to provide you with work. Your hours of work are not predetermined and will be notified to you on a weekly basis as soon as is practicable by your store manager. The company has the right to require you to work varied and extended hours from time to time."

But just to leave nobody in any doubt about the surrender of rights involved, Subway also make it a precondition of being hired that workers waive their rights (under European Working Time Regulations) to have the working week limited to 48 hours. So, you could be dragged in to work more than 48 hours one week, but literally no hours the next, and all along you are contracted to Subway, unable to get work with another firm, and only paid for the actual hours worked. Of course it's all perfectly legal.

Allegedly, workers on these contracts have the right to decline offers of work. The beauty of flexibility, we're assured. In reality there's absolutely no such choice. Numerous reports give accounts of people being starved of hours after they have said 'No' to a particular shift. They are frequently left with no work at all for weeks on end, because the employers can use ZHCs as a weapon to reward, reprimand or punish people according to their whim – the exploiters' ultimate dream of control.

As one Edinburgh woman reported, she'd been denied any work as a Home Carer for several weeks after asking for a day off for her child's medical appointment. I know a Home Care worker who got non-stop shifts for several months, sleepovers included, back-to-back shifts often, and then barely any work at all for months after she took a week's holiday (unpaid of course). In the end she gave up and left the job.

So it's a case of 'choose zero hours contracts, choose punishment'. And 'choose zero rights'. Such chaotic insecurity over hours, and therefore wages, are not the only consequences. Zero hours contracts also involve zero guarantee of sick pay, holiday pay, or redundancy pay. As Citizens Advice Scotland recently reported:

"We have advised people on zero hours contracts who've been denied taking any holidays, given no sick pay and therefore unable to go into hospital for necessary operations."

In the same CAS report, they confirm the pattern of punishment for workers who dare to differ:

"If they complain, it's far too easy for employers to simply stop giving them any work – basically dismissing them without any process being followed."

In other words, this form of enslavement without rights means the sack or redundancy, without an investigation procedure or redundancy packages.

Working zero hours contracts makes it virtually impossible to plan your life, particularly for workers with childcare responsibilities, or other care duties, not to mention the impact on family and social life. As one Edinburgh care worker explained:

"You basically have to take what hours you're given. So on any typical week I might have a Friday off when I'd rather be working, but then have to make up my hours on a Sunday when I want to spend time with the kids."

It makes it a nightmare to meet the bills and budget for daily life – and because there is no fixed, regular weekly wage involved, it makes it almost impossible to negotiate the benefits system, such as Working Tax Credits and childcare allowances. TUC research last year proved people on ZHCs are five times more likely to have varied wages than others, with at least one in three reporting they get no regular income. It's widely accepted that a major source of stress at work is lack of control over the job. These contracts are storing up an explosion of mental ill-health.

The one million-plus workers (120,000-plus in Scotland) subjected to this form of excruciating insecurity are also concentrated in the lowest-paid sectors of employment – and indeed that is one of the aims of these contracts. It's a low payers' paradise. The Tory government might claim it just blesses workers with infinite flexibility without reducing incomes. On the contrary. According to research by the TUC in 2014, workers on zero hours contracts earned an average £188-a-week, compared with £479-a-week for workers on permanent contracts. Plus they get an average of only 21 hours' work a week – compared to 32 hours for the rest. Only 23% of ZHC workers get more than 35 hours' work a week, compared with 60% of other employees.

Zero hours contracts workers are five times less likely to qualify for Statutory Sick Pay than employees on other contracts; a staggering 39% of ZHC workers (2014 figures) earn below the threshold of £112-a-week required. These figures also prove the simple, brutal truth: workers on ZHCs earn drastically lower hourly wages than other workers. Overwhelmingly, these contracts and the bare minimum legal minimum wage are two links in the same chain of super-exploitation. The STUC found that half of all on zero hours contracts earn less than £15,000-a-year... whereas, don't forget, the overall average wage last year was £27,200. The low pay and inherent uncertainty of these types of jobs also block workers from credit-worthiness or mortgages – adding to the downward spiral towards falling into the clutches of Pay Day Loan sharks, and reliance on parents for accommodation, or the grisly alternative of substandard housing, including with rent-racketeering private landlords.

* * * *

These contracts are not confined to the hidden undergrowth of the Scottish or British economy – nor are they the preserve of unscrupulous backstreet employers, or small firms struggling to survive, cutting labour costs. Quite the opposite. They are habitually chosen by the High Street cowboys as the preferred method of exploitation. The government's own Workplace Employment Relations Survey of late 2011 found that 6% of workplaces with less than 50 workers used them, whereas twice that proportion (11%) of workplaces with 50-99 workers did so – and a whopping 23% of workplaces employing 100 or more.

Household names exploit the power to dictate that ZHCs offer them. We've already mentioned Subway. Sports Direct has been exposed and shown 'the Red Card' by SSP protests against them hiring 20,000 of their 23,000 workers under ZHCs. Burger King uses them extensively to hand out low pay whoppers. Dominos Pizzas grabs a huge slice of profits by using them. Pizza Hut tries to deny using them, with smokescreens about "small business franchises deciding their own hours." Delegating their dirty work, more like. The truth behind Pizza Hut's weasel words was spelt out by one of their workers in Glasgow:

"It's all about 'business needs'. If I was on a shift and it's not busy, you're sent home. If you're off, and it gets busy, they phone you to come in. I once asked for a few days' holiday. I was told it wasn't possible. I came in to the shift and was sent home! You can refuse to go home but it damages your prospects. There's no respect for staff."

McDonald's, with 90% of their staff (82,000 in the UK) on them, dish out Big Mac starvation wages. JD Wetherspoon hire 80% of their staff this way. Others include Boots (4,000); Next; Cineworld; National Galleries; National Museums of Scotland; Tate Galleries; The National Trust; Buckingham Palace (one of the homes of the biggest family of benefit scroungers in the land); and the Kirk of Scotland's social care wing... to name only some of the ruthless exploiters of people's desperation.

Labour councils are up to their necks in this exploitation too: directly in some cases – and indirectly through work they've contracted out in a vast number of local authorities. A bad case of slave labour under New Labour. During the 2015 General Election, Labour politicians competed with SNP politicians in promises of 'tough action' and 'clamping down' on what both parties repeatedly called 'exploitative zero hours contracts'. On the very eve of polling day, it was confirmed that Glasgow City Labour council, and its arms length offshoots – ALEOS – employ 1,689 people on ZHCs. That's a giant 18% increase on the 1,436 they hired a year ago. Is that 'tough action', Labour style? Or are these not 'exploitative' versions of zero hours contracts? As if there was any other form!

That is perfectly predictable from the same party that spent 13 recent years in government doing absolutely nothing to scrap these pernicious contracts, but a hell of a lot driving forward the outsourcing, privatisation and public sector cuts that have driven hundreds of thousands into choosing between zero hours contracts and zero work. Nor are Labour the only guilty party. *The Herald* reported in August 2013 that at least twelve out of Scotland's 32 local authorities hire staff on zero hours contracts... subjecting well over 7,000 people in total to this insecure state of existence.

Ten out of Scotland's 14 health boards use ZHCs. Stuart worked in the Beardmore hotel, attached to the NHS-owned Jubilee hospital in Clydebank, which caters for patients' relatives from across the whole of Scotland.

"I had no fixed hours. I was told on the Friday or Saturday what rota I'd be on the next week. I worked there for eight years. But I was hired and then fired every twelve weeks to avoid employment rights! I'd work for twelve weeks, then get no hours and no pay the 13th week, then back on the rota the 14th week for another twelve weeks."

Education is colonised by ZHCs. Four Scottish universities – Edinburgh, Glasgow, Dundee and Napier – hire over 4,700 on them. Nearly 3,000 of them are tutors or support staff. In some cases the odium of zero hours contracts is thinly disguised by university authorities using a less contentious-sounding name: Hours To Be Notified (HTBN) contracts. As Shakespeare might have said, "What's in a name? That which we call a rose by any other name would smell as sweet" – or stinking, in this case.

One in four public sector employers use ZHCs, as do one in three voluntary sector employers. The ONS has confirmed that 35% of all education employers use them, as do 27% of all healthcare employers – with 100,000 people tied to this institutionalised uncertainty in the health sector alone. The union UNISON has proven that 41% of all home care workers are on them.

The areas of greatest concentration include hotels, catering and leisure; education, and healthcare. And the ruthless Michael O'Leary's Ryanair – the biggest airline in Europe – employs an incredible 75% of its 2,625 pilots on zero hours contracts, as part of a regime of bullying and sackings aimed at gagging these highly skilled workers from raising concerns and criticisms about the frightening breaches of safety in pursuit of skyrocketing profit.

* * * *

Are these forms of employment new? Why are they growing with such relentless speed? The media has only recently caught up with their existence, but ZHCs have been increasingly common since the late 1980s, and are indeed part of a much broader, deeper trend towards casual, insecure work since the mid-1970s. But what is new is the sheer scale of their use.

For about 30 years after World War Two, governments – both Labour and Tory – tended to aim at full employment, reluctantly tolerated the strength of the trade unions, and generally thought rising wages and secure employment was good for capitalism. It provided a growing market for their goods amongst millions of workers on better wages than their parents or grandparents – and the power of organised workers' unions won wages as their highest share of total national wealth on record by 1975. That changed with the first signs of crisis in their profit-based system in the mid-1970s, when UK governments began to claw back the gains working people had won in previous generations, so as to boost the flagging rates of profit for the capitalist minority at the time.

Thatcher's government in particular unleashed civil war against workers' conditions, seeking to smash the ability of trade unions to resist, deploying the weapon of mass unemployment to drive down wages. In subsequent years both Tory and Labour governments obeyed the orders of the bankers and capitalists, ripped manufacturing apart, concentrated far more on financial capitalism's interests and low-paid service sector employment.

Alongside deregulation of work and globalisation of capitalism, this swung the balance of power decisively to the employers, unleashing a reign of terror in workplaces, which accelerated in the wake of the miners' defeat in 1985.

New Labour governments carried on where the Tories left off in fashioning the conditions for maximum profit at the expense of workers' wages and conditions: neo-liberalism, what Tony Blair boasted was "the least regulated labour market in Europe."

Privatisation was a major driver, for instance fuelling local authorities' current hunt for the cheapest bidder through outsourced contracts for the likes of home care services, where a vast array of private companies bid for the care of as few as one elderly person, cutting costs to win the contract by hiring people on zero hours contracts. During the first three years of the 2010-15 Westminster Coalition government, half a million public sector jobs disappeared. These jobs were 'permanent'. These jobs butchers unblushingly claimed to have performed a latter-day miracle of Biblical proportions by reducing unemployment in the midst of a recession. But this apparent miracle is a mirage. It's explained by the fact that most of the jobs created since 2008 are either agency work, enforced part-time, zero hours contracts, and half of them are temporary.

That is the real context of the galloping growth of zero hours contracts. They are not a lifestyle choice for workers who prefer 'flexibility'. They are one major strand to the package of casualised, insecure, low-paid work that is imposed on desperate people, in pursuit of short-term profit boosts to the employers. A consciously fashioned device to drive down wages through horrendous and chronic job insecurity, accompanied by a reign of fear in workplaces to keep workers 'in their place'.

Back in the mid-1990s, when many of us who were the founders of the SSP were at the heart of building Scottish workers' solidarity (over a sustained period of three years, 1995-8) with the 500 locked-out Liverpool dockers, I often wrote and spoke of "casualisation being the curse of the modern working class."

That was a subject especially dear to the hearts of dockers, whose predecessors had fought fearlessly, and with terrible self-sacrifices, to end the casual labour system on the docks. A system that meant workers lining up in the dockers' pen of a morning, hoping to be picked by the gaffers for a day's work at a time, praying not to be one of the many slouching home in despair to their starving families because they'd not been given work. Left standing, deflated, in the pen, because their face didn't fit, they were too outspoken, or active in the unions.

Nowadays, instead of forming up in the pen, workers blessed with zero hours contracts sit by the phone or keep an eye on their emails, hoping to be offered work, never knowing exactly when or if the offer will arrive, nor for how many hours. Marion is a 20-year-old from Edinburgh who took a job in Next to save up to go to university.

"Instead of the regular hours I thought I was being offered, I had to check each night at 9pm or 10pm to find out what hours – if any – I was getting the next day. It made it impossible to plan medical appointments, holidays or a social life."

That is 21st century casualisation – a modern form of serfdom, where you're tied to an employer who in return offers absolutely no guarantees of work or other entitlements. The Institute of Directors praise this system as providing 'flexible labour', of being "a very attractive prospect." Bosses' organisations boast it is better to have 20 hours' work one week and none the next than to be unemployed.

If ZHCs are so good for the health of the economy, why bother having any laws whatsoever that limit the 'flexibility' of workers' exploitation? Why not repeal the 1874 Factory Act that banned work by children under-10 in factories? Or the 1847 Ten-Hour Act that limited child labour to ten hours a day? Or the 1841 Mines Act banning kids aged under-10 from working down pits? Why not just openly, honestly advocate a return to Victorian times?

Every minor or major improvement in working class conditions, at work or in communities, had to be fought for in the face of vicious repression from capitalists, their politicians, their media and their state agencies – because under the system of wage-slavery known as capitalism, better wages and conditions eat into profit margins. We need our eyes wide open to this historic truth in fighting to scrap zero hours contracts.

We can't passively rely on governments to outlaw exploitation. Successive governments have shredded workers' rights, in the crusade to shore up capitalist profit margins on the backs of millions struggling to cope with the miserly wages granted them. Self-organisation of the working class is pivotal to pounding those in power into reforms that would transform the lives of the million modern serfs on zero hours contracts.

Demands should not be restricted to the Westminster government alone, even though that's where power over employment legislation lies. The trade union movement, socialists and campaigners against this iniquitous form of precarious work should of course expose and embarrass individual employers using them, demanding secure contracts and union rights instead. But they should also hammer at the doors of councils and the Scottish Government to not only ban use of ZHCs in their own direct workforces, but also refuse contracts to any outfit using them, until such time as the jobs are brought back 'in-house', as part of a wider reversal of privatisation, in all its guises.

The trade union movement should launch a massive recruitment drive amongst unorganised workers, demanding the outright banning of all zero hours contracts, fighting instead for secure and permanent jobs for all – including full-time jobs for all who want them. Jobs with full union rights and recognition, so that workers have the collective power to negotiate and enforce genuine flexibility of working hours; family-friendly starting and finishing times; a living minimum wage; and equal rights to holidays, sick pay, redundancy – instead of employers having unilateral power to exploit an army of 'precarious workers' with the aid of the bosses' 'flexible friends', zero hours contracts.

Alongside the monster known as Zero Hours Contracts stands its little sister, Nominal (or Short)-Hours Contracts. They are both part of the growing, dysfunctional family of Casual Labour that haunts the modern working class. Nominal/Short-Hours Contracts are those where the part-time worker is only guaranteed a few hours a week: six, eight, or twelve hours being all too typical. From the employers' perspective this gives them the power to add an unspecified number of hours in a busy week for the business, but with absolutely no contractual obligation to do so every week, or even regularly. On top of the flexibility this affords employers, cutting the margins to maximise profits, it removes any need to pay overtime premium rates for the additional hours worked.

It is no accident that in one of the chief concentrations of low pay and part-time work – retail – one of the most frequent flashpoints between workers and management is over 'availability and flexibility'. Workers on low/nominal-hours contracts are expected to shunt around the rest of their lives to suit 'business needs'. To cancel family plans, or disrupt their sleep patterns, in order to work during peak business hours, with no fixed pattern of rotas. It's the same upheaval as faced by the army of zero hours contracts workers in retail, fast food joints and the care sector – except that they enjoy the guarantee of a minimal number of hours a week, commonly eight to twelve. Again, as with those on zero hours contracts, failure to be suitably available and flexible when the business demands it leads to pressure, conflict, and ultimately 'managed removal' from the job.

An in-depth survey by the TUC in April 2015 found that 700,000 reported themselves as being on ZHCs. A further 820,000 workers described themselves as underemployed, on 0-19 hours a week. Underemployed, short-hours contract workers are typically on much lower pay. The average for those on less than a 20-hour week is £8.40 an hour, compared with £13.20 for all employees. On this average hourly wage they'd have to work 18 hours before paying National Insurance Contributions. In 2014-15, the Weekly Secondary Threshold – the point at which employers must start paying NIC – was £153. Therefore, the average short-hours contract worker, on £8.40-an-hour, would need to work 18.2 hours before their boss would start contributing NIC. So employers are gifted an inherent incentive to offer fewer hours and lower hourly pay to avert NIC contributions.

Women account for 71% of the underemployed on nominal/short-hours contracts. Retail is the worst affected; 29% of all such workers are to be found in supermarkets, shops, warehouses and garages... nearly 250,000 of them. Education (accounting for another 16% of the underemployed); accommodation and food services (14%); health and social care (12%) make up other large chunks of those in these 'micro-jobs'. Zero hours contracts, short-hours contracts and low-paid, bogus self-employed jobs not only cut tax revenues, but have dragged down productivity in Britain.

Tiny contract hours like these may suit a tiny handful of workers. But for the vast majority on them, it's a case of 'little or nothing' – a few hours a week rather than no hours of work, frequently with the hounding, harassment and benefits sanctions that accompany the latter 'choice'. Surveys of part-time workers prove that an astonishing 40% of them want more hours – but can't get them.

* * * *

Not everyone wants a full-time job. Flexibility, both in the number of hours worked and the starting/finishing times, are an increasingly important aspect of working conditions which the unions need to organise for, allowing for care duties, travel arrangements and work/life balance in general. But right now, all the power to dictate the number of hours guaranteed per week rests with the employers, and they rip the profit out of a super-exploited army of workers on either literally Zero, or Nominal/Short-Hours Contracts.

The balance of power in the workplace and labour market needs to be transformed in favour of workers. Otherwise all talk of living in a democracy is empty chatter, false to the core, when there's no workplace democracy. That in turn requires vastly wide-ranging changes, including full rights to join and organise workers' unions; the constitutional right to strike after a simple majority vote; and ultimately workers' democratic control over day-to-day decisions. It was precisely elements of such workers' control that the employers and their government unleashed a class war against, in their showdown with the likes of the print-workers' unions in the mid-1980s. But one immediate reform that would lift the burden of insecurity from many part-time workers' shoulders, and transfer much of the power to workers in determining working patterns, would be to legally oblige all employers to guarantee a set minimum number of contracted hours per week – alongside the battle for a maximum working week (without loss of earnings) of 35 hours, as a step towards a four-day week.

In my own workplace, I managed to negotiate a package that not only scrapped the pernicious feature of shifts of less than four hours (which made it not worth the journey and cost of travel to work for three hours – or on occasion, 2.5 hours), but also means new jobs advertised now guarantee at least a 16-hours-a-week contract.

It's a complex issue: seeking to eliminate the precarious jobs sector that has ballooned in recent years, whilst achieving genuine flexibility for workers. The idea of legally obliging companies to offer at least a 16-hour week is worthy of serious debate in the trade union movement, with full involvement of members on zero hours and short-hours contracts.

It could be, and would need to be, accompanied by a clause that meant individual workers who wanted fewer hours in their contracts could waive the 16-hour minimum. In other words, opt out of it without any pressure to do so from the employer, and negotiate hours that suited them better. With union representation to ensure they are not bullied into lesser hours than they desire – and the legally-enforced guarantee of 16 hours a week if they want it. That would give some genuine flexibility to workers who don't want to, or can't, take on full-time jobs, but who want and need to escape the merciless insecurity and ruthless exploitation that are currently spreading like a modern plague – cheap, precarious, casual jobs, epitomised by zero hours and nominal-hours contracts… the capitalists' 'flexible friends'.

8

NATIONAL MINIMUM WAGE

Emily is a call handler, on the minimum wage, working for a well-known retail company whose profits surpassed £1billion last year.

"There are wee things other people might take for granted, like walking into a supermarket and thinking 'I'll buy this make of tomato sauce'. But then I think 'No, I might need to buy that cheaper one'. On my day off, me and my boyfriend might go out for the day, but realise we can't afford to go to that place for lunch. It takes the enjoyment out of life. You're never really on top of things, always chasing. Sometimes you feel judged by other people... who look at me and think I'm useless or not that clever. It gets to your self-confidence."

One of the multiple sources of poverty pay in today's Scotland is the pathetically low level of the National Minimum Wage, and the growing preponderance of workers living on or just above that level of hourly income.

Of course the concept of a legally enforced national minimum wage is something many of us fought for long and hard, through our trade unions and socialist organisations a generation ago. The problem is not the concept: the problem is who decides its level, who implements it. And the fact for capitalists and their governments that it's a necessary evil, a concession to a rising clamour for guarantees against super-exploitation, grudgingly given, dodged where possible, but (more importantly) set at the lowest level they can get away with.

The purpose behind this publication is not to trash or question the idea of a nationally guaranteed minimum wage – legally enforced, rather than being a purely voluntary option for employers. The aim is to change its level, transform it to a decent living wage, and thereby transform the lives of up to a million workers in Scotland – redistributing some of the wealth created by the working class in the process.

At the start of the 20th century, a section of the capitalists and their political wing accepted the idea of at least light-touch regulation of wages by the state. This featured the Trade Boards Act of 1909, which gave mild and partial guarantees on wages to a minority of the worst-paid trades of the time.

Winston Churchill, arch enemy of trade union struggle and working people, was hated by sections of the working class who knew his real history. This included him ordering troops into the South Wales coalfields in 1910 to counter strikes by 12,000 miners at Tonypandy, in the Rhondda valley. In response to strikers' pickets at the pitheads, Churchill, Liberal Home Secretary at the time, instructed the police, whose strike-breaking violence the army was there to back up, to "Drive the rats back down their holes."

The next year, Churchill again bared his fangs by ordering troops into action against the 1911 Llanelli railway workers' strike, when they opened fire and killed two workers. He continued this personal political tradition during the 1926 British General Strike, where he was in charge of recruiting and deploying the state's strike-breaking outfit – the Organisation for the Maintenance of Supplies (OMS) – as well as overseeing the terrified ruling class's propaganda machine.

So no friend of the workers, Mr Churchill! In fact when he died in 1965, whilst the BBC and government helped to canonise him through a televised state funeral, many older workers in the South Wales pit villages went onto the streets and openly celebrated his passing. As recently as 2010, councils in South Wales blocked plans to name streets after him because of his reviled reputation from a century before!

But even Churchill recognised the advantages, strictly from a capitalist viewpoint, of some degree of regulation of wages, of the labour market, rather than a complete laissez-faire free-for-all, an unrestricted race to the bottom. As he put it, speaking in support of the Trade Boards Act of 1909:

"Where you have what we call sweated trades, you have no organisation, no parity of bargaining, the good employer is undercut by the bad, and the bad employer is undercut by the worst."

Churchill was in part responding to the pressure of agitation against the horrors of 'sweated labour' – particularly of women and children, working horrendously long hours either at home or in unsanitary, unsafe sweatshops, on brutally low wages. The agitation for government intervention to protect these most vulnerable workers had been longstanding, since at least 1888. And because trade union organisation was deemed impossible due to the nature of most of these jobs, it was pursued by the National Anti Sweating League, whose ranks included the Fabian Society social democrats Sidney and Beatrice Webb.

But Churchill's concerns to introduce some kind of legal restraints on the worst excesses of slave labour – in 'the sweated trades' – wasn't born of concern for the conditions of the working class. It was more a desire to aid 'good employers', and restrain the growing unrest amongst those workers who were organised in the early years of the 1900s. This is demonstrated by the alternative model he sang hymns of praise to, in the same speech advocating the 1909 Trade Boards Act:

> "Where in the great staple trades you have a powerful organisation on both sides, where you have responsible leaders able to bind their constituents to their decisions… there you have a healthy bargaining which increases the competitive power of the industry… and continually weaves capital and labour closely together."

So there, in the confident tones of the callous enemy of workers in struggle, we hear a vision of collaboration between 'capital and labour', in the interests of industrial competitiveness and social peace – a view that 100 years later would now be called 'social partnership' by its latter-day advocates.

The Trade Boards set up through the 1909 Act initially covered a tiny share of the overall UK workforce. Whilst historians reckon at least 30% of Edwardian workers were slaves to the sweated trades, a mere 200,000 of them were initially embraced by the Trades Boards – in just four trades: tailoring, box-making, lace-making and chain-making.

Even when the trades covered were extended in 1913, it still only gave some measure of protection to about 370,000 workers (70% of them women). The Trade Boards consisted of representatives of employers, workers and 'independent' nominees of the government's Minister of Trade. The wage rates set – effectively sectoral minimum wages – were undoubtedly an improvement for these most downtrodden of all workers. However, as the British Journal of Industrial Relations commented:

"The wage rates set were not based on the cost of living, but on what individual trades could bear. On their own, they failed to eradicate Britain's long tradition of being a low pay economy."

The Trade Boards morphed into Wages Councils in 1945, and continued right up until the days of Maggie Thatcher, the spear-carrier for capitalist reaction, whose election in 1979 ushered in a regime of red-in-tooth-and-claw attacks on pay, to propel profits skywards. The 1986 Tory Wages Act weakened the impact of the Wages Councils, and workers aged under-21 were then removed from cover by them. Then, to complete the hatchet-job by the evangel of crude class warfare, Wages Councils were totally abolished in 1993 – leaving workers to the tender mercies of 'the free market' – that system that concedes workers full freedom to starve, but piles on mountains of legislation to guarantee gluttony for the profits, perks and privileges of the grotesquely rich.

* * * *

A feature of the 1960s and 1970s was that many trade unions – especially those in key industrial sectors that were highly organised and wielded powerful muscle as a result of their place in the production process – had come to see collective bargaining as their prime weapon to improve members' wages, rather than legislation. Unions such as those of car and engineering workers were vociferously opposed to a statutory national minimum wage, fearing this could drag down the wages they had used their bargaining power to achieve for skilled trades, and also in dread of the erosion of pay differentials gained by the skilled workers they represented.

From the mid-1970s onwards, right through the 1980s and 1990s, a steady, systematic, sometimes spectacular erosion of workers' wages was pursued by employers and governments. Their mission was to claw back the concessions granted in the aftermath of the mass destruction and mass radicalisation of World War Two, in terms both of actual wages and the social wage. They were out to recalibrate the share of national economic output going towards the rent, interest and profit of the landlords, bankers and capitalists. This consciously chosen path – planned poverty – condemned growing numbers of workers to impoverishment. A prime example were the millions of low-paid public sector workers herded into council depots, civil service factory offices, and NHS hospitals, subjected to real-term pay cuts by successive Tory and Labour governments in the 1970s.

It is no accident that this was the period where sections of the trade unions and their leaders raised a hue and cry in favour of a legal national minimum wage. As workers' unions had their ability to function and fight for wage increases restricted by several rounds of anti-union laws, they increasingly turned to political answers through a government-enforced minimum wage law.

It is no coincidence that the union leaders most prominent in this growing campaign – alongside socialists of the day – were the likes of Alan Fisher, leader of the National Union of Public Employees (NUPE) and his co-thinker Bernard Dix. They were at the head of a union populated by workers in some of the lowest-paid and often dirtiest jobs – binmen, street sweepers, hospital cleaners, gravediggers, school dinner staff, hospital ancillary staff, etc.

And very significantly, these unions demanded a minimum wage based on formulae linking it to median or average wages. At the 1973 Labour Party conference, NUPE argued for Labour to commit to a minimum wage set at 80% of average earnings. On other occasions their demand was for a statutory minimum valued as two-thirds median male wages, or sometimes two-thirds average male wages – a formula championed to this day by the Scottish Socialist Party.

Over the subsequent 20 years, a growing trade union demand for such a measure to halt the employers' offensive gained majority support in the TUC, overcoming the previous resistance and reluctance of the better-paid or skilled layers of workers. This came to fruition as they too were targeted by Thatcher's government in particular, in a concerted crusade to steal back the concessions in wages and conditions won by the previous generation of workers through their unions. Unions like the TGWU and craft unions swung round to supporting the call for a statutory minimum wage from the early 1990s onwards.

This drove Labour into actually doing something to implement a policy which on paper they had supported since 1906, but for 90 long years had done absolutely nothing to bring to fruition. Eventually, John Smith's and then Tony Blair's Labour leadership conceded to the growing clamour for this measure from beneath their own feet, in the form of workers and their unions – including affiliates to Labour – demanding action in a period when 13 years of Tory rule encouraged the employers to impose the gospel that it was 'better to have low wages than no wages.'

However, in pursuing this policy, the Blairites were ultra-careful to not offend the sensitivities of the profiteers, their carefully courted new 'social partners' in the big business boardrooms. They didn't want to undo the results of Labour's 'cocktail offensive' round the City of London in preceding years, designed to appease the fears of the spivs, speculators and capitalist money-grabbers that a Labour government might do something nasty like curb their excessive wealth, or concede to some of the wishes of a working class under siege from Thatcher and then John Major's Tories. Blair put Kirkintilloch-born Ian McCartney, Labour's new Minister for Trade and Industry, in charge of pacifying big business fears, in what McCartney boastfully claimed was "the most successful social partnership in the last three or four decades."

The subsequent form that the introduction of the National Minimum Wage took reflected this overweening desire to smooth the feathers of the capitalist class, whilst riding to office on the popularity of the idea of this measure – as well as an overwhelmingly anti-Tory vote for Labour – in the 1997 General Election.

In June 1998, I organised the only demonstration held in Scotland demanding a national minimum wage prior to its introduction, under the banner of the Scottish Socialist Alliance, forerunner to the SSP. We openly demanded it should be set at two-thirds male median earnings, for all over 16. On one of the wettest days in modern Scotland, we marched to Glasgow's George Square, where speakers included actor and film director Peter Mullan. He told the demonstrators the story of his brother, who emigrated to Norway after working in Fairfield's shipyard on the Clyde, as a caulker burner.

"He met a Norwegian girl and they moved to Oslo where he got himself a job as a labourer in a wee factory. Two days into the job and the shop steward comes up to him, tells him to put down his tools, that they're on strike. So he leaves along with the other workers and asks the shop steward what it's all about. The shop steward said: 'If we've told them once we've told them a thousand times, they either get that sauna fixed or we're out of here!' My brother told them that we too had confined rooms with slippery floors and steam rising – but we tended to call that the lavvy. It's all a question of self-worth."

This anecdote illustrates how backward conditions have been systematically imposed on workers in what used to be the shipbuilding centre of the world. How a class of parasites thrive on other people's lowered expectations.

When the National Minimum Wage was implemented in April 1999 it was a very welcome reform. It improved the wages of an estimated 1.3 million workers in Britain. It did at least something to overcome the situation described by the striking phrase of one worker in Northern Ireland at the time: "Living on the margins of degradation." To this day, Labour cling onto the kudos for introducing this, claiming credit for it as an earth-moving transformation of society.

Not quite! From the outset, Labour conceded to the screams of alarm and bloodcurdling scenarios of economic ruin shouted by the Tories and employers' organisations, including the CBI. We shouldn't allow today's Tories or bosses' organisations forget that they screamed blue murder in opposition to a statutory minimum wage in 1999. They threatened that the NMW would wipe out jobs, bringing the country to its knees.

Instead of facing down this economically illiterate blackmail, and mobilising trade unionists and other workers behind the introduction of a decent level of guaranteed wage for all over 16, the Blair government undermined the whole concept from its very birth. They introduced a string of exemption clauses that would have made the oiliest dodgy salesman blush, with lists of people not covered by the NMW, including the self-employed, workers under 18, au pairs. They allowed employers to include tips to workers in the likes of hotels, bars and restaurants to be included in the calculations of whether they were receiving the legal minimum; customers subsidising employers' legal obligations on wage levels.

Above all, Labour capitulated to the terror and threats from big capitalists by setting up the Low Pay Commission (LPC) to annually decide what level of minimum wage the government should consider. The Commission's remit was not to measure what income a worker requires to have a decent, if basic, standard of living; a living wage, taking account of other people's earnings and the cost of living in any given year. Instead, they were there to measure its (alleged) economic impact – code for how it would impact on profits, and therefore what amount the employers would graciously grant without a strike of investment.

That remit was made obvious by who was appointed to the LPC. From its very creation, it included three top company chief executives out of nine LPC members, accompanied by three high-income academics and 'independents', plus three appointed trade union officials (currently on salaries near or above six figures). For instance, one of the longest-serving members of the Low Pay Commission is John Hannett, the general secretary of Usdaw. In something of a stark distinction from the vast battalions of low-paid, part-time and zero hours contract workers in retail – who rely heavily on the level of the minimum wage to determine their incomes:

"The general secretary of the union was paid £89,896 in respect of salary and £49,818 in respect of benefits including employer National Insurance Contributions, employer pension contributions and the provision of a Union car." (Usdaw Annual Audit Report for 2014.)

The LPC, then and now, consults with the big business Confederation of British Industry, the Federation of Small Businesses, representatives of industries like hospitality, textiles, hairdressing – and a few massively-paid top union officials – but never the low-paid themselves! It has to be added, that far too many of the official union submissions to the LPC's annual review ignore, or even undermine, union national conference policies on what level of minimum wage members want.

Predictably enough, given that the Low Pay Commission didn't have a single direct representative of the millions on poverty pay on its panel, and that it had been appointed by a Labour government wedded to the profit interests of the handful who gain a fortune from minimising their wages bill, the National Minimum Wage was set at rock bottom level from its very birth. Its first level, from March 1999, was set at £3.60 an hour. It didn't even reach 50% of the average wage rate of the time. A full-time worker on the £3.60 took home £130 a week, whereas even the miserly measure of 50% of average wages in 1999 would have meant £170 a week.

Journalist Fran Abrams went undercover for three months in three separate low-paying jobs, which she recounted in her book *Below the Breadline* in 2002. She worked as a cleaner in London's Savoy hotel; as a pickle bottler in a South Yorkshire factory; and as a care assistant in a private care home in Aberdeenshire. In her words:

> "The National Minimum Wage was an old-fashioned political stitch up, set at a level which would ensure the lowest possible level of protest from employers without enraging the trade unions sufficiently for them to cause real trouble."

Unfortunately, most of the trade union leaders were far too eager not to 'cause real trouble'. In part because the pinnacles of the trade union movement live on salaries that put them on a different planet to their own low-paid members. And just as fundamentally because they have no vision of a different kind of society, and therefore accept the straitjacket of capitalism, the tight limitations on wages imposed by those in power. Union leaderships are all too frequently prisoners of 'social partnership' with the employers, rather than being proud protagonists of social justice for the working class members whose union fees fund the union.

The Low Pay Unit calculated that from its very inception, in 1999, the national minimum wage left 3.5 million working families in the UK – not individuals, but families – in poverty. This basement level of wages left the 1.3 million who'd thereby at least gained some kind of wage rise still struggling to survive their household bills. In addition to its abject failure to eliminate poverty, it did precious little to tackle poverty's ugly twin, inequality. The differential between the top 10% of wage earners and the bottom 10% remained static in 1999, and actually widened in the second year of the National Minimum Wage.

And that's only the differential within the wages league table – not the vastly wider gap in wealth as a whole. It doesn't even begin to describe the Grand Canyon separating the lowest-paid workers from the salaries, bonuses, share options, pension pots and downright stolen incomes through tax-dodging enjoyed by the chief executives and directors of those companies consulted by the Low Pay Commission in their annual review of the NMW.

One of the pivotal arguments for introducing the NMW, including in the mouths of Labour leaders, was to end state subsidies to poverty pay, in the form of top-up benefits to those on low wages. But size matters. The level set for the NMW meant the cost to taxpayers of top-up benefits actually more than doubled by 2001, from £2.4billion the year before the NMW was brought in, to £5.2billion two years later. Furthermore, a full one-third of the workers entitled to these top-up benefits didn't claim them. Of course this meant a win-win situation for big business and their business-friendly government. Employers avoided having to cut a sliver off their profit margins to concede decent wages, and the government saved on in-work benefits payments to 33% of the low-paid workers legally entitled to them.

From its inception, Labour's version of a National Minimum Wage was more a sop than a solution. The government and its appointed Low Pay Commission had at least one eye and ear – if not both – on the reaction and requests of big business, rather than the cries of anguish of millions languishing in poverty, still 'living on the margins of degradation'. Furthermore, it was enforced with the legislative equivalent of a feather, not the strong arm and iron fist of the law that is applied to people claiming a few extra quid on benefits. For starters, the Low Pay Commission's terms of reference meant, as Fran Abrams wrote:

"It is not currently charged with finding out whether or not employers are paying the NMW. Instead they have been asked to look at the effect of the Minimum on employment and competitiveness, on pay differentials and on the tax and benefits system."

From day one it also suffered a lack of rigorous enforcement measures or machinery. This was meant to be done by a HMRC inspection team. In the first year of the NMW they investigated 6,400 complaints, found 3,200 employers not complying – but only issued 349 enforcement notices, 62 penalty notices – and not a single prosecution! By way of contrast, they conducted a few high-profile raids on cash-in-hand benefit claimants hired and picked up in vans to work in sweatshop conditions, drastically below the legal minimum wage. Who doubts there's one law for the rich, another for the rest of us?

All manner of dodges, legal and otherwise, were deployed by bosses to undercut the legal minimum. For instance, sleepovers at nursing homes weren't counted as hours worked; workers' hours were cut; paid breaks were removed; some workers were given their jotters to avoid paying them the NMW.

Some of us at the time exposed and campaigned against the way the Wise Group – trumpeted by the Labour government as the model job-creation social enterprise, replete with a flying visit to its Glasgow HQ by Prime Minister Tony Blair – actually cut their hourly rate of pay to bring it down to the £3.60 legal minimum! All perfectly legal, of course, but utterly immoral. A reminder of the ethics of capitalism and its worship of the great god, Profit.

Sixteen years on, the National Minimum Wage has been tweaked, but still remains at a level – or rather, levels – that insult the intelligence of anyone committed to eliminating poverty in this rich country. It is still a source of poverty, not a solution to it.

For the first five years of its existence, workers aged under-18 were totally excluded from the minimum wage; they had absolutely no legally guaranteed rate of pay. The lower rate for workers aged 16-17 only started in 2005 – at £3-an-hour. Apprentices didn't enjoy any minimum wage cover whatsoever until 2010 – if today's £2.73-an-hour can be classified as 'cover'! The lower youth rates persist to this day. The 'adult' rate kicks in on your 21st birthday now, rather than your 22nd, as it did up until 2010.

But at its core, the National Minimum Wage is not only still stuck at rock bottom levels, but is discriminatory towards younger people. The rates since October 2014 are £6.50-an-hour for workers over 21; £5.13 'development rate' for workers aged 18-20; and a pathetic rate of £3.79 for workers aged 16-17. To crown this inglorious package of poverty pay, apprentices aged 16-18, and those aged 19 or over who are in their first year, are only guaranteed a National Minimum Wage of £2.73 an hour.

That's modern slave labour. And it's the rate paid to thousands of young apprentices across Scotland in the likes of councils run by various combinations of Tory, Labour and SNP councillors. These elected 'representatives' then have the effrontery to complain about youth disengagement from politics.

Nor should we sit back and relish the prospect of bountiful pay increases on 1st October 2015, when the new minimum wage rates kick in. The millions on or around the minimum wage could be forgiven for boycotting any champagne parties to mark the occasion, when the levels rise to £6.70, £5.30, £3.87 and £3.30 respectively.

* * * *

Even to this day, a minority of employers refuse to even cough up these derisory minimum wages, deploying a raft of ruses to avoid their legal obligations. The fine for such actions was increased in February 2014 from a maximum of £5,000 to one of £20,000. But what's that to a big profiteer, assuming the depleted army of HMRC inspectors catch him/her in the first place?

As a coldly calculated sop to the screams of fury at super-exploitation of workers, the Westminster government amended rules in October 2013 to 'name and shame' those employers discovered by the HMRC to be paying below the legal minimum wage. Since then, over about 18 months, the government's Business, Innovation and Skills Development department has named 210 employers stealing some of even the paltry minimum wage off their staff. In total they've identified workers short-changed by £635,000 in these 210 outfits – and fined the firms £248,000.

The most recent batch of 48 wage-robbers was named in March 2015. They owed workers £162,000 which they'd dodged paying to match the legal minimum. They 'suffered' fines of £67,000 for this criminal theft from the lowest paid; a fine that would barely impact on the owners' expenditure on lunches, let alone their profits. The list of contemptible thieves included hairdressers' chain Toni & Guy; French Connection; Footlocker/Freedom Sportsline, and – worst of all, as well as closest to home – Stefan King's G1 Group.

King owns about 45 venues – mostly upmarket clubs, restaurants, cinemas, hotels – plus over 100 leased pubs. He bought the old, iconic GPO building in Glasgow's George Square for £5million in 1999, and sold it in 2005 for £11million; that's one way to profit from former public assets. The G1 Group empire reported operating profits of £10.2million in 2013 – a leap of 36% on the healthy £7.48million the previous year. King is a multi-millionaire – 'worth' £54million back in the 2013 Rich List – whose last known residence was in Elphinstone Road, in Glasgow's leafy Southside, where some of the 17 mansions in the road first reached the value of £1million way back in 2004.

His 'classy' venues have faced legal challenges – for barring a disabled couple from the Polo Club in Glasgow; for installing spy mirrors for male patrons to peep at women in the bathrooms of the Glasgow Shimmy Club – and notoriety for opening a new Cotton Club, harking back to the racist traditions of the New York jazz club of the same name in the mid-1920s, with its 'whites only' admissions policy.

King's G1 Group was forced to pay back £411,834 to the Scottish Government in January 2015; public funding for a training scheme that they'd got under false pretences. His venues treat their (mostly young) staff with hooligan neglect, often making them work a 12-hour shift with just one 15-minute break, or none at all, and leaving them to walk home in the middle of the night after long shifts, refusing to pay for taxis to ensure staff safety.

But to add to their litany of crimes, they were exposed for robbing 2,895 staff in their Arta restaurant, in Glasgow's Merchant City, of £45,000 – by charges for uniforms and training being taken off their minimum wage pay!

The previous instalment in this serialised roll of shame identified Swedish-owned clothes chain H&M as the biggest company, with the largest number of workers (up until then) denied even the pitiful £6.50 hourly wage. Known for its fast fashion, cheap chic range, Hennes & Mauritz was founded in 1947 by Erling Persson.

The current company chairman is his son, Stefan Persson. He is the world's 24th-richest billionaire, with a personal fortune of £16.01billion. He gained mightily from last year's 25% rise in the stock value of his company, H&M. But he didn't do too badly from his other sideline, land ownership in England. In 2014 he bought Savernake Estate in Wiltshire; no crofter's strip of land, nor modest family farm, but a colossus of 8,700 acres... or about the size of 4,500 football pitches. And for Stefan's convenience, this latest acquisition isn't far from Linkenholt, a village in Hampshire – which he bought in 2009!

Despite this mind-boggling wealth, in the hands of Sweden's richest citizen, his company and primary source of wealth – H&M – dodged paying 500 of its staff the paltry £6.50-an-hour they are legally supposed to. Another classic case of billions for the bosses, buttons for their workers.

Whilst naming and shaming these wage-dodgers, who act illegally to steal money from the pockets of workers they employ, we shouldn't be distracted from the much bigger picture. Even if a vast army of HMRC wage inspectors was hired – and it should be, instead of being slashed by half – to enforce the legal minimum, how in hell can anyone be expected to have a decent standard of life, with full access to all aspects of modern society, if the minimum remains at such a pitiful level?

You could be forgiven for thinking the theory behind the national minimum wage is that it is only the MINIMUM guaranteed income, with plenty of scope for higher rates. That's what the label on the tin says: 'minimum'. But the label lies! Far from being merely the minimum, with the promise of progression, for millions of workers it has become the norm, the standard rate, an almost fixed level of pay for the foreseeable future, regardless of length of service or level of skills, proficiency and experience.

It's fast become a way of life for vast battalions of workers, especially in sectors like retail, cleaning and hospitality. The Low Pay Commission itself reckoned that in late 2013, no less than 1.386 million workers were paid the NMW, 750,000 of them in the three sectors just mentioned. Nor is it a passing phase for workers. The London *Times* on 23 October 2014 reported:

> "More people are flat-lining on poverty pay too. A decade ago, among those who had been on the NMW for at least five years, 10% found themselves stuck here for the whole of that period; today the figure is 23%."

Other reports identified that nearly three-quarters of workers classified as low-paid in 2002 were still in that category a decade later, in 2012. And last year, a whopping 2.6 million earned less than 50 pence above the legal minimum. Or as the Resolution Foundation Report stated in October 2013:

> "For parts of the UK's minimum wage workforce – in particular women, part-time workers and those who ended up or remained in wholesale and retail roles – the minimum wage has been a reality for an extended period of time."

Their research discovered 1.9 million (one out of every 13 workers) earned within 25p of the National Minimum Wage in 2012, twice the proportion hovering round this basement level in 2002. They found a massive 320,000 workers had languished on this low-level minimum wage for over five years. So much for the much-vaunted 'upward mobility' we're told to rely on as a means of bettering ourselves. And nearly 100,000 workers had been on or near the minimum wage for the entire first 13 years of its existence. Lucky 13 for some – employers, that is.

* * * *

In part because the National Minimum Wage is not calculated by any formula that fixes it at a percentage of average or median pay rates, it serves to further drag down overall wages, rather than dragging them up for the lower-paid. It's like a boulder hung round the necks of workers swimming in a sea of poverty pay, their chins barely above water. When employers have a massive 'reserve army of labour' (as Karl Marx defined them 150 years ago) desperate to get a job, any job – including those hounded and sanctioned by the benefits authorities to take any job on offer – employers will joyfully offer the bare legal minimum as often as possible. And that's not even taking account of the growing use of Workfare; working for literally nothing on pain of loss of benefits, passed off as 'work experience', in reality providing companies and services with zero-cost labour.

John McArthur is an electronics specialist from Motherwell. During 2010-11 he worked for the social enterprise, LAMH Recycle, which repairs computers and recycles tin and cardboard. He did so under the previous Labour government's Future Jobs Fund, and was paid the national minimum wage. John says he was happy to do so, but then in late 2014, at the age of 59, he refused to obey the DWP when he was ordered to go back and do the same job in the same LAMH for precisely nothing, literally no wages, under the Tory/Lib Dem Coalition's Community Work Placement.

Despite meeting the imperious demands of the benefits system by applying for 50 jobs a week, without joy, he was ordered to work for zero wages for 26 weeks. When he refused, his benefits were sanctioned by the DWP, leaving him to survive on a monthly pension of

£149. LAMH confirmed to the *Guardian* that they had 16 people working for them under the CWP scheme – government forced labour, free labour, imposed on desperate people issued the 'choice' of 'work for no wages or starve.'

This is but one tiny example of a system that is running rampant through the economy, with hundreds of thousands of people forced onto jobs or placements without pay, working for their miserly benefits, often for months on end. Numerous businesses and charities – including the British Heart Foundation, Marie Curie, Scope, Barnardo's, Sue Ryder, etc. – have exploited this government compulsion, grabbing literally free labour to prevent them having to bother hiring waged workers.

The Tories regard this brutal treatment of people unable to find a job, living on subsistence level benefits, as a strand to 'making work pay', part of 'The Big Society'. It's actually straight, simple, old-fashioned slave labour, making people work for no pay, using the threat of literal starvation as the weapon to force workers into producing 100% profit on their labour. And why would profiteering businesses spurn such a brilliant chance to exploit workers for literally every penny they produce?

* * * *

That trend – using the 'reserve army of labour' to slash wages – has escalated during the recent economic crisis, post-2008, but was working its way through the system well before the recession handed the profiteers a blunt instrument to hammer down wages and thereby push up profits. One stark statistic proves this trend at work: the Joseph Rowntree Foundation's annual report in November 2014 declared that average wages for men working full-time had plunged in real terms from £13.90 an hour in 2008 to £12.90 in 2013. The equivalent drop for women full-time workers was from £10.80 to £10.30 an hour.

Whilst we were subjected to relentless claims of an economic miracle in job creation by the 2010-15 Tory/Lib Dem Coalition – apparently confirmed by the paradox of falling numbers unemployed during the 2008-13 recession – we need to stop, look, and see the types of jobs created, the levels of wages on offer. Median (middle) wages for these 'new' workers plunged from £8.42 an hour in the 3rd Quarter of 2009 to £7.51 in the second Quarter of 2012.

So a ready, willing, even desperate pool of would-be workers selling their labour-power on the capitalist markets in a period of economic decline was the perfect prospect for low-paying, profiteering bosses. It helped to drag down wages.

Indeed, mass unemployment was the weapon of choice, wielded with all the subtlety of a ten-tonne sledgehammer, to smash to smithereens the wages of those "lucky enough to have a job", since at least 1980s Thatcherism. This assault on living standards was made infinitely easier by the failure of the huge majority of trade union leaders – and the entire Labour machine, oiled by union members' money – to resist and organise a fight to counter the planned poverty in the wage packets of growing numbers. So the recession was good for some people: the employers, in their hunt for cheaper labour.

The National Minimum Wage, set annually by the government after recommendations by a Low Pay Commission that never goes near a low-paid worker, institutionalises low wages rather than increase workers' share of wealth. It reinforces poverty pay, rather than remove it.

* * * *

Britain, and Scotland, can lay claim to being one of the most developed countries in the world. But it also 'boasts' a clutch of particularly ugly features on its face. One of the lowest minimum wage levels in the advanced capitalist countries. Some of the steepest falls in real pay in Europe since 2010. One of the worst concentrations of poverty wages in the world. According to figures from the Office of National Statistics, published in January 2014, the UK has the second-highest rate of low pay in the entire 32 OECD countries – twice the rate of some other advanced economies. Britain suffered an average fall in real wages of 5.5% from 2010 to 2013, compared to the average fall of 0.7% in the 27 EU countries, making it the fourth-worst decline in real wages in the EU (only better than Greece, Portugal and Holland).

International league tables of national minimum wages make equally grim reading. They make Scotland and the UK look more of a Bathgate than a Barcelona in the European wages league! For instance, in January 2014, the respective national minimum wages for EU countries were €11.10 in Luxembourg; €9.53 in France; €9.11 in Holland; €9.10 in Belgium; €8.65 in the South of Ireland; €8.50 (pending it's subsequent introduction) in Germany... and €7.43 in Britain.

But, you might understandably object, surely those figures take no account of the varying cost of living in these countries? Fair enough, let's look at what these national minimum rates mean in comparison to the cost of living in each state; in what is called 'Purchasing Power Standards', PPS, instead of in Euros. In fact, Britain remains at a poor seventh in the EU table of comparisons, using this more useful PPS measure. Luxembourg was still at the top with a minimum wage equivalent to 9.01 PPS; followed by France (8.74 PPS); Germany (8.37); Belgium (8.32); Holland (8.27); Ireland (7.33)... with Britain trailing on 6.55 PPS.

To ram the message home even deeper, let's glance at the respective national minimum wage levels of European countries as a percentage of their respective full-time workers' median wage. Without turning this into a maths lesson, the median is where you take ALL the wages paid to each and every worker (in this case all full-time workers) and see how much the person in the middle of the wages league table is paid. In other words, half of all workers get more than the median wage, half get less. On this measure, advanced capitalist Britain slides down from seventh to an appalling tenth place in the EU countries – in what is a measure of the legal minimum wage as a tool to counter wage inequality. The less the National Minimum Wage is as a percentage of that country's MEDIAN full-time wage, the less effective it is at helping to lift the lower-paid out of relative poverty.

In France, the NMW is worth 62% of the full-time worker's median wage; in Slovenia it's worth 60%; Portugal (58%); Hungary (54%) ...right down until we find the UK's NMW is only equivalent to 47% of the median (middle) wage earned by a full-time worker in this state. And it's consistently sat at 46-47% of Scotland's full-time median wage since 2007, right up to the present.

Turn this battery of figures round another way: even if the National Minimum Wage in Scotland was raised to the less-than-generous 62% of the median full-time wage that prevails in France, a worker over 21 trying to cope on £6.50 an hour in 2015 would instead be guaranteed £8.58 an hour! Not a king's ransom, but a vast improvement nonetheless, for millions of workers.

9

THE LIVING WAGE

Much is said nowadays about 'the Living Wage'. It's an increasingly popular idea, as workers seek a lifeboat to rescue them from a rising, treacherous sea of poverty pay. It's a notion that has the official support of not just trade unions, but governments too.

Even the upper-class David Cameron declared in 2010: "The Living Wage is an idea whose time has come." But before you get too carried away with relief or astonishment, Cameron didn't trumpet so loudly the fact that by 2014 – a full four years later, under his Coalition government – the number of workers earning less than the Living Wage had rocketed skywards by 50%. Nor did he care to announce that whereas in 2007 a disgraceful 420,000 Londoners earned less than the London Living Wage, and despite that city enjoying an unimaginable economic boom in subsequent years, by 2014 an absolutely outrageous 640,000 workers there were being paid less than the London Living Wage... under the mayoralty of his classmate at Eton, Boris Johnson.

In the next chapter, we expose the scurrilous theft of our language by Tory Chancellor George Osborne, when he called £7.20-an-hour from April 2016 – for those aged over-25 – a 'National Living Wage'. Not content with robbing workers' wages and desperate people's benefits, this upper-class charlatan has sought to rob the terminology of those with the decency to confront poverty by demanding a genuine living wage. Particularly, as we spell out in the same chapter, when this exercise in distraction was designed to throw a blanket over his theft of in-work benefits. By use of the term 'National Living Wage', Osborne, Cameron and the 'compassionate Conservative' Iain Duncan Smith were putting the lie into headlines!

Labour has oft-repeated its support of the Living Wage, although numerous Labour-run councils have failed to pay it, or in even more cases dodged direct blame for not paying it by offloading responsibility to the arms-length companies and contractors that increasingly run council services. In virtually all Scottish councils – Labour, SNP and various combinations of the 'mainstream parties' – they lay claim to the kudos of paying staff the Living Wage, but exclude hundreds of apprentices in each local authority, giving these young workers as little as the slave-labour legal minimum of £2.73-an-hour.

The SNP Scottish Government officially supports the introduction of the Living Wage by employers, and funds staffing in the Poverty Alliance to pursue this. They announce every new Accredited Living Wage Employer with a fanfare, and set new targets. At the time of writing, the number of companies thus awarded the official Accreditation has risen to 380 across Scotland, with a target of 500 by Christmas announced by Nicola Sturgeon's government.

* * * *

So what is the Living Wage? Where has it come from? What does it mean to workers? How is the level of the Living Wage decided? How is it different from the National Minimum Wage? What are its advantages? What are its shortcomings? How does it relate to the demand for a £10-an-hour minimum?

The concept of a Living Wage has a long history. It goes back as far as Victorian times, when trade unionists, socialists and social reformers fought the sweated labour described in all its inglorious degradation, indignity, filth and starvation for millions by Charles Dickens and others. The demand for 'a Living Wage' emerged in the 1870s when early trade unions demanded that workers be paid enough to cover food, clothing and shelter for themselves and their families. As one supportive Liberal MP put it in 1894:

"A Living Wage must be sufficient to maintain the worker in the highest state of industrial efficiency, with decent surroundings and sufficient leisure."

So right from the outset, some of the more 'enlightened' capitalists and their political representatives saw this as an issue of 'industrial efficiency'; of the 'enlightened self-interest' of the capitalist employing class, rather than some kind of selfless devotion to the well-being of workers. They saw the dirt and degradation endured by whole swathes of the working class as an obstacle to having a fit, healthy, productive workforce, physically capable of producing profits for the minority class of industrialists represented at the time by the Liberal party, and in turn increasingly by the Tories – which had previously been more the party of the landowning class and aristocracy.

Social reformers of the Victorian age included Joseph Rowntree – businessman, chocolatier, Quaker and philanthropist – from York, in North Yorkshire. He developed the family business into one of the top-100 in the UK at the time. He sought to improve workers' conditions in Rowntree's cocoa and chocolate factories. In part spurred on in his beliefs by witnessing first-hand the effects of the 1840s famines in Ireland, Rowntree provided his workforce (which peaked at about 4,000 workers) with an eight-hour day, wage increases, a library, resident dentist, resident doctor and pension scheme. When his son Benjamin Seebohm produced a damning report on the abject poverty and hovels inhabited by the majority of workers in the town of York in 1901, Joseph Rowntree bought land outside York and built a model 'garden village', New Earshaw, which housed workers and managers in brick houses with gardens and fruit trees.

As we've explained elsewhere in this publication, the predominant wing of capitalist politicians, epitomised by Winston Churchill, began to see the sense of curtailing the worst excesses of 'bad employers', those in 'the sweated trades', who threatened to undercut and undermine the efforts at profiteering by more advanced sections of the same class. They introduced minimum standards for the low-paid, including women working at home, through the 1909 Trade Boards Act, which ushered in Wages Councils in several sectors and industries.

In that same period, one of the enlightened industrialists, the aforementioned Benjamin Seebohm Rowntree (son of Joseph) conducted unprecedentedly comprehensive social research into the causes of poverty, in the working class of York, challenging two major assumptions of the time. Firstly, he proved that poverty was not exclusive to

London, as most sociologists and politicians claimed. Secondly, and even more importantly, Rowntree proved that the single biggest cause of poverty was low wages – not the 'fickleness' of the working class, 'bringing it upon themselves', as most other capitalists of the time insisted was the case.

Seebohm Rowntree developed a toolkit to calculate a 'Living Wage', or what he called "the human costs of labour." His efforts, and his father's reputation as a benevolent employer, lives on through the Joseph Rowntree Foundation, still one of today's pre-eminent research institutions on the whole issue of poverty and solutions to it.

As a footnote to the story, the more recent fate of Rowntree's chocolate factories perfectly encapsulates the ruthless monopolisation of the economy over recent decades, and its utter lack of social responsibility: it was taken over by Nestlé in 1988. That's the same multinational food giant notorious for its far from philanthropic practices in the likes of Africa. In the 1970s, Nestlé was at the heart of a scandal for causing illness and death amongst infants, through promotion of bottle-feeding instead of breast-feeding – using Nestlé salespeople dressed up as nurses to push the virtues of buying their powdered baby-milk.

* * * *

The Independent Labour Party – which included many of the famous Red Clydesiders – adopted the idea of a Living Wage as their official policy. They proposed a Living Wage Bill in the House of Commons on 6 February 1931. In a powerful speech that cut to the core of capitalist exploitation, and its crazy internal contradictions, the ILP MP for Glasgow Bridgeton, Red Clydesider Jimmy Maxton, declared:

"The ILP has over the years worked out a complete scheme of social reorganisation based on the assumption that overproduction and under-consumption are two facts of the present time. The scheme is all-embracing. It involves the necessity of more adequate maintenance for our aged, for widows, for the unemployed. It involves the setting up of a new social service termed 'family allowance'. It involves the national ownership and control of the key industries – banking, power, coal and transport; national control of our import and export trade. But this proposal for a Living Wage is a pivotal proposal round which all the others are arranged. We are trying to provide a cure that is in conformity with the disease. When we are told there is overproduction, we reply that there is only overproduction in the relative sense... only in comparison with the purchasing power that exists to consume the goods produced. There are masses of the population who could be and ought to be consuming far more of all the essential things in life, who require better and more food, better housing, better furnishings inside their homes, better illumination of those homes and better sanitation. I have just left my own town of Barrhead, where my intimate friends are practically all engaged in the work of sanitary engineering, making wash-hand basins, baths, water closets, etc. They are all working short time. They are also very anxious to get coals for their fires. I leave Barrhead where my friends are unemployed because there is no demand for baths and wash-hand basins, and I go to South Wales where I find the miners want wash-hand basins and sanitary equipment and they are unable to get them. These miners are unemployed, because my engineering friends in Barrhead are unable to buy coal."

The ILP's Living Wage Bill was seconded by Maxton's fellow-Red Clydesider, Davy Kirkwood, former union convener at the giant Parkhead Forge – when it was the biggest steelworkers in Scotland, employing 20,000, not a shopping centre staffed by low-paid retail workers! He told the House of Commons:

"During the war [1914-18] my class, my trade, the engineers, sacrificed all their trade rights. I asked them not to sacrifice their trade rights, and I was imprisoned and deported for so doing. What have the engineers, the shipbuilders, the miners, the cotton and woollen operatives, the agricultural workers – the working class, who produced all the wealth in this country – got in return? They are the great producing class of the country. They are 'up against it' not because we have a famine in the land, but because we have not yet produced statesmen who can see that there is superabundance, who have the courage to give the people the power to buy back what they produce."

The ILP Living Wage Bill was defeated, despite being proposed during a Labour government.

For the next 70 years the whole concept of a living wage was buried from sight in the world of politics, rarely if ever mentioned, except by socialists who steadfastly fought on against the system whose very bloodstream is profit at the expense of pay. It vanished from prominence, including press coverage, until its current phase of life was ignited by a group of people in London's East End in 2001. A group called London Citizens was created that year. The founders were East End parents who simply couldn't cope, despite working two or more jobs on the National Minimum Wage. Their motivation was deepened further by the fact they found themselves left with no time for family life, or involvement in their local communities, after working long, hard hours to try and make up for their miserable hourly rates of pay – especially in the context of the horrendously high cost of living in London, which has since become the most expensive city in the world.

As the property bubble inflated to bursting point, enriching a tiny minority of spivs and speculators, the cost of housing for working-class Londoners rocketed to crisis point, leaving many barely able to keep a roof over their heads, or those of their children. These were the real citizens of the real city of London, living 'the other side of the tracks' from the engorged yuppies and financial wide-boys of the City of London. The parents who founded London Citizens were joined in their pioneering campaigning by other communities, campaigners and faith groups, and after several high-profile protests, won wage rises for some of the lowest-paid.

Just glance at two illustrative examples of the struggles workers were forced to prosecute. In 2005, cleaners in the Houses of Parliament went on strike for the London Living Wage, £6.70-an-hour at the time. These workers – many of them migrants with good qualifications, who had settled in the self-styled 'mother of democracy' in hope of a better life – were only paid a few pence above the statutory minimum wage of £4.85, only got twelve days' holiday a year, and were denied sick pay or pension contributions by the contractors used by the parliament to cover up their own dirty work. One of the strikers told journalists how he had two cleaning jobs at the Commons to make ends meet – cleaning kitchens during the night, clearing up rubbish during the day, working a 64-hour week.

These courageous fighters staged protests and strikes, descending on parliament, with placards and mops aloft, warning the MPs and Lords they could clean their own rooms unless their demands were met. After two 24-hour strikes and numerous protests, the cleaners won in February 2006, gaining a staged pay increase to £6.70-an-hour, 28 days' annual holiday, and sick pay. Above all they won dignity through struggle.

Subsequently, cleaners on London Underground, led by the RMT union, staged several strikes over a period of two whole years before they were conceded the London Living Wage (then £7.85-an-hour) by Transport for London bosses in mid-2010. Their anger, determination and bravery in taking action was further fuelled by revelations at the time that bonuses to bosses on the London Underground had doubled between 2007 and 2009, to £5.3million. These workers, hidden from view, refused to be forgotten and fought against the odds to win.

So nothing was gifted to workers, including not by the political authorities in London who profess their undying devotion to the idea of a Living Wage.

* * * *

This pressure from below won a big breakthrough when, in 2005, the Greater London Authority established its own Living Wage Unit to calculate the level that would constitute a London Living Wage. The idea spread. Soon the Centre for Research in Social Policy at Loughborough University offered its expertise to calculate a Living Wage for the rest of the UK, outside London. This is based on their Minimum Income Standard, which measures the incomes required for households to have "a minimum acceptable standard of living, including food, clothing, rent, Council Tax, fuel for heating, and childcare." They then calculate the minimum incomes required for each of nine different types of households – for example, single person; childless couple; single parent and different numbers of children; pensioners, etc – and then work out an overall average, with the minimum each household member needs per hour to cover such a basic standard of living.

The Public and Commercial Services union (PCS), which has a proud record of fighting for decent levels of wages (and decent benefits for those who encounter PCS members in the JobCentres) defines the Living Wage as:

"The hourly wage needed to achieve an adequate level of warmth and shelter, a healthy palatable diet, social integration and avoidance of chronic stress."

Following on from the battles by London parents for decent wages in the early 2000s, London Citizens has developed into Citizens UK, which in turn established the Living Wage Foundation in 2010 as a project to promote and pursue the aims of a Living Wage. Campaigning umbrellas include the Scottish Living Wage Campaign, linked with the Poverty Alliance, backed by several trade unions and the STUC. These bodies and institutions have provided invaluable information and research, lobbied politicians and businesses, and generally raised the awareness of not just poverty pay, but also the concept of a decent living wage. They produce case histories of the impact on workers' lives when they achieve 'the Living Wage', produce forests of research, and keep the issue alive in the media with regular commentaries and stories.

From the outset, the modern revivers of the Living Wage campaign sought after "non-statutory solutions to in-work poverty", to quote the Scottish Living Wage campaign. In essence, having used various toolkits to calculate what they deem to be a Living Wage for London, and separately for the rest of the UK, they lobby and cajole employers to implement that hourly rate. The rate is upgraded annually, in November. The current (2015) Living Wage rates as defined by these bodies are £7.85-an-hour outside London, and £9.15 for London.

But it is entirely voluntary, with no legal obligation on employers to either start paying it, or indeed continue to pay it, including after its annual uprating. There is absolutely no legal mechanism to enforce the Living Wage. It's entirely left to the whims and fancies of employers to decide if they want to sign up as Accredited Living Wage Employers, and thereby get bestowed the logo and certificate, with the kudos that accompanies this.

The whole Living Wage Campaign relies on powers of persuasion to cajole companies into signing up to pay this vastly improved rate. There isn't so much as a hint of deploying and mobilising the collective will of workers to achieve this modest redistribution of wealth to wages compared to profits.

Allow me to illustrate this point with a personal anecdote. I briefly considered applying for a job as Living Wage Accreditation Officer with the Poverty Alliance. As the Usdaw union convener in a huge multinational retail company, I've campaigned on and off for four years through union members and lobbied our company to pay a living wage – admittedly, arguing that it should not just be £7.85, but for the past year, £10-an-hour! They have just announced (in July 2015) their intention to pay the Living Wage across the UK and Ireland from April 2016 – though at the semi-official £7.85 rate, rather than the £10-an-hour I've advocated. But still, a substantial pay rise for a significant minority of the 8,000 of us they employ, after our shop-floor efforts to push for it.

So I thought the job with the Poverty Alliance, funded by the SNP government, would be a chance to spread that attempt to win at least some level of 'Living Wage' – through the campaigning efforts of workers' organised unions – to the rest of this nation of rotten pay. But I rapidly abandoned the pursuit of the job on reading the job description. There wasn't a single word about linking up with unions. It mostly mentioned 'business breakfasts' with employers to persuade them of the merits of a Living Wage for their company. All fine and dandy, but not exactly a recipe for empowering workers to improve their own share of the wealth they produce for their own employers, and of national wealth – let alone encouraging a bigger struggle to win working class control over the main centres of economic output!

In fact, this job description encapsulates an important shift in what's happening. Initiated by poverty-stricken wage-earners in London's East End, growing into vigorous campaigning by working class people and their allies across the UK, the Living Wage campaign is now apparently being incorporated into an arms-length extension of the Scottish Government.

On the one hand, we should welcome the Scottish Government funding the staffing of the Poverty Alliance in pursuit of the target (by Christmas 2015) of enlisting 500 employers in Scotland to pay this Living Wage. But on the other hand, it's not such a clear challenge by the Scottish Government to profiteering, low-paying big business as would be a statutory minimum Living Wage – legally enforced, unavoidable, not just voluntary on the part of companies.

This is classic SNP, it has to be said. Looking good to workers desperate for a substantial pay rise, by preaching the virtues of a £7.85 Living Wage – whilst studiously avoiding any offence to big business with even a hint of immediately, here and now in 2015, making such a wage a legally enforced national minimum. Outbidding their tribal opponents in Labour during the 2015 Westminster elections by promising a minimum of £8.70... but not until 2020!

Meantime the same SNP voted down a Motion in the Scottish Parliament for a £10 minimum – even though it was only proposed for introduction five years later, in 2020. Facing in two opposite directions, all at the same time. Being all things to all classes – seeking to please the wealth creators, and the profiteers who steal that wealth off working people's wages.

Of course, it's to the credit of all those 380 Scottish employers that have uprated the minimum rate of pay for their employees from the miserly, miserable National Minimum Wage of £6.50 (for over-21s) to the £7.85 Living Wage. It's stating the blindingly obvious that any worker, any trade unionist, let alone any socialist worth their salt, would welcome the 21% increase on the government's statutory minimum rate that this Living Wage figure amounts to. On gross hourly pay, that is, as it means a far lesser real rise in income for the worker involved, after taking account of loss of various in-work benefits.

Several surveys of workplaces that have started paying the Living Wage demonstrate beyond all doubt the social, economic and human advantages of a decent wage. For instance, the Scottish Living Wage Accreditation Initiative compiled information on the impact of its introduction – from employers. They reported a 25% fall in the rate of worker absenteeism compared to before paying the Living Wage. A massive 80% of employers reported "enhanced quality of work by staff", and 66% of firms found a "significant positive impact on recruitment and retention of staff." PriceWaterhouseCoopers reported: "Turnover of contractors fell from 4% to 1% since they adopted the Living Wage."

The human progress it means for workers previously condemned to the minuscule Minimum Wage is well documented. John is a security guard. He explained his modest expectations and the big boost to his life after getting the Living Wage:

"Instead of every penny that comes in having to go out again, it has given me a little extra to spend on my wife and kids, and that brings joy to my life. It means we can have a proper family life. We can do things together like going to the cinema or a play centre."

Or as the Scottish Living Wage campaign summarised it:

"Better psychological well-being; more time with family; rest; looking after health; participating in society; with a boost to the local economy through increased spending power."

Welcome though it is when any additional companies sign up as Accredited Living Wage Employers, we need to never lose sight of its two fundamental flaws: the fact it's entirely voluntary, not legally enforceable, and the fact that the level it's set at is still not worthy of the term 'Living Wage' in a proper, meaningful sense. Behind the wel-

come headlines announcing a growing number of Living Wage firms
lurk a few stark, sobering statistics. They underline the weakness of
a system based on companies voluntarily offering this wage, rather
than being obliged to by a combination of the collective power of organised workers' unions and government legislation.

In Scotland, in early 2014 only 23 employers were recognised Living Wage payers. By December 2014 the Poverty Alliance and Scottish Living Wage Campaign were able to boast that the numbers had
trebled during the recent months of high-profile campaigning – to
94 companies in total. New adherents to the Living Wage included
the Scottish Parliament (only then!), Hearts FC (the first Scottish
football club to do so) and the first cleaning company in the whole
of Scotland to do so, Strata Cleaning.

More sobering still is the fact that the same report admitted that
after examining the 32 new companies signed up in the final months
of 2014, 38% of them are micro-businesses, employing less than ten
workers each. Another 70% of the 32 newly-accredited companies
employ less than 50 workers each. Plus, although no breakdown of
such detail seems available, it's fair to assume that at least some of
the workers in these micro-businesses and small businesses were already earning more than the £7.85 Living Wage, which highlights
just how modest the numbers gaining from such voluntary improvements really are.

This educated guess is confirmed by the fact that one of the biggest
Scottish firms to sign up, (in October 2014) and the first in the
household goods retail sector, was PerfectHome. Although they employ 700 staff in 67 stores, a mere 51 of their workers enjoyed a pay
rise when they became Living Wage employers (17 part-timers and
34 full-time staff).

Now, by October 2015, there are 380 Accredited Living Wage Employers in Scotland. Progress, undoubtedly, and very welcome too. But
to keep these advances in perspective we need only recall a couple of
harsh, stubborn facts. As of November 2014, Scotland has a total of
2,270 large businesses, each employing over 250 workers. There are a
further 3,705 Medium Enterprises, those with 50-249 workers each.

And a massive 337,135 registered Small Enterprises – those with 0-49 workers employed. So 380 Living Wage employers, only 16 of them employing over 500 workers, and a minute twelve others employing 250-500 each, make up a devastatingly small proportion of the grand total of companies in Scotland, many of them relying on the minimum wage (or worse!) to harvest the profits and dividends for their owners and shareholders. In cold, undeniable figures, 380 employers make up an almost invisible 0.1% of all Scotland's registered companies!

* * * *

At UK level, by the summer of 2015, just 1,800 employers had volunteered to pay the Living Wage. Again for perspective, not a single, solitary retail company was on the list at the time – a telling omission given the huge concentration of low-paid workers in that sector. In fact according to the April 2015 Citizens UK report:

> "Sales and retail assistants make up the largest single group of people in the UK economy on less than the Living Wage – 760,000 of them!"

Just to focus on three of the many more retail giants who even now (October 2015) have NOT signed up for a basic wage of £7.85: Tesco, ASDA and Sainsbury's posted combined profits last year of £3.8billion, but still tell us they cannot afford to become Living Wage employers.

The general picture across big business is little better: the number of FTSE 100 companies sporting the Living Wage logo rose from a derisory four to a paltry 18 during the course of 2014. By October 2015 that figure has crept up to 29. In signing up, Nationwide's Head of Corporate Citizenship(?!) Stephen Uden let slip the cynical motives of those big corporations who have promised the Living Wage. On 3 November 2014 he blurted out:

> "We hope consumers will see more of the Living Wage logo over the next year, as further businesses accredit. People will be able to show their support with their feet and their wallets."

It was Oscar Wilde who defined a cynic as someone who "knows the price of everything and the value of nothing." For some big businesses, increased sales and profits through the kudos of displaying a logo for paying an extremely modest wage is the price they'll pay. They don't care one iota about the value of an improved life for those who work to produce their profits.

Most telling of all about the limitations of relying on an entirely voluntary Living Wage is the briefing by Oxfam, in December 2014. This reminds us that whilst there are over 5.24 million UK workers earning below the Living Wage, those who have had their wages raised to that figure through their employers becoming recognised Living Wage employers only amounts to a puny total of 60,000 workers. And as if it couldn't get any worse, even Oxfam's claim of 60,000 is seriously challenged by another report; one the same month, December 2014, by an institution that we must surely assume should know about these things – the Living Wage Foundation itself!

In reporting the previous month's rise on the Living Wages' hourly rates to £7.85 and £9.15 (London), and the fact that during 2014 the numbers of UK employers accredited with paying those Living Wages had doubled to over 1,000, they hid away a tiny bombshell in their statistics. They wrote: "This improves the pay of 35,000 workers employed by over 1,000 Living Wage accredited organisations." 35,000! A mere 35,000 workers – or in the extremely unlikely event of Oxfam knowing the figures better than the Living Wage Foundation itself – 60,000 in the whole of Britain, from a potential pool of over 5.24 million workers who would gain a pay increase if the £7.85/£9.15 Living Wages were applied across the board. And half a million of those who have not gained this modest rise, through the voluntary scheme that is the Living Wage, live and work in Scotland.

That's a reminder of a simple guiding truth: employers who are in business to make profits – which after all is the very essence of capitalism – do not readily volunteer to surrender a larger slice of the cake to workers' wages rather than their own profits and dividends.

A further health warning is required in reading about Living Wage employers: there are in effect two types of lists recognised by the

Scottish Living Wage Accreditation and its ilk. There are companies accredited because they not only guarantee the Living Wage to their own direct employees, but also insist on the same for any contract workers they employ through another company (the likes of cleaning, security or catering firms being common examples of this). But there are other employers accredited whilst only paying their own direct employees the Living Wage, but granted a phased accreditation on the promise of only hiring contract companies who pay the Living Wage when those contracts next come up for renewal.

When the Living Wage Commission conducted a year-long study from June 2013 onwards, they reported the Scottish Government as one of only 23 employers in Scotland paying the Living Wage at the time. But the *Daily Record*, in 2013, exposed the fact that sub-contracted cleaners at Scottish Government buildings were being paid less than £7-an-hour! So the Scottish SNP government itself was one of many employers who glowed with the glory of signing up as Living Wage bosses, but delegated their dirty work of hiring workers on buttons to a third party, in an attempt to hide their shame. An all-too-common cover-up, which also applies to the use of zero hours contracts.

* * * *

The fact that it is not legally enforceable is one fundamental flaw of the Living Wage. The little-known fact that it only applies to workers aged 18 or over, and excludes not only the youngest staff but also trainees and interns, is another blemish on what is widely perceived as its spotless face. However, perhaps its much more profound fault, its true Achilles' Heel, is the level it's set at by the bodies who measure and uprate it annually – the London Living Wage Unit and the Centre for Research in Social Policy, used by the Living Wage Foundation. The current hourly rates of £7.85 and £9.15.

Not a single one of the half-a-million workers in Scotland struggling on less than £7.85-an-hour would spurn the so-called Living Wage, which is 22% better than the legal National Minimum Wage of £6.50 (if you've celebrated your 21st birthday, that is! The percentage increase for younger workers would be massively more). But that's where any bacchanalian celebrations should pause, for a sober look at whether these figures really do merit the label 'Living Wage'. Behind the fanfares and fuss made by employers, political parties and governments who demand public acclamation for supporting or implementing this semi-institutionalised 'Living Wage', lurk a few dirty secrets, not known to the viewing public.

For starters, the annual calculation of how much to increase the Living Wage by has a self-imposed cap. First, they use focus groups to measure "a socially acceptable minimum standard of living for a range of [nine] types of households", in turn calculating an average hourly figure applied to all household types. Then the UK Living Wage (that set outside London) is limited to a rise of no more than two percentage points above either the rise in average incomes or median earnings, whichever is the greater.

According to the Resolution Foundation, in terms of hard cash, the difference between the actually required Living Wage and the level imposed by this cap is stark. In 2012, the true rate should have been £8.80-an-hour here in Scotland, instead of the £7.45 decided upon. In 2013, Living Wage researchers calculated the required Living Wage was £9.08, which they then capped at £7.65.

* * * *

Still more of a bombshell for those who just accept the figures trotted out as a 'Living Wage' – because that's what we are constantly told it is by the Living Wage Campaign, Poverty Alliance, Scottish Government, and its other advocates – is the fact that even the researchers and institutions that calculate these figures do not actually regard them as the true level of wage required to be called 'a Living Wage'!

Let me explain this critical fact; for fact it is, and one at the heart of our case for a £10 living minimum wage. A fact that has never hit the headlines, nor even the News In Briefs columns of a media that would much rather workers didn't get too uppity in their expectations and demands. As was explained in – amongst other even more obscure places – the Resolution Foundation's document of January 2013, *Beyond The Bottom Line*, the figures calculated for the 'Living Wage' make a huge assumption. They assume a full uptake of in-work benefits – including Child Tax Credits, Working Tax Credits and Housing Benefit – or otherwise the figures would be far, far higher.

One startling illustration of the difference, as calculated in the same document, is that if dependency on taxpayer-funded top-up benefits was removed from the calculations, London's Living Wage for November 2012 would not have been the £8.55-an-hour that it was, but instead a massively different £10.70-an-hour! And that was close to three years ago.

In the recent furore surrounding the bogus 'National Living Wage' invented by Tory Chancellor George Osborne – to throw dust in people's eyes and blind them to the actual cuts to workers' incomes carried in his July 2015 Emergency Budget – the Living Wage Foundation admitted the current £9.15 London Living Wage would need to be £12-an-hour if state benefit top-ups weren't included in their calculations.

As another illustration of the same key point, BBC Scotland was recently given access to a focus group actually used, in real life, to help determine the level of 'Living Wage'. Broadcast in May 2015, this programme provided several insights. It televised the comments of Tracey, who explained how she gets paid on a Thursday, and often runs out of cash Tuesday or Wednesday, and then sits in the dark in her house until pay day. It showed viewers the heart-breaking account of another Scottish woman who has always worked, but on the minimum wage, and whose one big dream is to have a holiday abroad, which she's never managed. One modest week's holiday in Scotland had left her broke for years since. It broadcast the debate within the focus group on whether they thought a television was a necessity, or an unnecessary luxury, as part of their calculations of the wage required for a basic but acceptable standard of living!

Leaving aside your opinion of some of the quality of what is broadcast, for many of the poorest a TV is the only affordable source of entertainment for themselves, or their kids; often the only means of reaching the outside world, given the cost of transport, or the cinema, or of going to the pub. Also, although they are being displaced by smartphones and tablets for some people, a TV is for many a route to the internet or email. It might be a source of the world wide web, but it's hardly asking for the earth! But crucially, despite the miserly expectations being considered by this focus group, their conclusion was that rather than £7.85, the Living Wage would need to be £9.20-an-hour to afford people the rock-bottom basics of life.

* * * *

Coming back to our original source on this central criticism of what, frankly, is a sanitised version of a genuine living wage, the Resolution Foundation wrote in January 2013:

"Both Living Wages of £8.55 and £7.45 [London and the rest of the UK, as of January 2013] are premised on the full take-up of tax credits and other in-work benefits. Without state support they would be FAR higher. So Living Wages do NOT precisely do what they say on the tin."

That's one of the several reasons we need a legally enforced living wage of £10-an-hour, in 2015 figures. That's the real level of living minimum wage that is essential to escape dependency on state benefits. To escape the poverty trap of a wage rise not really being a wage rise after loss of in-work benefits, some of which remove up to 86p for every £1 wage increase. To end dependency on the self-interested 'goodwill' of profit-hunting employers who only volunteer a pay rise if they think it enhances their overall market share. To guarantee workers a decent share of the wealth the working class creates, in the form of a wage that is a real and guaranteed route out of poverty.

A £10 minimum wage wouldn't be the route to a life of luxury. Workers getting it wouldn't exactly be taking time off work to wallpaper their living rooms with £10 notes! But at least it would guarantee access to the bare necessities of modern life – in fabulously rich 21st century Scotland. Is that too much to ask?

10

TORY TRIPLE THEFT

July 2015 was the month of the Tory Triple Theft. The newly 'elected' Tory dictatorship of the obscenely rich announced a Trade Union Bill that aims to steal the last vestiges of workers' rights. They want to crush workers' rights in order to crush our wages and public services. The Tory Emergency Budget announced a raft of measures that steals even more of our wages and benefits.

But perhaps most pernicious of all in this Unholy Trinity of Theft by the Tories was the Chancellor's theft of the English language. Whilst announcing a series of vicious cuts to low-paid workers' incomes – and those of their families, children included – George Osborne caught the gullible and/or willing media's attention with bogus claims of a 'National Living Wage' of £7.20, for those aged over-25, from April 2016.

Standing at the Dispatch Box was a man well used to twisting words and their meaning to suit his own interests. Born the son of Sir Peter Osborne, 17th Baronet, and Felicity Alexandra Loxton-Peacock, the aforementioned, humbly-named 'George' would like us to believe he's a man with the common touch. That's a pretence he sports in common with his fellow-member of the exclusive, upper-class, male-only Bullingdon Club of binge-drinking restaurant wreckers and rioters at Oxford University, 'Dave' Cameron. Actually, George is a man with an estimated personal fortune of £4million, including about £2million worth of shares in his father's wallpaper and fabrics empire, Osborne & Little.

George obviously knows all about the housing problems faced by the 'commoners' he seeks credibility and votes from, including that oft-mentioned category, 'hard-working families'. He has a mortgage on his £2million London house, with the oldest, most elite bank in Britain – C. Hoare & Co, which was established in 1672, only has 10,000 of the very richest as customers, expects each to deposit at least £500,000 in their heavily-protected portfolio, and has liveried doormen guarding the entrances to their two branches – which contain a grand piano inside one manager's office, a well in the basement, and a private garden.

So George won't have to traipse down to the Spartan decor of the local RBS or Bank of Scotland branch, nor eat up his phone bills waiting for a response from a (low-paid, harassed) call-handler in some remote call centre. His bank guarantees a direct line to a 'relationship manager' any time he wants! But whilst being one of the architects of the brutal bedroom tax, and ruthless author and executioner of the welfare benefits cap, George has some considerable experience at milking the system – at taxpayers' expense.

In 2000, he bought a Cheshire farmhouse for £445,000, without having to bother with a mortgage. Three years later, he seized advantage of the benefits loophole available to scroungers on Westminster's green benches: he 'flipped' his claim for public funding of an MP's second home allowance, from his London pile to the Cheshire farmhouse. He took out a mortgage on the latter (remember, he could afford to buy it cash-in-hand, without a mortgage, three years earlier) and claimed £1,900 a month interest payments off you and me, the taxpayers.

So it hardly merits 'exclusive' headlines to say Tory Chancellor Osborne is not only a brazen liar, but also a thief. In his July 2015 Emergency Budget he stole hundreds, indeed thousands of pounds off low-income families, the vast majority of them working families – and lied through his aristocratic teeth with headline-grabbing claims to be introducing a 'National Living Wage' from April 2016.

This theft of the noble term 'Living Wage' has largely served its purpose; it's thrown a fog of confusion into the discussion about what workers need as a real living wage that guarantees a decent, though basic, standard of living. So let's cut through the fog with a spotlight on what the first Tory Budget since 1996 actually meant for working class people.

Osborne's Budget unleashed naked class war on the working class, whilst conjuring up a con-trick that a master magician would eat his heart out for. The headline-grabbing 'National Living Wage' cynically attempted to throw dust in people's eyes, to blind them to the Tories' theft of incomes from low-paid workers, young people and parents with the audacity to have more than two children.

This Budget was a bloodcurdling awakening to anyone who thinks 'class' is an outdated, antediluvian concept. From behind all the recent bullshit about the Tories being 'the party of working people', 'blue-collar Conservatives', 'One Nation Tories', leapt out a Budget that made the bankers, billionaires and big business even more bloated in their opulence, by robbing the rest of us. It declared undiluted class war, camouflaged by the confusing guff about 'a National Living Wage'.

Before dealing with the issue of wages, let's glance at a few features of this first Tory Budget in 19 years. First, some of the winners. Corporation Tax on big business was 28% in 2010, when Osborne first took up his rent-free residence in 11 Downing Street. Now it's set to plummet to 18%, the lowest business tax in any country in the world – apart from Estonia and Ireland. By contrast, for example, German corporations are taxed at 30%; those in France 33.3%; and 40% in the USA.

Even before this bounty to big business, analysts at the University of York have shown that in 2012-13 the government gifted big business £58.2billion in subsidies, grants and Corporation Tax benefits – whilst only collecting £41.3billion in Corporation Tax that year. Now Osborne's shamelessly capitalist government is set to give big business an obscene £93billion in such handouts. That means every household has been forced to pay – without even being asked their leave to do so – an average of £3,500 in subsidies for big corporations. And the winners include many Corporation Tax-Dodgers.

Another major set of winners are those in receipt of inherited properties worth £1million, who won't have to fork out any Inheritance Tax. One figure quoted is that 26,000 such estates gain a giant £2.5billion. And just to update the story of Osborne's housing scams: he and his wife – Honourable Frances, daughter of former Tory Minister Lord Howell – bought a six-bedroom mansion in London, which they've rented out for £10,000 a month since ensconcing themselves, rent-free, in 11 Downing Street. Valued at around £2.3million, the Osbornes would gain £140,000 courtesy the slashed liability to Inheritance Tax on their London property alone. Who can deny this is government by the rich, for the rich?

Those profiting from war and death – the military industrial complex – can sleep peacefully in the knowledge the Tories agreed to jack up defence spending to the 2% of GDP demanded by NATO. The Tory warmongers didn't want to make their pals in the City of London feel left out in their handouts to the rich: contrary to the headlines, they'll gain from the replacement of the bank levy by the less 'punitive' 8% bank profits tax.

A small minority were winners from the Tory Budget, but they gained £billions. In contrast, millions were losers – overwhelmingly the 'hard-working families' we hear such repeated, hypocritical prattling about from Tory (and Labour) politicians, especially in pre-election periods. Whilst handing out £93billion to big business, the Tories stole £35billion from working class people in benefits – especially in-work benefits.

Over 5.3 million public sector workers – half a million of them in Scotland – have suffered pay cuts since 2010. According to UNISON, a miserable 3% pay rise in the past five years, whilst inflation rose by 17%. Now they are condemned to another four years of a 1% pay cap. That's not a decade of suffering a Pay Freeze, it's a modern Ice Age for workers in the NHS, councils, education and the likes.

Disabled people deemed fit to work stand to lose £30 a week. Young people will have all their benefits withdrawn if they decline unpaid work placements. Grants for working class students are to be scrapped in favour of loans. Housing benefit is to be wiped out for people aged 18-21.

Council and housing association tenants are to be given a miserly 1% cut to their rents, but if their household income is above £30,000 (and the official average wage per person last year was £27,200, don't forget) they will have to pay the full market rent. And the risible rent cuts to some tenants will mean 14,000 fewer social sector houses being available for affordable rent. Furthermore, as part of driving people into the money-grabbing embrace of the private rented sector, the tax threshold for landlords letting rooms was raised from £4,250 to £7,500.

Nearly all working age benefits are to be frozen until 2020, despite forecasts of rising inflation by then. The household benefit cap is to be slashed from £26,000 to £20,000. In a measure that King Herod would have blushed and baulked at implementing, the multi-millionaire George Osborne is to deny any additional Housing Benefit, tax credit or Universal Credit for any more than two children per family. As the Children's Commissioner, Tam Baillie, was moved to comment:

> "Parents and carers must feed and clothe all of their children, not just the first two. This is denying millions of children their basic human rights."

An estimated seven million children face savage cuts to their families' incomes from the overall Budget. And Osborne's rule about 'two kids only' smacks of class hatred and a form of eugenics; only the rich are allowed to breed, it seems.

One of the biggest component chunks of cuts is that suffered by low-paid workers through attacks on tax credits, including Working Tax Credits. A horrendous £4.5billion is to be robbed off some of the poorest-paid this year alone.

* * * *

But that's where Osborne the ruthless thief became Osborne the shameless liar. To distract and confuse those outraged at his daylight robbery of the incomes of workers, students, disabled people, young people and parents, he perpetrated the monstrous lie that "Britain needs a pay rise and Britain is getting a pay rise." Stealing not only our incomes, but also our language, he then played dirty, disgraceful tricks with the term 'Living Wage'.

To unmask his lies, it's useful to recap a few simple facts. The current National Minimum Wage, since October 2015, is £6.70-an-hour – once you're aged 21. And, crucially, it's legally enforceable. The current Living Wage Foundation figure for (entirely voluntary) Living Wage is £7.85 an hour, outside Greater London. It will be uprated in November. This figure is based on the very important assumption of full uptake of all forms of in-work benefits, including tax credits and Housing Benefit. Otherwise, its own authors admit, it would have to be far, far higher.

There's the rub, the essence of the God Almighty lie perpetrated by Osborne and the Tories. It's a Biblical case of George giveth, and George taketh away! Osborne manufactured media headlines – in a masterly distraction ploy from his slaughter of benefits and wages – by talking of 'a National Living Wage' of £7.20 by April 2016, "with an ambition of this rising to £9 by 2020." None of the media mentioned, let alone exposed, that weasel phrase, "an ambition." But leaving that aside, one key point is that £7.20 in April 2016 is a mere 50p up on the newly-announced National Minimum Wage, in itself derisory. Furthermore it is well below the current 'Living Wage' of £7.85, even before that is uprated this November. Perhaps most critical of all, it disguises the theft of tax credits which will mean low-paid workers will lose, not gain, from Osborne's sham 'National Living Wage'.

* * * *

To shine a piercing light of truth through Osborne's fog of lies, let us quote a few calculations by various economists in the wake of the Budget baloney about "Britain getting a pay rise."

A couple, with two kids, both working full-time on the current £6.50 minimum wage would gain £1,560 in wages, but lose £2,200 in tax credits. Two workers, both earning £9.25 an hour, with two kids, would be £850 a year worse off. A family with two at work, currently earning £20,000, would have a fall in their income of £2,057 a year. A single parent now earning a pathetic £10,000 would lose £1,455 of that under Osborne's deceitful package. The IFS estimates that a family earning £7,000 a year, with two or more children, will have their family income cut by £1,724.

Mark is an Usdaw union rep, working 35 hours a week as a driver for Tesco Extra in Port Glasgow. His partner Agnes works on the checkouts in the same store, 18 hours a week. They have three young children. Mark demolished the mountain of lies from the Tories by explaining his own family's situation:

"Our standard of living has been going backwards since 2010, with in-work benefits either cut or frozen. The Chancellor's so-called National Living Wage means nothing to me. I already earn 57p-an-hour more than his £7.20, although Agnes is currently on £7.39-an-hour. But the cuts to Working Tax Credits, the reduction in the threshold from £6,420 to £3,850, and the increase from 41% to 48% in the amount the government cuts your tax credits over a certain limit, will take around £40 a week out of our household budget. It makes you think does work pay? It's pride that's keeping us at work; we don't want to live on benefits."

The National Institute of Economic and Social Research concluded that three million families will lose more in tax credits than they gain in wages or changes to the Income Tax threshold, and that the Budget will only benefit childless and non-disabled individuals working 40-hours-a-week on the National Minimum Wage. The equally eminent Institute for Fiscal Studies (IFS) reckon 13 million families in Britain will lose an average of £260 a year – with 3.2 million of these households being an average of over £1,000-a-year the poorer.

In Scotland, over 500,000 children (60% of the total) currently live in families that rely on tax credits to supplement their paltry pay. Research by the Scottish Government shows that at least 250,000 families here will be on average £1,000 a year worse off as a consequence of the July 2015 Tory Budget's assault on tax credits.

And those are just sample figures for workers who qualify for Osborne's grossly misnamed 'National Living Wage' by dint of being aged 25 or more. Over two million workers in Britain aged under-25 are to be denied the Tories' bountiful 'increase' – including a full one-third of retail workers, in what is one of the prime concentrations of low pay. Far from being a route to 'a high wage economy', this Budget is, amongst other things, a recipe for replacement of older workers by under-25s as a source of dirt-cheap labour.

The SSP has never favoured a pathetically low, legal national minimum wage. Nor have we restricted our fight to support for a voluntary, unenforceable 'Living Wage' – especially one which is not actually a genuine living wage at all, since it depends on top-ups, which in turn come out of the pockets of workers' taxes. Since our formation, the SSP has demanded a decent living minimum wage, legally enforced, based on the formula of two-thirds male median earnings. In 2015 figures, that means we demand a national minimum wage of £10, here and now.

And critically, the SSP's demand has always been that this applies to all workers and apprentices aged 16 and over. Not just to the over-18s as applies to the (voluntary) Living Wage. Not only the over-21s as applies now to the statutory National Minimum Wage. Not merely the over-25s as Osborne plans, in a further ploy to divide the working class and furnish employers with a ready-made army of cheap, desperate labour. And not accompanied by cuts to in-work benefits.

The fact is, a £10 minimum – right now in 2015, not five years hence – would constitute a genuine living income, and is the level required to remove workers from reliance on state top-ups, which constitute a £30billion annual subsidy to bosses who pay their workers peanuts in pursuit of ever-higher profits. The trade union movement and socialists need to cut through the crap perpetrated by the Tories on this issue, and mobilise workers in struggle for a living minimum wage of £10 now, for all over 16, with equal pay for women.

The Tories' July 2015 Budget was enough to make anyone's blood boil in anger at the bitter class war by the rich it represents. But it should also put fire in our bellies and steel in our resolve to fight back.

11

WHY DEMAND £10 NOW?

Why advocate and campaign of £10 Now? Is it just because it's a nice round figure, easy to remember? Absolutely not! Before too long it will become outdated, lagging behind needs, the cost of living, and relative earnings. It's the method behind the demand that counts, not its neatness. Its radicalism, not its roundness.

The Scottish Socialist Party has fought for a decent level of national minimum wage since its formation in September 1998 – as did the SSP's socialist predecessors. We have consistently demanded it be for "all over 16", thereby including the central policy of scrapping the lower youth rates, which have always existed since the national minimum wage legislation was first implemented in April 1999. In fact for its first six years, up until 2005, there was no legal minimum wage at all covering workers aged 16-17, and the derisory apprentices' legal minimum was only introduced five years later still, in 2010.

Unless, as an aside, you happen to migrate to the UK Crown dependency of Jersey. There, in 2012, their Employment Forum declared against a lower youth rate, giving younger workers the full £6.78 minimum wage, which Jersey (along with Guernsey and the Isle of Man) has the power to decide on. We await news of economic collapse and social catastrophe from this profligate Channel Island 'dependency'!

We see no justification in lower pay for young workers. When someone under 21 goes to buy bread and milk they don't get a discounted youth price. When they eat in a fast food restaurant, served overwhelmingly by young workers, they're not asked for ID to qualify for an under-21 price discount. When they shop in retail stores – staffed by huge numbers of workers under 21 – they don't encounter sales banners declaring 'Special Youth Discount'.

Working class people aged under-21 are classed as old enough to marry, vote, and fight, kill and die in bloody wars for bloodthirsty imperialist powers. But their 'special youth discount' wages frequently mean they can't afford to rent their own accommodation, let alone get a mortgage, which leads to a growing pattern of living at home with their parents for years longer than either family generation would freely choose.

On top of that, lower youth rates for the government minimum wage is a recipe for divide-and-rule tactics, hiring cheaper younger workers in preference to older, more experienced ones – who, critically in the world-view of capitalist employers, are also more expensive to buy labour-power off. Just take a look at the fast food joints and coffee shops that have spread to every corner of Scotland in the past ten to fifteen years: they're heavily populated by younger, cheaper workers, usually not just on zero hours contracts, but also on the below-basement level 'youth development' minimum wage.

* * * *

Likewise, the SSP has always attached the further demand "with equal pay for women." This is a critically important – if succinct – phrase, as the gender pay gap has been an obnoxious, inbuilt feature of capitalism for as long as that form of class exploitation has existed, including throughout the 45 years since the Equal Pay Act was made law in the UK. The gender pay gap closed slightly for a period in recent years compared to 1997, when records began. Back then it was 17.4%. So when a woman worker got £100 in wages, a man in the same type of work would get £117.40. By 2010, on the 40th anniversary of the Equal Pay Act, the Fawcett Society reported the gender pay gap was still 16.4%.

But the same organisation's August 2014 research claimed that by 2013 the shortfall had risen again for the first time in five years, to a staggering 19.1%. That's the equivalent of a workplace where full-time male workers are paid all year round, but females work for free from about 22 October!

In contrast to these figures, the government's ASHE report of November 2014 claims the gender pay gap has narrowed to 9.4%. But even if true, that still means a woman only getting 90p for every £1 earned by a man in the same type of job. Several other analyses of the unprecedented nose-dive in all workers' wages between 2008 and 2014 would suggest that – if indeed the ASHE survey is accurate – this narrowing of the gender gap has more to do with men's wages falling even more drastically, rather than women's wages rising.

To quote just one of many such statistical surveys, the Joseph Rowntree Foundation (November 2014) concluded that average real wages for men had fallen between 2008 and 2013 from £13.90 to £12.90 per hour, whilst women's had also fallen, but by a lesser amount, from £10.80 to £10.30 an hour. The figures for 2014 reveal that 26% of women worked for less than £7.65-an-hour, whereas 16% of men suffered that slave-wage status.

* * * *

Several mechanisms create this double exploitation of women workers. Women are often corralled into low-paying sectors of employment, such as retail, hospitality and the care sector. Women workers all-too-frequently land in jobs seen by employers as an extension of domestic tasks and domestic drudgery, such as elderly care, childcare, cleaning and catering. And despite the socially invaluable role of such jobs, they are given low status and even lower wages by those in charge of capitalist society.

The main concentrations of low-wage, low-status jobs – hotels, restaurants, retail – frequently also offer little career opportunity. Primary responsibility for childcare, especially in the child's early years, plus the dire lack of affordable childcare, serves to cut off many women's career paths, trapping them on the lower rungs of the jobs ladder. It's at the typical child-bearing age range that women's pay inequality hits hard, and then remains in subsequent years. Of course on top of that, there is straightforward, unadulterated wage discrimination; witness the tens of thousands of claims for equal pay settlements by women workers against local authorities, NHS boards and ASDA, to name but some. The end result is, as the Poverty Alliance reported in December 2014, that a monumental 64% of those on low pay in Scotland are women – and a full 40% of the overall low-paid total is women in part-time jobs.

Furthermore, things got even worse for women workers since the 2008 bankers' crisis. The Fawcett Society found that nearly twice as many women in Scotland are in low-pay, low-status, insecure jobs as were before 2008; in part, for the brutally simple reason that those are overwhelmingly the types of jobs created in recent years. The same Fawcett Society survey found 50% of low paid women feel worse off now than they did five years ago, and 10% of them have taken out a Pay Day Loan in the last twelve months – a sure road to the financial gates of Hell! So the SSP is unashamedly persistent in the demand "with equal pay for women", including as an integral part of the case for a living minimum wage.

* * * *

But why the figure of £10... "for all over 16, with equal pay for women"? When the Labour government conceded a minimum wage law in 1999, they refused to base its level (actually, levels, plural) on any clear and consistent formula. It wasn't – and still isn't – based on any percentage of average pay or median earnings, for instance. Its levels are determined by the incumbent government annually, after recommendations from the Low Pay Commission.

From its very birth it was, as we've written earlier, a 'classic political stitch-up'. A balancing act between appeasing some of the clamour for a living income from anti-poverty campaigners, the organised trade unions and that amorphous entity 'the general public' – whilst on the other hand, sustaining the profit margins of capitalist employers, whose influence overwhelmingly prevails during the deliberations of the Low Pay Commission and governments.

The figures are arbitrary, the arithmetic more political in its calculations than mathematical. How small an increase can they get away with? What token annual increase will avoid alienating the voting public? How little will workers and their unions accept without a revolt? That's the politically-influenced arithmetic used, not some sci-

entific measure of the wage required for workers to have full access
to all the basics that modern society has to offer – in their country, at
any given moment in history.

In contrast, in order to try and use a statutory minimum wage as a
major weapon in an unashamed war on poverty – but also on inequality – socialists in the SSP and its predecessors have always used a formula to calculate what the legally enforceable minimum wage should
be. Concretely, in keeping with many past generations of socialists and
trade unionists – and indeed many non-socialist campaigns and institutions to this day – the SSP has persistently adopted the formula
of 'two-thirds median male earnings' to calculate the figure that should
be put on a living minimum wage any particular year. That's where
the £10 demand comes from, here in Scotland, here and now in 2015.

* * * *

We have no fixation with this particular formula, but it's as good
as any for several reasons. Let's break down the formula 'two-thirds
male median earnings' into its component parts, to show why it's a
very reasonable, modest demand, but also a radical challenge to the
cruel exploitation suffered by workers under the ruling capitalist system of economy.

Firstly, 'median'. That's not the same as the average wage, which
would actually be higher than the median wage. It's where you list
every single wage paid in this country and take the one in the middle
of the whole lot. In round figures, if there were two million workers
in Scotland, when you list the hourly wage of each and every one, in
a league table from highest rates to lowest, the median wage will be
that of the one-millionth worker on the list. Put plainly, half of all
workers earn MORE than the median wage, the other half earn
LESS than the median wage.

Secondly, 'median male'. We've opted for this because the gender
gap in pay means male wages on average are at least 9-10% higher
than women workers' wages, in comparable jobs – or actually 19%,
according to the Fawcett Society's calculations for 2013, as quoted

above. We could just as easily decide to call for a minimum wage based on a percentage of median hourly pay for ALL workers. But a formula based on the median wage for MALE workers is not only higher in absolute money terms, but has the crucial advantage of at least modestly helping to combat wage inequality between male and female workers. Women make up far greater numbers of the lowest paid (64%); conversely they will gain much more from a legally enforced minimum based on a percentage of the MALE median wage. It helps with a bit of catching up; helps reduce the gender gap.

Thirdly, 'two-thirds median male earnings'. We could argue a powerful case for the minimum wage to be set at 'median male earnings', which by definition would increase the hourly rate of pay for exactly half of all men in work, and substantially more than half of all women workers. So calling for just 66% of that is an extremely modest demand, hardly asking for the earth, let alone the moon and the stars. Whilst exceedingly modest, it is also a radical departure from the pathetic levels of minimum wage which millions have been subjected to over the past 16 years in this country. Right now, the official claim is that the 'adult' rate, that for workers over 21, amounts to 47% of the median wage. It's consistently sat at 46-47% since 2007. So right away you can see the leap in incomes the '66% of male median earnings' formula – a £10 minimum wage – would offer millions of working people across Scotland and the UK.

* * * *

Furthermore, variants of this 'two-thirds median' formula are widely accepted by institutions a million miles removed from the SSP and socialism! The world-wide Organisation for Economic Cooperation and Development – the OECD – sets its measurement of a Low Pay Threshold at "two-thirds of gross median hourly earnings for all full-time employees." The Resolution Foundation uses the slightly lesser variant of "the relative Low Pay Threshold, defined here as two-thirds median pay for all employees." That's lower in hourly rates of pay than the OECD's formula, because of the Resolution Foundation's inclusion of part-time workers – whose hourly pay is persistently, substantially lower than that of full-timers. For instance, the November 2014 Report by KPMG found that 43% of all part-timers earned below £7.65-an-hour, whereas 13% of full-timers suffered such rotten hourly rates.

If we look at the implications of the OECD's measurement of poverty wages, it is a devastating condemnation of the state of affairs in 'modern' capitalist Scotland and Britain, even compared with countries not noted for their progressive regimes. For the years 2009-11, the OECD's Labour Market Statistics reveal that the percentage of workers earning below 'two-thirds median full-time' hourly rates for each particular country is at its worst in South Korea and the USA; 25% in both cases.

Next in this league of shame is Israel, where 22% of workers are below the OECD threshold, followed closely by Hungary and Britain – both with 21%. So workers in Britain are five percentage points more likely to fall below the OECD's measure of poverty pay than the (16%) average for all the OECD countries. And we are five times more likely to fall below that threshold than workers in Belgium; twice as likely as our counterparts in Italy. To amend Shakespeare's Hamlet, "Something's rotten in the state of Britain."

* * * *

The definition of poverty matters profoundly to those stuck on low incomes! Conversely, it also matters massively to those hell-bent on scooping up maximum shares of wealth for themselves in the form of profits, perks and privileges. That explains the history of shifting definitions of the threshold for low pay and poverty, as accepted by various governments and institutions. Most Tories and many employers are in denial about the whole concept of relative poverty. They would much prefer if we simply compared absolute incomes in 2015 to those in 1915, or the Hungry Thirties – easing the path to them boasting how well off the current generation of workers are by comparison, in terms of absolute wages. Or when it suits them, they will remind workers in this country how 'privileged' we are compared with those millions in the developing world, suffering literal mass starvation and death from preventable diseases induced by indescribable poverty. In a world where, according to Oxfam, 805 million people haven't enough food to lead a healthy active life; where hunger kills more people every year than malaria, AIDS and tuberculosis combined; in such a world of mass death through poverty, it's hardly a stunning revelation to state people in Scotland are better off, in absolute terms, than hundreds of millions in Africa, Asia or Latin America.

But it misses the point, entirely. In Scotland, a country awash with wealth, a nation of mass abundance, the fact a huge minority of the population is completely denied access to that wealth is a criminal indictment of the class-ridden system that we need to rid ourselves of. It's not the amount of wealth produced in Scotland that causes poverty; it's the ownership and distribution of the wealth that condemns whole swathes of the population to exclusion from the socially accepted norms of life and living standards.

* * * *

The first measure of relative poverty in this country was conducted in the late 1980s, courtesy the Households Below Average Incomes (HBAI). For most of the 1980s, the HBAI used the full range from 50% to 90% of MEAN (average) household income to measure relative poverty. The lesser-value MEDIAN was only chosen and preferred by the HBAI as recently as the late-1990s. After much debate throughout this period, the formula of '60% of median household incomes' was only eventually adopted by the HBAI statisticians in 1999.

Likewise, it was only the year before – 1998 – that the same relative poverty threshold was used by the Statistical Programme Committee of the European Union. And 1999 was the year when Tony Blair declared the goal of "eradicating child poverty within 20 years", making it the first time a government had adopted '60% of median household incomes' as the measure of (relative) poverty. As eminent academics Stewart Lansley and Joanna Mack, who have conducted the Breadline Britain surveys for the past 30 years, wrote:

"60% of median household incomes was a statistical compromise after much debate between 50% and 90%, with little evidence as to WHY 60% is the best place to draw the line."

And the figure of choice makes a devastating difference to official measures of poverty. For instance, in 2012-13, a scandalous 21% of all people in the UK lived below the '60% median household income' threshold – whereas if this was uprated to anything below 70% of the median, a whopping 29% of the population of Britain would have been thereby categorised as living in poverty.

Whilst governments and many research institutions swallowed whole the arbitrary '60% of median household incomes' as the accepted measure of relative poverty, other comprehensive research found this threshold to be far too low. For instance, as recently as 2011, the Joseph Rowntree Foundation assessed requirements for different sectors of the population to meet Minimum Income Standards. They discovered that a pensioner couple could only meet this modest level with 64% of median household incomes, and all other sections of the population with 66-67%.

Lansley and Mack also puncture the profound shortcomings of this whole formula ('net household incomes') as it fails to take account of debt repayment, changes in the cost of living, and is based on all forms of household income BEFORE the deduction of housing costs. In the real world of massively inflated housing costs in recent decades, this formula becomes a hopelessly unrealistic measure of real standards of living – and of poverty.

* * * *

This is but one example of the downgrading of the poverty threshold, as measured by contemporary capitalist governments, in this country and others. Perhaps one of the most pivotal examples of statistics being used as a weapon to make people submit to lowered expectations, as a prelude to lowered wages, is the EU Commission's European Decency Threshold. Up until 2004, this concept was used as a central reference point by many of us in the trade union and socialist movement, vigorously campaigning for a national minimum wage matching the Council of Europe Decency Threshold. Why? Because the Decency Threshold at the time was set at "68% of the average gross national earnings" in any member state in the EU; almost exactly corresponding to the 'two-thirds male median earnings' figure.

But in 2004 all that changed, removing a powerful campaigning weapon from the hands of those of us championing a guaranteed, decent, living minimum wage for all. The 68% formula was eliminated, as governments across Europe sought to dilute and dismantle the reforms of the Social Charter – that aspect of the EU which for a time shielded workers from some of the worst excesses of class war by Thatcher and her continental counterparts.

Governments of the traditional, conservative right were joined by social democratic parties lurching to the right, in a convergence of capitalist political forces desperate to claw back the reforms and concessions to the working class granted in the social upheaval of the post-WW2 period, and the subsequent era of international capitalist boom-time, which could afford such concessions, from 1950-75. Reformism morphed into counter-reformism; social democracy into neo-liberal capitalism.

That process was reflected at EU level. The Decency Threshold was hedged by a forest of qualifications and caveats that made it almost impossible to measure, as the crystal clear '68% of average gross earnings' was replaced by "60% of net earnings", renamed the European Social Charter Adequate Remuneration Threshold – ESCART.

Aside from the blatantly obvious reduction in real value this represented – 60% compared with 68% – a dense woodland of other caveats and obstacles to a radical improvement in guaranteed pay accompanied this EU change to its own Social Charter. For starters, the measurement of 'net earnings', as pointed out by the Scottish Low Pay Unit:

"Meant bonuses and gratuities are to be taken into account. But low-paid workers don't usually get these and therefore the resulting figure wouldn't be reflective of the position of the people it was intended to assist."

Furthermore, measurements of 'net earnings' are not produced by the UK government, making it just about impossible to work out what 60% of their average would be for a minimum wage. And that's not the end of it. The European Committee of Social Rights went on to define what they mean by "60% of net earnings" in language that would make a fortune for lawyers and provide a lifelong campaign for the Plain English Society!

"That is, after deductions of social security contributions and taxes, of the total wages, in principle both monetary and in kind, paid regularly by an employer to a worker for work carried out. Account shall where applicable be taken of bonuses and gratuities not paid regularly with each pay packet."

Over to you for the translation! Suffice to say, it's up to the European trade union movement and genuine socialist parties across Europe to define and then demand a real and measurable European Decency Threshold minimum wage, to combat the spreading cancer of poverty pay across the continent. Restoration of the pre-2004 formula of "68% of average gross wages", or some similar measure such as "two-thirds male median earnings", for each nation state within the EU, would be as decent a starting point as any.

And vast numbers of workers would stand to gain, immensely, from a successful battle for a European minimum wage set at such levels. A hint of this was provided by social researcher Thorsten Shulten, who in October 2014 wrote that a European minimum wage set at 60% of national median wages – not the 68% or 66% I've proposed, but just 60% – would improve the wages of 28 million workers across Europe; 16% of the total European workforce.

* * * *

There are forces and traditions much closer to the hearts of socialists and trade unionists than those institutions which recognise some version of 'two-thirds male median earnings' or 'two-thirds median full-time earnings' as the formula required to guarantee the bare necessities of life. In the 1970s, the leaders of the union organising many of the lowest-paid workers, NUPE (National Union of Public Employees), adopted precisely this formula in pursuit of a national minimum wage. NUPE leaders Alan Fisher and Bernard Dix pursued this policy within the TUC, STUC and Labour Party, initially facing stiff opposition from many other trade union leaderships, especially those with the better-organised, skilled and better-paid workers, who used the collective bargaining power and industrial muscle of workers at key points of production to squeeze wage concessions out of the employers.

These skilled and semi-skilled workers' union leaders – including the two giants of the time, AEEU and TGWU – rightly saw the collective, organised power of workers as the chief weapon in the relentless war between pay and profit, labour and capital. But they mistakenly dismissed the value of a guaranteed, statutory minimum wage – in part for those workers possessing less bargaining power in the production process – in an erroneous belief it would undermine the wages of skilled workers. It took the best part of two decades of battling within the unions, and then putting pressure on Labour, before the statutory minimum wage was legislated for and introduced in April 1999.

In the modern crusade to transform the minimum wage into a legally enforced living wage, the SSP has played an outstanding part. Not only on the streets, agitating and educating people on the case, but also through and within our unions. For instance, SSP members have written, presented, and successfully argued for the policy of a national minimum wage based on 'two-thirds male median earnings' in several trade union conferences, including the civil service PCS union, and the Scottish Trades Union Congress. We have also won support for this policy in numerous local branches and Scottish bodies of other unions, including Unison, Unite, FBU, Usdaw, CWU, NUJ and GMB.

The biggest recent breakthrough in fighting for a living minimum wage was undoubtedly won through the efforts of the Bakers, Food and Allied Workers' Union (BFAWU) at the 2014 congress of the TUC. They proposed the Motion at the TUC congress in Liverpool which agreed "to campaign for a £10 per hour minimum wage for all workers." The key weapon thus forged for those wishing to eradicate poverty pay is the fact this policy was passed unanimously – without a single vote or voice against – at the TUC conference of delegates representing 6.5 million unionised workers throughout the private, public and third sector. Every single union voted in favour of it.

The potential power behind the policy rests in the hands of the various union leaderships. If they are at all serious or sincere in voting for the £10 minimum for all workers they should be trumpeting this policy in every workplace, holding forums for union reps to equip them with the arguments in favour of it. The union leaderships should be submitting wage claims with this £10 minimum written into pay demands, popularising the case amongst members – and making serious preparations for collective industrial action in pursuit of such pay claims where necessary. They should be targeting non-union workplaces with materials seeking to recruit workers around a serious fight for £10 Now!, offering experienced organisers to service new recruits in pursuit of workplace rights and a living wage.

To their eternal credit, the Bakers' Union is doing precisely that. They've been spearheading the Hungry for Justice campaign aimed at fast food workers, around the central fighting demands of union rights, an end to zero hours contracts, and £10 Now! Although the fear of reprisals that has been whipped up by employers for years makes this a difficult struggle, groups of fast food workers have begun to join the BFAWU and campaign. They are driven by the material need to struggle or starve, and inspired by the example of fast food and retail workers who are storming heaven in the US, with courageous mass walkouts and marches for $15 Now!

12

'LET'S BE REALISTIC'
– SAY THE PROFITEERS

But surely £10-an-hour is not realistic? Surely employers couldn't afford it? Even some people outraged at the depths of poverty suffered by far too many of our own kind, the working class, express such doubts and worries. Of course the mainstream media, 'mainstream' (read 'pro-capitalist') political parties, and a predicable cacophony of big business voices are raised in thundering outrage at such a proposal.

Let us soberly examine some facts. Let us put the call for a decent living wage of £10 Now! – not in 2020 or some other distant date, but now, in 2015 – in proper perspective. After looking at some facts, our demand looks mild and modest, easily affordable. But like any other bit of progress ever made for the working class majority population, a £10 minimum living wage is only 'realistic' if enough of us organise, demand and fight ferociously for it. Against the equally ferocious resistance of precisely those classes of people and institutions who tell us Scotland couldn't afford such a guaranteed minimum income.

Some of the most hard-line opponents of a living minimum wage of £10-an-hour are people who wouldn't get out of bed for anything less than £1,000-an-hour. Socialist exaggeration? No! In 2014, a phrase was coined: Fat Cat Wednesday. This captured the outrageous fact that assuming the chief executives of the FTSE 100 companies returned from the Christmas holidays on the first Monday of the New Year, by midday on Wednesday they would – on average – have raked in the £27,000 that it took the average worker in Scotland the entire previous year to earn.

The following year, 2015, a new phrase had to be coined, to keep up with the skyrocketing incomes of the bosses of big business: Fat Cat Tuesday. Why? Because this year they'd grabbed the equivalent of the average worker's annual wage – which had crept upwards to £27,200 – in the first TWO days of the year, by the Tuesday evening.

They didn't even have to toil onwards into Wednesday morning! Even if we make the naively generous assumption that these boardroom dictators work a 12-hour day, only take ten days' annual leave, and work three out of four weekends (none of which assumptions there is an ounce of evidence for!), that still means they are on £1,200 an hour. Their annual average income for 2014 was £4.72million – each! Whereas the average worker's wage 'rose' a paltry £200 in 2014, the FTSE 100 chief executives awarded themselves an average increase of £500,000, each.

Yet these are the people who dictate disgustingly dirt-cheap wages to workers, and use their ownership and control of the mass media to demonise trade unionists who dare to stand up for a pay rise, and denounce demands for a £10 living wage as madness at best, or treason at worst. The big business CBI's outgoing president John Cridland called the Tories' planned, pathetically low £7.20-an-hour 'National Living Wage' a gamble. His successor, Paul Drechsler, has gone further, with hair-raising warnings of it shedding jobs, ending the hiring of workers and slashing profit. "In one big company it would wipe out all of their profits", he claimed. So we can begin to imagine the blood-curdling venom these captains of industry reserve for proposals of a genuine living wage of £10, including for the under-25s.

We're told £10-an-hour is 'unrealistic' for workers, but £1,000-an-hour is a gross underestimate of what the top bosses of British capitalism actually pay themselves. Do you still think we can't afford a £10 minimum wage?

* * * *

The incomes of the FTSE 100 CEOs are not some aberration, bucking the trend in the boardrooms. In fact the pay of ALL company directors in this country rocketed by 21% in 2014, in the wake of even bigger rises the previous years. Yet for millions of workers that was the 4th, 5th or 6th year without a pay increase, or a derisory 1% 'rise'.

It's widely accepted the bankers' greed was central to the financial meltdown of 2008, for which working people have paid twice over: first through the plundering of £1.3trillion of taxpayers' money to bail out the banks, and then through the seven years of famine faced in workers' jobs, pay and public services to compensate for the bankers' feast.

Since the financial crisis of 2008, hundreds of thousands of bank workers have lost their jobs, joining the massed army of casualties in other sectors – the victims of crises caused by the bankers' and billionaires' system. The giant Wall Street banks alone have shed 50,000 workers since 2008. Britain's Big Four – Lloyds, HSBC, RBS and Barclays – slashed their world-wide workforces by 189,000 between 2008 and 2013. That included 4,000 RBS staff and 5,500 in Barclays in the UK. Subsequently, Barclays announced a further 9,000 UK job losses by 2016, and HSBC recently declared the death knell for 25,000 jobs, 8,000 of them in Britain.

Meantime, on the other side of the gaping class divide, a gang of 2,600 senior bankers in London grabbed an average income of £1.3m, each, in 2014. So this small group of 2,600 economy-wreckers had a combined income substantially larger than the entire block grant from Westminster to the Scottish Government – which of course was cut yet again, because 'we have to balance the books', and 'tighten our belts'. I know whose necks I would like to tighten my belt round! Straight away we can surely see one simple way to pay for a decent £10 minimum wage for all workers: tax the rich, the tiny elite, those who in the wake of the anti-capitalist Occupy movement of the 2000s are known as 'the 1%'.

Every year since 1989, the *Sunday Times* has compiled its Rich List. In 2014, the richest 1,000 individuals in Britain almost doubled their combined wealth compared to five years before, to a Himalayan Mountain scale of riches, £519billion. A short year later, the 2015 Rich List showed this mountain of personal wealth had exploded further to £547billion.

One of a package of measures the SSP would favour in a radical redistribution of wealth, a far-reaching offensive against poverty, and inequality, would be a wealth tax. Imagine, for instance, a modest 10% wealth tax. Even if we take the figures for the richest 1,000, that would raise £55billion across the UK this year. The equivalent of over

£2,200 for the wages of every one of the 25 million employees in Britain. But why stop at 10%? Would these people even notice 20% or 30% being lopped off their monstrous mountain of wealth? And why would a wealth tax merely apply to the richest 1,000 who sit atop such a fortune? For starters, there are about 34,000 millionaires who should be made to contribute to society, rather than salt their hoardings away in the vaults of banks in overseas tax havens, dodging even the puny taxes they are currently liable to pay.

* * * *

The stink of hypocrisy on this issue is overpowering if you enter the realms of the rich and their attitudes to workers' pay, or to a guaranteed living wage. Multitudes of low-paid workers, and people sinking in poverty on benefits, pour into Primark in search of cheap clothes. Primark is owned by Associated British Foods. That outfit's top dog, George Weston, was awarded a £5million Christmas bonus for meeting 2014 targets, on top of his £1million salary and £900,000 annual bonus. And subsequently it's emerged that Galen and George Weston – owners also of Selfridges – enjoyed a £3.7billion boost to their wealth last year, making them 'worth' £11billion.

Yet Primark stubbornly refuse to pay its workers the modest so-called Living Wage of £7.85. So it would take a Primark worker on the £6.50 minimum wage, working full-time, a total of 354 years to match George Weston's 2014 income. How 'realistic' is that?

For now, one other example. If you've grabbed a bag of what amounts to throw-away, wash-once, disposable clothes in Primark, because you worked a few hours overtime, or struck lucky at the bingo, and got a bargain flight with easyJet, you'll also be boosting the income of Carolyn McCall. Not a household name admittedly, nor someone you feel morally obliged to give money. Nor is she one of the hard-pressed, modestly-paid cabin crew, under orders to sell you Lotto tickets and extortionate thimbles of coffee before you even take off. She's easyJet's chief executive. If you're lucky enough to earn the average worker's wage it will take you a modest 283 years to match her annual salary.

But if you are on the 'economy class' legal minimum wage, expect delays! You'll need to stretch your working life out to 592 years to earn what this high flyer earned in 2014 alone. How 'realistic' is that?!

* * * *

In January 2015, Christian May, Head of Campaigns at the Institute of Directors, chastised us for daring to raise these issues. Showing the gap between the pay of CEOs and average or lowest-paid workers, he complained:

> "is verging on the politics of the playground. Voyeuristic gawping at the salaries of the successful doesn't do much to promote the politics of prosperity. It adds to a creeping anti business mood that could damage the long term prospects of the economy."

Notwithstanding Mr May's whingeing on behalf of 'the successful', we make no apologies for asserting that these gaping chasms between the incomes of company bosses and workers are perverse. The Institute of Directors obviously exists to promote the politics of the prosperous – at the expense of no prosperity at all for the rest of the population.

In the first days of 2015, TUI Travel announced their chief executive Peter Lang was paid over £13million in 2014 – the same year that the authorities admit over a million people relied on food banks for food handouts, many of them in jobs. Modern capitalist Britain violates the human right to food, in the Third Millennium. As Olivier de Schutter, the UN Special Rapporteur on the Right to Food puts it:

> "Except in situations of natural disaster or civil strife, the right to food is not the right to be fed; it is the right to feed oneself with dignity."

Modern capitalist Britain spectacularly fails on that count – not for lack of food production, but due to the outrageously lop-sided distribution of wealth between workers and employers, between chief wealth-creators and chief executives. And modern capitalist Scotland exhibits the same obnoxious contradictions between plentiful food production and swathes of its own people being denied the human right to food – "the right to feed oneself with dignity" – reduced to indignity, destitution and reliance on charitable food parcels.

In May 2015, the Scottish Government boasted of rocketing levels of food and drink exports, valued at £5.1billion in 2014, with food exports alone surpassing £1.1billion for the first time ever. And that's only the food exports that were sent through Scottish ports and airports – with unquantifiable mountains more Scottish produce shipped off from elsewhere in the UK. These figures were trumpeted by the Scottish Government with triumphant declarations about:

"Scotland's distinguished heritage as a food-producing nation... a wonderful natural larder that lends itself to some of the best produce in the world... in demand across the globe."

The celebratory announcements coincided with this being the Year of Food and Drink. It was also the year when 117,689 Scottish citizens swallowed their pride, unable to 'feed oneself with dignity', resorting to food banks for handouts to avert starvation – many of them workers, whose wages deprived them of the ability to eat properly in this food-exporting nation.

It's blatantly obvious the top company chiefs who decry and deny a decent living wage for workers couldn't even begin to imagine what it's like to live on £100-an-hour, let alone £10. They'd regard themselves surviving on £100-an-hour even more 'unrealistic' than they think £10-an-hour is as a minimum wage for the rest of us.

If governments had the powers, principles and desire to redistribute wealth and combat not only absolute poverty but also the divisive, destructive inequality that blights Scotland, they could do worse than – as a first step – tax these bloated boardroom bosses.

The apologists for low taxation of the boardroom barons and the rest of the unspeakably rich have a lot of explaining to do. Top rate taxes in this country are at an all-time low – 45%, set to plunge further to 40%, on incomes over £150,000. Under Ted Heath's Tories, in 1973, it was 75%. On being elected the next year, Labour increased this to 83%, and levied a further 15% surtax on investment income.

On gaining power in 1979, Thatcher's Tory regime slashed the top rate to 60%. Perhaps most incredibly though, given her infamy as an opponent of wealth redistribution and state intervention, Thatcher retained the 60% top rate tax for a full nine years, only eventually cutting it to 40% in 1988. In other words, in the period after defeating the miners and tangling up the trade union movement in chains of repressive legislation.

If low taxation of the minute minority on stratospheric incomes was the route to economic success, Britain today should be a world beater on all fronts, including the well-being of its people. Far from it. Compared with the period when top earners' taxes were 83%, or even 60%, the numbers here in dire poverty has literally doubled, and the UK economy has been driven to the outer edges compared with key competitors. Restoration of the top personal tax rates to pre-Thatcher levels would harvest a small fortune for the national economy, and afford a major drive to improve the health, education and general wellbeing of millions of children and adults.

However, the salaries, bonuses, share options, pension pots and tax dodges of those who dictate poverty pay to the rest of us are not the only source of banishing low wages; not even the main source. It's when we look at the one word that nestles in the heart of the capitalist beast that the fabulous potential for decent pay for all workers glares out in flashing neon signs: PROFIT.

Bear in mind the fundamentals: the source of profit for capitalist employers is the unpaid labour of the working class; the hours worked per week over and above the hours it takes to produce enough to cover the cost of workers' wages. An extreme example of this process of capitalist exploitation took place in the British Leyland car plants in the 1970s, when economists showed that workers produced enough cars, of sufficient value, in one single week to cover the wages bill – and the salaries of the office staff – for the entire year!

So in this real (if more extreme) example, substantially less than one hour of a 40-hour week's work covered wages; the rest were 'the unpaid labour' or 'surplus value' that piled up the profits of the owners of British Leyland. And as the chairman of British Leyland at the time, Lord Stokes, infamously but honestly blurted out to the media:

"We are in business to make money, not cars."

Retail is home to one of the biggest concentrations of low-paid workers in modern Scotland. It's no accident that Glasgow is a cluster of low wages: it is also home to the biggest UK retail sector outside of London, and one of the largest in Europe. If we look at a few retail companies, their profits and their pay, it becomes clear that these multinational giants could readily afford a living wage for their staff and barely notice the difference – if it wasn't for the great god Profit, worshipped by the entire capitalist congregation.

Tesco is the second-largest retail firm in the world, both in terms of sales and profits. In the UK they have conquered 29% of the market. Chief executive Philip Clark 'self-served' himself £7million a year. For the 24,000 who work for Tesco in Scotland alone, (500,000 across the UK), the basic rate of pay is £7.39 – and they are not paid for breaks.

Yet the same multi-billioned octopus – whose tentacles spread into virtually every street corner and village – last year whinged about a fall in their profits. As the BBC reported in September 2014:

"Shares in Tesco reached an eleven-year low in August 2014 after the firm cut its full-year profit forecast to £2.4billion from £2.8billion."

That truly heartbreaking prediction of 'only' £2.4billion profit came hot on the heels of their actual pre-tax profits of £3.1billion in the year up to February 2014. "Every little helps", as they say.

A month later, the next-ranking supermarket giant, ASDA, complained of a "weak 2% rise in turnover"... to £22.5billion! But their profits (figures for 2013) weren't quite so 'weak': they rose by 5% to £718.6million, the same year that they'd slashed their workforce by over 1,000, despite opening 15 new stores. Another example of profits being boosted by squeezing more work from fewer workers. And ASDA's hourly pay rate – as of August 2015 – is £7.25-an-hour.

But just in case you slump in despair for poor Tesco, or imagine massive profits are a rarity, untypical, and that 'Scotland/Britain can't afford a pay rise', here's a simple summary of the situation on the profits front:

> "UK companies are at their most profitable since 1998." – *Guardian*, 14 November 2014.

Or to add the report and opinion of the august (London) *Times*, for over a century the chief mouthpiece of British capitalism:

> "British business currently is just about the luckiest in the world. Lower Corporation Tax than America. More open borders than Australia. Competitive exchange rates, unlike much of the Eurozone. Lower borrowing costs than at almost any time in the UK's history. And the world likes what it sees. Last year investment in the UK hit a record £975billion."

But what does the world see? What attracts overseas investment? The very same *Times* article inadvertently tells us:

> "But the proceeds of growth have to be more fairly distributed. Average wages have fallen £50 a week since the start of the Great Recession. That's the biggest drop since the 1860s."

So there you have it, straight from the horse's mouth. There's been a recession in wages, but no recession in profits. Even sections of the capitalist commentariat are fearful of the consequences. On the one hand, sustained poverty pay amidst plenty will slash spending power and thereby undermine profits; part of the problem for the Big Four supermarkets recently. On the other hand, such rampant inequality could fuel a revolt that these circles of the ruling elite dread, because, in the words of the revolutionary poet Shelley, "we are many, they are few."

The facts and figures that show just how modest the demand for £10 Now is – if only the glut of profits was curbed, let alone eliminated through a system of public ownership of the main sectors of the economy – are carefully hidden from the view of the working class majority. Knowledge is power, and the capitalists who hoard profits made for them by workers' efforts also hoard information. But mind-boggling facts on profits are buried in obscure corners, to be found like dirty secrets if you dig deep enough.

The rates of profit enjoyed by different sectors of the British economy – the percentage made by owners of the means of production, distribution and exchange, after all overhead costs including wages – tell a tale of plenty for the few who own big business. In 2013, as reported by the BBC, the profit margins for five main industrial sectors paint a picture of plenty that punctures all the pleas of inability to afford the level of guaranteed minimum wage we're advocating. In the pharmaceutical companies, profit margins averaged at 19%, but peaked at 42% for the largest drug company. Banks grabbed an average profit margin of 19%, with one making 29%. The car industry ranged from 3-10% (6% average); oil and gas companies up to 24%; and the media industry earned 12% profits on their investments on average, with up to 18% for each company.

In the third quarter (i.e. July-Sept) of 2014, profit rates were:
• all companies excluding Continental Shelf (i.e. oil and gas) companies: 12% rate of profit
• private non-financial corporations: 12% rate of profit
• manufacturing companies: 10.9% rate of profit
• service companies: 16.8% – the highest rate of profit on record for this sector
• companies in North Sea oil and gas: 16.9% – incredibly, the lowest rate of profit for these Continental Shelf companies since records began in 1997, but still 16.9%

Again, to prove this is not just a one-off – a blip on the curve of profit margins that I've chosen to prove a groundless case for a living hourly minimum of £10 – an outfit called Consensus Forecast reported on the ups and downs of corporate profits in the UK in recent years. They found the 'ups and downs' were all ups!

Year-on-year UK company profits rose by 4% in 2010 compared to 2009; by 7.1% in 2011 compared to 2010; by another 4.3% in 2012;

and a further 5% rise in 2013 above the profits of 2012 – with them estimating an additional 6.1% growth of profits during 2014 (as predicted on figures available in November 2014). Those years straddle both the post-2008 recession and subsequent 'boom' years. Maybe when Labour Chancellor Gordon Brown boasted 'the end of boom and bust' he only meant in the piles of profit devoured by the capitalist corporations! Because it was certainly all 'boom' on that front.

Just think how that compares with successive years of zero, or 1-2% pay 'rises' for workers. Not to mention – in several cases at the height of the recession – the actual, absolute pay cuts, as workers were presented the choice of deep pay cuts or even deeper job losses. To repeat the point, there was a recession for wages, jobs and public services, for the working class – but a massive boom for profits and the profiteers.

Another obscure source, Trading Economics, sums up the facts, stubborn facts, about the QUARTERLY profits (remember, these are NOT annual figures) enjoyed by UK corporations. As Harry Enfield's obnoxious satirical character in the Thatcherite 1980s used to say, waving his wad of cash in your face, there's "Loadsamoney!"

Trading Economics report that over the years 1955-2014, the average quarterly profits of UK companies were £29.289billion. According to my rough calculation, that's an average profit for every three months of £1,200 produced by each employee in Britain. Last year Trading Economics reported:

"Quarterly profits reached an all time high of £99.632billion in the second quarter of 2014."

In fact, for the four quarters of 2014, the eye-swivelling sums amassed in UK Corporate profits were £96.563billion, £99.632billion, £97.308billion and £97.026billion. That's over £390.5billion harvested in profit just in the one year of 2014, proving there's definitely a boom going on in the economy. But a boom that workers haven't seen any of the benefits of. After all, pay rises for 2014 officially averaged 1.7%... and still a piffling 2.4% after factoring in bonuses.

And there's no let-up in this collision between booming profits and stagnating pay. Just prior to the Tories announcing another 1% pay cap for 5.3 million public sector workers for a long, dark four years, the same Trading Economics issued a new announcement on the profits front:

"UK Corporate profits reached an all-time high in the first quarter of 2015, at £100.941billion."

There's one serious qualification we need to add to all these profit figures: big corporations hire armies of accountants and lawyers to fiddle the figures, to downgrade their reported profits, so as to dodge Corporation Tax. So the bountiful profit margins quoted above – already enough to make your blood boil when contrasted with the abject misery imposed on millions in and out of work – seriously understate the loot grabbed by the capitalist overlords of Britain. They 'export' profits to other national branches of multinational companies so as to pay lower company taxes in low-tax countries. They habitually record investments as losses on the profit and loss balance sheet, when everyone knows most investments are a deferred form of income, which they get back in later sales and profits. They set up shell companies with bogus company headquarters in the likes of Lichtenstein and Holland to dodge taxes on their profits in this country.

Diageo, who in 2009 plunged Kilmarnock deeper into devastation by closing the iconic Johnnie Walker plant, which had been in the town since 1820, is but one of many profiteers that use this tax-dodging device. Diageo is typical of most multinationals; drunk on profits, greedily guzzling £2.6billion in profits in the year they wiped out 700 jobs in Kilmarnock. They were presided over by a chief executive on a £2.3million salary, plus £6million in shares, plus £8.26million pension pot. But that still wasn't enough for these rampaging profiteers. Diageo, the world's biggest drinks company, gave a whole new meaning to the expression 'going Dutch'. Whilst firmly based in England, with their office headquarters there, they set up an impenetrably complex series of front companies based in Holland, thereby enjoying the tax-free life given to foreign companies by the Dutch authorities. This gifted the profit-guzzlers an extra £100million a year, every year, in business taxes avoided in the UK.

It would take a whole separate booklet to describe the depths these capitalist gangsters stoop to in order to maximise profits, minimise taxes, and simultaneously minimise wages. Mostly 'all perfectly legal' of course, as they devise the laws in the first place, through a myriad of interconnections between government departments and company representatives.

The fundamental point proven by this mere summary and sample of the profits creamed off by the profiteers is that we are swimming in a sea of wealth that could be dipped into to fund a decent living wage for all, starting with a minimum of £10-an-hour, here and now. Or to borrow the phrase of the poet Coleridge in *The Rime of the Ancient Mariner*, there's "Water, water, every where, nor any drop to drink."

Our task is to organise those parched by poverty pay, and quench their thirst by dipping into the bottomless well of profits to boost pay.

13

SCOTLAND LTD – PROFITS UNLIMITED

Capitalism works – for a minuscule elite. It works wonders for the wealth of a few – at the expense of the many, who pay for profits out of unpaid labour. Even in periods of recession for the rest of us, profits boom for the billionaires, banks and big business. And Scotland is no exception. A report by Grant Thornton on Scotland's top 100 companies, entitled Scotland Ltd, was published in November 2014. It's a devastating rebuttal of the arguments of anyone who is in denial about profits being 'the unpaid labour of the working class'; or doubtful about the potential for hefty pay rises for those who produce the nation's goods and services if the impediment of private profit was removed.

Firstly, there's no belt-tightening to get the top capitalist owners through hard times. That's just for the rest of us! Profits for the top 100 limited companies in Scotland last year rocketed by nearly a third – 32%! Most workers last year didn't enjoy a 3% pay rise, nor even 2%, let alone 32%. Forty of the 100 top companies enjoyed a rise in profits of over 10%.

In total, these 100 outfits enjoyed £882million in Operating Profits. Given that they employ a total of 103,807 workers, that means on average every worker provided their respective employer with a clear profit of £8,560 last year, after taking account of all wages, operating costs, overheads. That's £8,560 'unpaid labour' per worker going straight to the coffers of the owners and dominant shareholders, on top of the workers producing goods and services to the value of their wages and other running costs. As an important aside, just in case you fall for the line that the SNP is a socialist party, hell-bent on tackling such profiteering, note the response to this Report from SNP Business Minister Fergus Ewing:

"Our latest Budget includes £4.5billion of investment in infrastructure in 2015-16 and continued support for business through the delivery of the most comprehensive business tax environment in the UK."

It's also interesting to note the types of business this publicly-funded infrastructure and 'comprehensive business tax environment' is being provided for. As the Scotland Ltd Report coyly words it:

"There's still a place for heavy industry [in the top 100 companies] but retail and wholesale, and food, beverage and leisure dominate – with 42 of the top 100 companies being in these two sectors."

Dig a little deeper into the detail in the Report and you will find some sign of the extent of profit-provision by workers to their employers; proof of the golden eggs laid by these particular geese, through the mechanisms of capitalist 'surplus value', unpaid labour. The food, beverage and leisure sector of Scotland's top 100 accounts for 21 companies, which between them last year notched up £442million in 'operating profit'. A total of 20,637 employees produced that bounty for the owners of the 21 companies. Their average salary is reported as £24,383; which obviously includes the fat cats at the top, given the pitiful averages we all know about for frontline workers in that sector.

But here's the nub of the question: the average salary might be £24,383, but by my calculations the profit produced by the staff averages at £21,418 – each! So if the craving for profit for the owners wasn't built into the very bone-marrow of capitalism as a system of economy, each worker's wage could be near-as-damn-it doubled – from £24,383 average, to one of £45,801. And that's taking no account of the real pay of the vast majority, drastically below the current average, and therefore the percentage rise they'd gain if it wasn't for 'the unpaid labour of the working class' that is the source of profit.

Of course we need to qualify these sums by one other truth: even in a socialist democracy, with production for public need rather than private greed, not all these amounts would just go in wages. Some would be set aside for investment and modernisation, some paid into the pot that is 'the social wage' – the provision of public services like health, education, transport. But the central point remains. Under capitalism, with profit maximisation as its core driving force, and the private acquisition of profit being derived from the collective production of that wealth by workers, the real wealth-creators never get back 'the full fruits of their labour' – neither directly in wages, nor indirectly in social, collective service provision, the 'social wage'.

Looking more briefly at some of the other sectors within Scotland's top 100 limited companies, the 25,231 employees in 'others' – manufacturing, oil and gas, transport, logistics, freight, land and rural – each produced an average of £9,988 in profit for the 28 companies' owners. Those in auto and motor retail averaged £8,259 each in profit production. And despite it being a bad year for the sector, retail and wholesale staff added £2,965 each to their employers' profit margins, on top of their wages.

* * * *

These few facts and figures are devastating enough in their depiction of the workings and consequences of the profit-making money machine that is capitalism, here and now in Scotland. But behind the cold figures stand the flesh and blood of the people involved and affected. On the one side stands a vast army of Scotland's working population, carrying the burdens of poverty pay, job insecurity, anxiety for the future of their kids, overloaded by work as companies scale down their wages bills, squeezing more work out of fewer people.

Workers on zero hours contracts, nominal/short-hours contracts, temporary contracts, Agency staff... battalions of workers with little or no job security, blighted by worry and record levels of stress. People who get up at all hours of the night and day to work the shifts dictated by this crazed, consumerist crusade to maximise market share and profits in the 24/7 'must have' society generated by those in power. Covering the cleaning, catering and cash-desks which jingle up sales for the giant shareholders.

People with back-breaking jobs and/or mind-breaking jobs, where recent (November 2014) surveys by YouGov found two-thirds of workers are expected to do more work than five years ago; over one-third are expected to do unpaid overtime; two-thirds either dread going to work or are at best ambivalent about the prospect; one in four worry they might lose their job in the next year; 40% think they have no prospect of progress in their job.

The Health and Safety Executive found nearly 500,000 workers in the UK suffered work-related stress, depression or anxiety in the past year, half of them being brand new cases. As Frances O'Grady, general secretary of the TUC, summarised the fate of far too many workers:

> "Employers and politicians talk up the flexible labour market, but for too many it means being treated as only slightly more important than what is in the stationery cupboard."

Those are the features of life for one set of people in Scotland; the wealth-creators, the providers of the profits sampled above. But standing miles apart from this vast crowd of workers is a minuscule minority, the recipients of those profits, that fabulous wealth; the owners of big business. Theirs is an entirely different world.

For starters, an increasing majority of the big employers – of the top 100, and indeed of all those employing 500 or more workers in Scotland – are from overseas. The rapid demise of the British empire, upon which native Scottish capitalism overly depended, has wiped out much of the native capitalist ownership of the biggest enterprises. By last year, foreign firms controlled 64% of all Scottish employment in large companies, and 78% of their turnover. Even as long ago as 2003 a mere nine out of the top 100 companies in Scotland were owned by Scottish families, and a whopping 56 of the 100 were wholly owned by overseas capitalists.

But the distance between the workers who collectively create the wealth of Scotland and the tiny, tiny handful who skim off the profits they produce is not just a geographical gap. Even those indigenous Scots who own and control some of the firms may as well live on Pluto, or some other as-yet-undiscovered planet, for all they have in common with the workers they employ.

One of the few growth industries in modern Scotland – alongside food banks, and stress at work – is billionaires. Their number has just grown from seven in 2014, to nine now. And the wealth they possess, as measured by the *Sunday Times* Rich List (which, don't forget, excludes anything they have stashed in their bank accounts!) is mind-boggling; frankly beyond human comprehension.

As shown earlier, the top 100 companies in Scotland are now heavily colonised by those in the food, beverage and leisure sector. So it's more than sheer coincidence that the two richest billionaires in Scotland currently are the Grant-Gordon whisky family, and Mahdi Al-Tajir of Highland Spring. They enjoy wealth (excluding bank accounts) of £2.15billion and £1.67billion respectively. Between the nine of them, Scotland's billionaires sit on a pile worth £12.1billion – plus their bank accounts! To keep that in some kind of perspective, the entire Scottish Government annual budget for over 5.3 million of us is £30billion.

If you extend the count to the richest 100 Scots – hardly enough of a crowd to squeeze into and fill a (preferably very hot) school classroom, their gluttony adds up to combined personal wealth of £27billion. So we're "all Jock Tamson's bairns", are we? It would seem old Jock has disowned and disinherited the vast majority of us, to the benefit of a bloated handful of his 'bairns', the billionaires and big businessmen (mostly men) who harvest and hoard the wealth the rest of us create.

14

IMMIGRATION: THE MONEY MYTHS

One of the cruellest con-tricks used by the indescribably rich to keep workers in mental chains is their 'divide-and-conquer' tactics.

Past generations of the rich in Britain first practised this in Ireland, their first colony, laughing all the way to their banks, landed estates and mighty industrial profits as they divided Protestant and Catholic peasants and workers. On many occasions they added the brute force of armies to the bitter poison of sectarian propaganda, when the masses united and rose against their holy writ, demanding control over the land, or better wages and conditions, or an end to sectarian discrimination, or an end to sectarian threats, divisions and killings. And back in Britain, in the mid-19th century, the socialist thinker and activist Karl Marx was moved to write:

"The ordinary English worker hates the Irish worker as a competitor who lowers his standard of life. In relation to the Irish worker he feels himself a member of the ruling nation. This antagonism is kept alive by the press, the pulpit, the comic papers – by all the means at the disposal of the ruling class. This antagonism is the secret impotence of the English working class... it is the secret by which the capitalist class maintains its power. And the latter is quite aware of this."

This divide-and-rule weapon was spread from Ireland (and Britain) across the four corners of the globe as the British empire conquered lands, mineral wealth, slave labour, trading routes, market monopolies, military bases, power, prestige and profit. We still reap the bitter fruits of these brutal methods of dividing people along lines of colour, creed, ethnicity or national origin to this very day, with communal conflicts and killings in the likes of the Middle East, the Indian subcontinent and many corners of Africa. But the conscious incitement of enmity, hatred, even violence between people with everything else in common, except maybe their colour, or creed, or country of origin, is not a discarded relic of past methods deployed by the rich and powerful. It is alive, rotten and rife right now here in Scotland and the UK when it comes to issues like immigration, jobs and wages. How many times have you encountered the comment "It's all these immigrants who cause low wages", or "We can't get jobs because of the blacks/Poles/foreigners"? These comments predominantly come from the mouths of some of the most desperate people, ones 'without two brass farthings to rub together' as older people would say.

But their opinions are neither ones they were born with, nor are they original, nor are they based on facts! Babies aren't born screaming "Get the foreigners out" or "Keep me away from that foreign-born midwife or doctor or nurse." Little children play happily together with complete 'colour blindness'. It's only a bit later in life they begin to hear frankly racist comments, which in turn originate from sections of the media and those politicians who scapegoat people of a different colour, creed or country of origin for the ills in society. To cynically build up a popular base of support for themselves by trotting out trite, easy-sounding 'explanations' for the problems their target audience are suffering.

* * * *

Prime examples of this method right now is the monstrous mainstream media message that immigration is causing unemployment among the indigenous population, and pushing down wages for us all. There's a flood, they tell us. It's out of control. It's only common sense that more people in the country means higher unemployment and lower wages, we're taught and told to think.

The facts say otherwise. The factors surrounding immigration, jobs and wages are certainly complex. But there is no body of evidence whatsoever backing up the claims – made openly not only by fascists, racists and UKIP, but also relentlessly by the Tories and Labour – that immigration into Britain and Scotland is adding to unemployment or poverty pay for the indigenous population.

For starters, this myth is based on the notion that people uproot themselves and travel hundreds or thousands of miles to land in the Nirvana of plentiful pay and generous state benefits that is Britain. Britain has some of the worst levels of pay in the whole of Europe, certainly Western Europe.

As part of a pay struggle in the South of Ireland in early 2014, Unite the union produced a document with devastating comparisons between what is called 'Employee Compensation' in the private sector in 15 different EU countries. 'Employee Compensation' means the combined total of actual wages paid directly to workers (basic wages, overtime, bonuses, etc) plus employers' contributions to the social wage, social insurance – National Insurance Contributions and the likes, towards the NHS, pensions, sickness and unemployment benefits. Unite's study of the hourly rates of 'Employee Compensation', based on the latest available data from Eurostat (2011) showed Denmark at the top of the league with €39.61-an-hour; Sweden in second place with €39.28; Belgium €38.65... plummeting right down to Ireland at eleventh place on €24.57 an hour.

But, you've guessed it! Mighty Britain, powerhouse economy, currently rated as the fifth-biggest economy on earth, comes in at a dismal 13th out of 15 EU countries, with hourly 'Employee Compensation' of €18.95-an-hour, only outstripping Greece and Portugal in this league table of shame. So the notion that immigrants flock to Britain as a haven of high wages, with milk and honey on tap, is to say the least, 'challenged'! Of course people fleeing the appalling deprivation of many Eastern European countries – economies suffering the wreckage caused by the triumphant restoration of capitalism 25 years ago – will often enjoy a substantial wage rise on arrival here. But does that mean these migrant workers drag down the wages of the indigenous workforce?

One of the myths that the lies are based on is that there's some fixed 'lump of labour' in a country. A set, unchanging amount of work, which in turn means immigrant workers battle it out against indigenous workers to get this finite number of jobs. Taking the economy as a whole, this is utter nonsense. As well as supplying their ability to work – their labour-power – immigrants also add to the demand in the economy. Newcomers to Scotland need food, clothing, housing, household goods, public transport, public services, the same as any other citizen does – which in turn means a need for more work to be done to supply these basic essentials. Only an economic system as crazed and contradictory as capitalism could see a problem with the arrival on Scotland's shores of overwhelmingly young people, many of them highly skilled or educated, eager to work, fit to produce far more in goods and services than they could ever personally consume, thereby adding to the overall wealth of the nation.

If there was anything sane about the system, more people in Scotland means not just more skills and more labour-power for sale – and therefore more competition in the marketplace for jobs. It also means more demand for goods and services, more output growth, more goods and services produced, and therefore the requirement of more jobs. When there are more jobs on offer, more demand for workers' labour-power – as with any other commodity for sale – that tends to raise the price paid for workers' unique commodity: their ability to work and produce surplus value above and beyond the cost of hiring them to work. In other words, it tends to produce higher wages – and much more so if workers' unions have the muscle to demand higher wages in a period of increased demand for workers' labour-power.

* * * *

Contrary to the divisive myths that the country is swamped by people living in the lap of luxury on state benefits, stealing our jobs and slashing our wages – presumably doing all these things simultaneously! – migration has been integral to the entire history of humanity and its progress.

Historians reckon the first 'immigrants' settled in Britain 25,000 years ago. Early agricultural techniques – in other words, humanity's progressive development of its ability to feed itself – were developed by immigrants to Britain about 10,000 years ago – Celts, Picts and Romans. Germanic tribes colonised the south of this island, the

Vikings the north, then the Normans from 1066. Immigration continued in the 19th and 20th centuries. A new wave was actively encouraged by both Labour and subsequent Tory governments to meet labour shortages after the 1939-45 World War. Many of the most vital, but most strenuous or dirtiest jobs were filled by workers landing from the Caribbean and Indian sub-continent.

Meantime, right across several decades of the 20th century, Irish workers met labour shortages in Britain, including Scotland, and frequently laid down their lives to build canals, tunnels, roads, as well as pouring into Scotland's docks, mines and factory production lines. Right here and now the country is enriched culturally, and has had added skills sets provided by newcomers in a period when there's a chronic skills shortage, created by decades of failure by employers and governments to properly invest in apprenticeships and skilling-up the workforce.

Contrary to one of the central scaremongering lies that relentlessly pound our ears, from the media and most pro-capitalist politicians, the overwhelming reasons people arrive in this country are to work, or study, and to join families already settled here – not as 'benefit tourists'.

By far the biggest proportion of non-EU immigrants are students, actively pursued by University authorities hungry for their fees. Witness, for instance, the growth of mini-Chinatowns in university districts of Glasgow and Edinburgh, where Chinese students pile into halls of residence and fork out about £20,000 a year in student fees. And non-EU immigrants have to pay an Immigration Health Surcharge of £200 a year each (£50 for students), even if they never once use the NHS. So no free-loading or 'benefit tourism' there, then.

In the case of EU migrants, 228,000 of the 560,000 total who came to Britain in 2014 did so for work-related reasons; a further 177,000 to study; and 83,000 to unite with immediate family members.

Again, to obliterate one of the vicious myths used by the rich and their propaganda machine to divide us, immigrants are not tearing up their family and cultural roots to land in Scotland for our 'generous' state benefits. As a major study commissioned by the *Sunday Mirror* in September 2014 proved, indigenous workers are 43% more likely to claim benefits than immigrants who arrived since 2000. Far from being a burden on the state, EU immigrants between 2000 and 2011 contributed £5billion more in taxes than they took in benefits and through use of public services, combined.

* * * *

But could immigration still not dampen down wage levels? Numerous in-depth academic studies have been conducted on this issue in recent years. In a review of 18 of them, although three of the 18 concluded immigration has had an (extremely marginal) impact on wage levels for the long-standing population, the rest of these pieces of extensive research concluded the opposite. The common conclusion from these studies, despite the slight variations in their exact figures, is that the impact of immigration into Britain and Scotland on wage rates for the 'native' population ranges from none to negligible. Research in 2008 by Nickell & Salaheen, surveying data for 1992-2006, concluded that: "In the unskilled and semi-skilled service sector, a 1% rise in the share of migrants reduced wages by 0.5%." Reed & Lattore (2009) researched the period 2000-2007, concluding "a 1% increase in the share of migrants in the UK working-age population lowers average wages by 0.3%."

On the other hand, an extremely comprehensive study of the years 1997-2005 by economists Dustmann, Frattini & Preston (2013) drew the conclusion that "an increase in migrants corresponding to 1% of UK-born working-age population led to an increase in average wages of 0.1% to 0.3%."

These latter economists' detailed research document carried figures from a period in which the immigrant population rose by the equivalent of 3% of the UK-born population; a very significant increase. But their document also carries figures that really do put the whole claim that 'immigration depresses wages' in clear perspective. They found that immigration had lowered the wages of the poorest-paid 10% of UK workers by an average of 0.7p an hour; raised the hourly wages of middle earners by 1.5p; and increased those of the top wage-earners by 2p an hour! So even for the lowest-paid tenth of workers, that would signify a wage reduction of 28p over the course of a 40-hour week! Hardly the root cause of the horrendous and long-term decline suffered in workers' pay packets.

Even the staunchly capitalist mouthpiece, the *Financial Times*, reported this study under the headline "Immigrants Help Raise Average Wages." A headline they could safely publish for the business people that largely make up the readership of the 'FT', and which at the very least challenges the idea that the same employers get away with lowering wages by encouraging immigration.

But a headline we're not about to see emblazoned on billboards and in the tabloids, the mass readership red-tops, who serve the pernicious purpose of keeping working-class people divided and distracted from the real causes, and the real villains, when it comes to workers being chained to poverty pay. One thing can be claimed with absolute certainty: there is no body of evidence of a substantial or significant reduction of pay rates due to immigration.

Furthermore, guess which set of workers have been hardest hit by the negative impact of immigration in the small minority of studies that have found ANY impact at all? Previous immigrants! That was the clear findings of, for instance, Manacorda, Manning & Warsworth in their 2012 study of wages data covering the 30-year period of 1975-2005. And it's not that difficult to see why. Some of the lowest-paid jobs that both new and previous immigrant workers all-too-frequently land in are unskilled, and/or don't require language fluency or local knowledge. Many of them will be the dirtiest, least attractive jobs. Also often the least unionised.

Of course, these in-depth statistical studies seem to contradict 'common sense'. But commonly held beliefs are moulded by the propaganda of those in power, who aim to divide and rule the working class. And they would never be so silly as to let the facts get in the way of a good propaganda weapon!

Having said all that, there are plenty of instances of migrant workers being treated like a sub-human species by super-exploitative employers. People trekking across countries, continents or oceans to flee poverty, war and persecution are prone to take the worst-paid jobs with the worst conditions. Such people, desperate for a better life, frequently highly-educated people at that, are used to squeeze the very last drop of profit out of them. In flagrant breach of the law all too often; or by employers exploiting the multiple loopholes left in minimum wage legislation by our business-friendly governments.

Let's take a few random examples of the way immigrants are treated like dirt when they arrive on our shores, offering to use their ability to work to boost the wealth of Scotland/UK. And I don't mean asylum seekers; they're not even allowed to work, by law.

Adverts were carried in Romania last year offering pay of £650-1,000 a month in the UK, only for those who made the journey to find they have to pay travel and accommodation charges out of that sum, or pay for their uniforms or work equipment, as ways of dodging the legal £6.50 hourly minimum.

Agency EasyPoland carried adverts declaring "Accommodation: must bring bedding." This relates to the practice of 'hot-bedding', with migrant workers sleeping in shifts in overcrowded hovels, or forking out rent way above the legally-permitted maximum (£34.37 a week) that can be deducted from wages under Minimum Wage legislation. The fact that the 1997-2010 Labour government of Blair and Brown stubbornly refused to extend laws on gang-masters to cover construction and hospitality, leaves migrant workers prey to brutal exploitation in these sectors.

The prestigious Hilton hotel, whose previous management had responded to protests by Citizens UK and some of the Hilton's staff by entering negotiations on wages and conditions, was then taken over by Blackstone private equity company. The new owners proceeded to sack the more receptive managers, and introduced a system of paying the cleaners (most of them migrants) by the number of rooms cleaned, with a workload that makes it impossible to reach the hourly national minimum wage.

In a graphic, heart-rending report in the *Observer* (May 2015), we glimpse another example of the horrendous super-exploitation of migrant workers in London's vast hospitality sector, and their courageous fight-back through the unions, in this case with the support of Unite.

A group of room attendants (chambermaids, in a former age), all Polish, meet in a café to plan strike action. They recount how four months before, they were still hired by Hotelcare, paid the £6.50 minimum wage to clean 13 rooms in the four-star Park Plaza Hotel, in an eight-hour shift. Then another cleaning company took over: WGC, who boast of "servicing over ten million hotel rooms a year" on their website and brochures. WGC demand that they clean 15-17 rooms in a 7.5-hour shift. They are constantly watched, timed, shouted and screamed at by supervisors to go faster, faster, faster all the time. When guests are late in departing their rooms, these women are forced to work extra hours, unpaid. If they're sick, they're told to go home, with no pay. Their work is lonely, repetitive, under constant harassment to go faster, bullied – and most have long commutes to work, leaving them tired, long hours apart from their children, and unable to find time to develop their skills or mastery of English.

All this is happening within a five-minute walk from the Palaces of Westminster. Where Lords of the realm pick up £300-a-day for simply 'clocking-on' in the Upper Chamber, and MPs enjoy a salary (before all the expenses) of £74,000.

Hospitality is the UK's fourth-largest industry, worth over £60billion a year. London alone has 136,000 hotel rooms. Accountancy giant PwC has calculated that with 84% occupancy, and an average charge of £145 a night, the owners stand to gain £122 per room per night. But the room attendants get between £2.30 and £3.75 a room for their back-breaking toil, under stress and duress. Some of the women preparing to strike against their treatment by WGC have previously worked elsewhere (illegally) for piece rates, paid £2.17 a room, 25 rooms a day. As one of the women bravely concludes to the *Observer* journalist, "We want what is fair, so we have to strike."

* * * *

One of the key factors that prevents immigration being used to drive wages down even further – alongside the indispensable contribution of the trade union movement – is the existence of a statutory minimum wage. If it wasn't for that – a measure as socialists we have vociferously fought for, whilst demanding a vast improvement on its present pathetic levels – the employers could and would undoubtedly play all manner of divisive tricks to further drive down the prices paid for labour-power in the jungle of the capitalist market.

And it wasn't immigrants from Eastern Europe, or Africa, or anywhere else – any more than previous incomers to Scotland from Ireland, Italy, Pakistan, India, Lithuania, or indeed England – that decided the national minimum wage should be set at basement levels. It was a succession of Labour, Tory and Tory/Lib Dem Coalition governments who set these wages – under the imperious demands of profiteering big business, capitalists who recognise the bleedin' obvious: every penny on workers' pay is a penny off their short-term profits. Again, it's worth noting that new immigrants are ten times more likely than long-standing citizens to not be paid even the pathetic, legally-required minimum wage.

We're all familiar with the vans arriving in the middle of the night, collecting flower pickers, seasonal agricultural workers, cockle pickers or sweatshop factory labourers from Eastern Europe, Africa, or elsewhere. These people, usually desperate to escape persecution, war, torture or at least dire poverty in their native country, are often superexploited by gang masters, or have accommodation charges docked from their wages – for living in overcrowded hovels or cold, dilapidated caravans hired out by big farmers.

Or the skilled chefs and waiters who get £2 or £3-an-hour – cash in hand, under the counter, in cafés and restaurants: a ghost workforce, never registered with the authorities, and with no cover for accidents or death at work. The criminal lack of effort by the government to resource enforcement of the payment of the minimum wage – compared to a mighty machine of sanctions, persecution and prosecution for those relying on pitiful state benefits – means thousands of workers right now don't get their legal entitlements.

According to the government's own Office of National Statistics (ONS), 299,000 jobs were paying below the national minimum wage, in 2014. This scandalous theft of wages is aided and abetted by the

25% cut to HMRC budgets, which led to a halving of the number of wages inspectors, expected to monitor and enforce the legal minimum wage. The ONS also reported that the dismal failure to inspect minimum wage enforcement is especially prevalent in sectors with substantial numbers of migrant workers. A grand total of two employers have been prosecuted for breaking the law on the legal minimum wage in the last three years!

It wasn't immigrants who caused that, it was decisions by successive governments, including loopholes in the minimum wage law that allow accommodation charges to count towards calculations of the hourly rate, for instance.

Such legal loopholes not only open the door to employers ripping off immigrant workers in the cleaning and catering sectors, but also for councils right here in Scotland to rip off care workers – indigenous Scots and newcomers alike. Witness the case being pursued by Unison Scotland over care sector union members denied the legal minimum wage by the trickery of not counting sleepovers as time at work – with their (often lengthy) travel time to work also disregarded, unpaid.

* * * *

Of course inside most lies there nestles a grain of truth. Whilst there is no evidence to back up the claims of immigration driving down wages in Scotland or the UK, there are plenty of cases of employers taking full advantage of so-called 'globalisation' to maximise their profits at terrible cost to workers across the globe – including here. They indulge in a ruthless race to the bottom, chasing after the biggest short-term profits available, in a global economy where the restraints of labour market regulations have been shredded by governments world-wide.

Workers create capital, not the other way round. The work of those employed and paid a wage produces more wealth than they get back in their wages – that's capitalism! The unpaid labour of the working class is what produces profit for the owners of the means of producing goods and services. And whenever these owners invest some of those profits in new machinery and modernised equipment – capital – they do so purely to make more profit, and so the cycle continues.

But capitalist globalisation – a term invented in the 1960s, made a buzz word the last 20 years, but identified and described by other names by Karl Marx as far back as the 1840s – means the capitalist overlords shift their capital investments round the globe to get the biggest profit margins in whatever country offers it at any given time. Whilst they whip up vicious outrage at the free movement of people (labour) they actively pursue, and declare as a virtue, the free movement of capital.

When working class people feel tempted to blame minorities of a different colour, creed or country of origin for their low pay or job insecurity, they should remember a simple fact: the employing class couldn't give a toss what colour, creed or country you're from, so long as they can squeeze the maximum work for the minimum pay out of you. Look at the huge percentage of Scottish and UK companies now owned by shareholders from abroad. Do they care that their profits derive from the exploitation of Scottish workers – or English, Welsh or Irish? No, it's the colour of their money that counts, not the colour of the skin, or the creeds of workers. But they're past masters at making workers scapegoat people like themselves for the problems created by the masters of capital.

* * * *

Globalised capitalism is consciously designed to produce a 'race to the bottom' on wages and conditions for workers. The masters of the universe whose whole creed is greed, profit maximisation, will stop at nothing to slash the share of wealth going to wages. Indeed, long before the term 'globalisation' was ever coined, capitalists imported cheap foreign labour to undercut indigenous workers' wages, and frequently to openly break strikes. That method was frequently deployed, whether it was people from Scotland and the rest of Britain drafted into the USA, or Irish workers imported to break strikes or undermine wages in Britain, to cite but two of vast numbers of past examples.

The International Working Men's Association – the First International, involving Karl Marx, Friedrich Engels, and British trade unionists and socialists amongst many others – played a critical, dynamic role in organising to stop workers of various countries being used to scab on strikers and/or undercut wages as long ago as the 1860s.

In recent decades, we've witnessed several attempts to drag desperate people in to undermine the wages and working conditions of others. Close to home, during the 1993 Timex strike in Dundee – which the mostly female workforce of 343 heroically staged for a full seven months – people from across Tayside were literally bussed through the strikers' picket lines. Strikers' shop stewards were threatened with jail if they went near the picket lines. A diluted version of apartheid South Africa's pass laws outlawed several strikers from parts of their native city. Police violence included crushing workers up against the perimeter fence, and breaking a woman's arm during arrest, then holding her for 27 hours before release – without charge!

Over 500 police officers from several forces across the UK – including undercover cops and snatch squads – were deployed to escort buses through the mass pickets of up to 1,000 strikers and their allies from other unions. These strike-breaking vehicles ferried scabs in to keep up the pretence of normal production – a pretence that Timex bosses eventually abandoned, shutting down the Dundee plant in August 1993. Those driven through the picket lines, often prostrate on the bus floor to avoid being recognised by Timex strikers, were desperate people, usually recruited through the Job Centres.

The ruthless regime of benefits sanctions imposed in recent years would leave the unemployed infinitely more prey to being frog-marched into playing a strike-breaking role nowadays. Current plans by the Tories to repeal the ban on use of Agency workers to replace workers during strikes – a ban in operation since 1973, including right through the Thatcher years! – would make such methods all the easier for employers. It would mean dragooning desperate, insecurely-employed people to undermine fellow-workers' wages, jobs and conditions – and thereby their own – with a legal gun to their heads, offered the 'choice' of either 'scab or be sacked'.

But the capitalist employers have sometimes shipped people in, rather than bussed them in! One of the issues the maritime workers' unions (RMT, Nautilus, Unite) have had to confront over the years is the use of overseas crews on ships, from the likes of the Philippines, including use of 'flags of convenience', to undercut the pay and conditions agreed by these unions with the employers through negotiations and collective union struggle.

Currently, similar methods are being deployed in the North Sea offshore industry by contractors. Workers from as far afield as South Africa and the Philippines are being drafted in as divers and other trades, on as low as 45% of the going rates won through hard battles by the offshore unions in Scotland. In these situations, the unions have rightly fought to defend nationally-agreed terms and conditions, rather than descend into xenophobic attacks on workers from abroad.

It's not workers from other countries that have created these attempts to smash down wages in a race to the bottom. Rather, they've been exploited for their desperation to find work, by employers hellbent on getting the biggest possible slice of the cake for themselves, delighting in any scraps they can incite between workers of different countries over the remaining crumbs.

* * * *

A profoundly rich lesson on these issues was learnt in the power construction and oil refinery industry in January 2009. At the huge Lindsey Oil Refinery in Lincolnshire, construction contract workers were issued with 90-day redundancy notices in November 2008. Just before their notice period had expired, they were confronted by the arrival of a new Italian contract company, IREM, which explicitly advertised that no UK workers could even apply for the jobs, hiring instead hundreds of workers from Italy and Portugal – on far worse wages and conditions. These migrant workers were housed offshore on barges in Grimsby harbour, to segregate them from the indigenous, unionised workers, who were rightly infuriated at being banned from even getting an interview for a job.

The locals, from all contract companies, held union mass meetings, immediately went on strike – in defiance of every anti-union law on the statute books – and triggered equally illegal mass solidarity walk-outs across the UK, including at Grangemouth oil refinery and Longannet power station. Contrary to the confusion and chauvinism portrayed in the media at the time, this was not an anti-foreign worker strike. The pickets chased the fascist BNP when they turned up with their demands for 'British jobs for British workers'.

On the contrary, as the SSP advocated from day one of the strikes, local union leaders proposed and won unanimous backing for a set of demands that included union rights for all workers, including immigrant labour; union facilities for the Italian and Portuguese workers to make them an integral part of the trade union movement here; and for implementation of the national construction and engineering industry agreement on the rate for the job, hours of work, breaks and conditions for all working in the UK – including the Italians and Portuguese.

Workers, and particularly their rank-and-file shop steward leaders, rightly saw the Italian company as their enemy, not the Italian or Portuguese workers that they'd shipped in. They rightly identified this as an attempt by European companies to exploit EU court rulings and the EU Directive on Posted Workers to crush union organisation and demolish hard-won rights and wages. These Directives and rulings in essence mean national agreements can be ignored by companies based or registered abroad, in keeping with the EU's adherence to global deregulation of the labour markets – otherwise known as ripping the maximum profit out of workers who've been left legally defenceless in the bosses' and billionaires' global race to the bottom.

Most importantly for the future, this marvellous display of militant trade unionism, in mass collective defiance of the battery of anti-union laws designed to permanently chain workers to poverty, resulted in outright victory. Informed by solidarity and internationalism, initially by their shop stewards and other union activists, these skilled industrial workers forced the Italian firm IREM into a complete climb-down. They won 50% of the jobs for UK workers, but with no layoffs for the overseas workers, and full implementation of the industry's national agreement on wages, hours and conditions. A complete victory which showed the indispensable value of socialist trade unionists giving direction to fellow workers when faced with attempts to use workers from another country to drive down even further the share of wealth going to wages.

Furthermore, this inspirational struggle was rich in other lessons and potential solutions to the threats from globalisation. As I wrote at the time, for the SSP's website:

> "We also need to raise demands such as trade union registers of un-employed workers in the industry as the pool for employment when jobs are on offer – at least a small step forward to the days when unions had elements of control over hiring and firing in a few of the better-organised industries, such as printing. That would help counter the conscious 'race to the bottom' of conditions by companies at home and abroad, by use of cheap, disorganised workers to undermine the rights won by unionised workforces. This dispute highlights the broader issue of ownership of the power and energy industry, where multinationals seize advantage of the deregulated, cheap-labour EU market – championed by Blaire and Brown – to maximise profits – and the SSP's counter-proposal of public ownership and democratic control of the industry, where workers' elected representatives would have a direct input to all aspects of employment, production and planning."

* * * *

On the types of occasions just described, globalised capitalism ships in labour to undercut and undermine the wages and rights at work, won through hard struggle and union organisation. On other occasions the profit-maximisers ship capital abroad to achieve the same aims.

When Volvo, Amazon, Motorola, Diageo, BT, a string of electronics companies, or numerous textile firms decide to shut down – or drastically reduce – their operations in Scotland in order to relocate to the likes of Poland, Hungary, Romania, Mexico, Philippines, China, India, or Ireland – as they've done – they are not doing so because they love the peoples of these other countries any more than the Scots. It's their love of profit that drives them abroad.

They are doing it to grab state development grants, or take advantage of low business taxes, tax holidays, or to get closer to new, expanding local markets, and especially to seize temporary advantage of highly educated workers who are on dirt cheap wages compared with those in the country the capitalists are abandoning in their race to the bottom of the wages league.

When capitalists declare closures or wholesale redundancies in Scotland to hunt for cheaper labour abroad, we should demand that the Scottish Government confiscate their assets, including factories, offices and capital equipment, to retain jobs and production in Scotland, utilising the skills and experience of the workforce to plan useful local production, instead of allowing globalised capitalism to leave a desert behind and call it progress.

* * * *

It's not immigrants who cause poverty pay, but the division whipped up around the issue of immigration undoubtedly can and has driven wages down further. A divided working class is a weakened working class when it comes to striving for a bigger share of national wealth going to wages. When people on poor pay are distracted by the pernicious prattling of racist forces like UKIP and sections of the media – and full-blown acceptance by the Tories and Labour of the same false claims of immigration being 'a problem' – they are falling for one of the oldest tricks in the trade: blaming the victims.

Instead of recognising that it's the bankers and capitalist billionaires who impose poverty pay, workers' combined resistance to daylight robbery by the rich is undermined when they allow the profiteers to set the victims of low pay at each other's throats.

It is not an accident of geography, or due to something different in the DNA of the population, that the average wages of workers in the same jobs in Northern Ireland have been consistently lower than in virtually every other nation or region of the UK for decades. Frequently up to 20% lower. For instance, according to the Office of National Statistics, the median weekly wage of full-time workers in the UK in 2014 was £518 – with Scotland getting exactly that figure too – but was only £450 in Northern Ireland. The late-19th and 20th centuries were littered with examples of the landlords and capitalists consciously sowing and inciting sectarian divisions between Protestant and Catholic workers in Ireland, deliberately weakening their potential power to win improved wages and living standards for workers of all religions and none through united, collective struggle.

Some of the biggest concentrations of poverty pay in Scotland, such as fast food outlets, retail, catering, hotels, and cleaning, are populated by workers of many and varied national and ethnic origins. For instance, in the retail multinational where I work, those who have joined the union include workers born in Scotland, England, Ireland, Poland, Slovakia, Bulgaria, Iraq, China, India, Pakistan, Spain, Nigeria, Belgium...

Instead of blaming each other – along lines of race or nationality – for poor pay, it makes infinitely better sense to unite in action to demand wage increases for all, regardless of background. The efforts by some workers' unions to reach immigrant workers with material in their own languages, hiring and training organisers from amongst them, is to be applauded and extended.

* * * *

One of several challenges we need to issue to those who blame immigrants for low pay is this: would they demand the expulsion from the country of all native-born Scots who are unemployed, or hired as agency workers – to prevent them being deployed as weapons against the wage levels of other Scots in jobs? And if not, why then effectively demand that other ordinary people – keen to work, at that – should be barred from entering the country?

Should we whip up a campaign to 'drive the Irish out of Scottish jobs', decades or centuries after their ancestors first arrived on Scotland's shores? Or shouldn't we instead welcome the fact that in many regions, people of Irish descent – or indeed first-generation Irish immigrants to Scotland – make up disproportionately large numbers of devoted, determined trade union activists and socialist fighters, to the benefit of people of all colour, creed or country of origin?

By the same logic, since women's wages are drastically lower than those of men in similar jobs, is the solution to demand the expulsion of women workers from their jobs – or even from the country! – in order to stop employers exploiting them to cheapen average wages? Historically, that outrageous proposal was actually supported by a minority of workers terrified of their jobs and wages being undermined by women being drafted in, for instance during and after the two World Wars – especially during the deep recessions of the 1920s and 1930s.

For instance, the city of Sheffield has recently conducted a crowd-funded campaign to erect sculpted statues, concerts, exhibitions and other celebrations of 'The Women of Steel'. This is a belated act of respect and recognition for the army of women, including many in their 20s, who were conscripted into the dangerous and downright frightening work of the steelworks during both World Wars, churning our armaments whilst the men of the city fought on the war-fronts – but on only half the pay rates enjoyed by the men. After the cessation of each World War, the women were summarily ejected from their jobs, as the men returned to the steelworks – without so much as an acknowledgement of their efforts for the subsequent 70 years.

In the inter-war period of bleak crises in the economy, the number of women in work in this country drastically declined compared with the war years of 1914-18. Whilst the trade unions sought to recruit women around the fight for equal pay during the War years, with female union membership peaking at 1,342,000 in 1920, they largely shelved earlier efforts to win equal pay post-1918. The result was that by 1931, average pay for women had plunged to the pre-War crime of being only 50% that of men in equivalent jobs.

Further to that neglect by most unions, in the more privileged craft unions the leadership actually argued for strict limits on the number of women allowed to work – such as in teaching, the civil service and other new professions. The unions feared women would be used to lower wages, and in many cases pushed for stricter application – or even the introduction – of the 'marriage bar', whereby women in many sectors were barred from working after they got married.

In the case of the Union of Post Office Workers, by 1935 it argued for a total exclusion of women from jobs in that service. These marriage bars were only opposed within some unions from as late as the mid-1940s onwards, and only dismantled in several sectors from 1944 up until as recently as the 1960s.

Nobody today would advocate or tolerate such a response to the systematic driving down of wages. No reasonable or self-respecting person – men included – would see a call for the exclusion of women from work as anything other than medieval and a monstrous outrage against basic human rights. So why should anyone advocate the equivalent for people of a particular colour, or creed, or country of origin?

Surely the best weapon against capitalists and their governments slaughtering wages as a share of overall wealth – with the use of 'a reserve army of labour' as a blunt instrument to enforce poverty pay – is to unite workers in action to win decent jobs and wages for all – regardless of gender, age, creed, colour or country of origin? Workers can't afford to be divided and driven down into even deeper poverty, by employers whose only loyalty is neither to creed, colour nor country, but to their one true god: Profit.

15

CAPITALIST SUBSIDY JUNKIES

We live in a state infested by subsidy junkies.

No, this is not the opener for a *Daily Mail* rant against the poorest, designed to demonise the victims of paltry state benefits – of £60-70 a week – and divide different layers of the working class from each other. Nor is it conceding even a centimetre to the inflammatory lie – oft repeated not only by tabloids but mainstream capitalist politicians – that this country is a favoured destination for 'benefit tourists'. That is one of the most squalid and absurd claims, designed to whip up xenophobia and racist division so the rich can laugh at us as they pick our pockets. A sick joke, considering the UK has one of the lowest levels of state benefits for anyone unfortunate enough to be jobless, long-term sick, disabled, or simply retired.

An even sicker lie considering immigrants to the UK have been proven to be net contributors to government funds, in taxes over and above any state benefits they receive, to the tune of £8.8billion in 2013 alone, as analysed by Manchester University. Not to even mention the huge contribution of immigrants to the health and wellbeing of the population, considering the NHS would collapse without the 40% of all nursing staff and 30% of its doctors that come from abroad.

Nor is it an echo of the scurrilous lie of that calculating, viciously right-wing Tory, masquerading as a lovable buffoon – recently elected MP Boris Johnston – when he declared:

"Londoners are forking out for things in Scotland."

Nor the ill-informed, and subsequently retracted, opinion of Labour's former London Mayor Ken Livingstone, who also infamously maligned the people of Scotland when he said:

"We need Crossrail to keep London's economy ticking over so that we can continue to pay for the Scottish to live the lifestyle to which they are accustomed."

They indulged in a cheap, inflammatory lie designed to win favour from the hard-pressed working class of London – conveniently ignoring the hard facts that Scotland has been a net exporter of taxes to Westminster for every one of the last 35 years – to the tune of £4.4billion in 2011-12 alone. Or that from 1981 until 2013, Scottish taxpayers contributed £222billion more in taxes to Westminster than if Scotland's cash contribution per head had been the same as the UK's per head of population; a £45,000 subsidy from Scotland to the British state from every man, woman and child!

No, those addicted to state handouts, greedily dipping into a bottomless barrel of taxpayers' money, are the capitalist owners of giant corporations. They have an insatiable hunger for state largesse, which clashes sharply with their professed opposition to 'state interference' in their capitalist 'free market'.

The very same class who denounce and deny the enlargement of social provision for the mass of the population in the form of free, universal public services – not to mention their apoplectic opposition to the expansion of social ownership of the means of producing society's wealth – are relentless in their reliance on state handouts for their own privileges and profits. They have systematically pounded successive Tory and Labour governments into slashing state spending on benefits to the poor, sick, disabled, unemployed or retired, while they themselves devour state handouts like they're hooked to an incurable addiction. Which of course they are: pure, unadulterated greed – the cocaine of the capitalists!

* * * *

At its peak, 20% of the British economy was nationalised, owned by the state. That was the case in the 1960s and 1970s. But that did not signify an egalitarian socialist democracy. For starters, such partial public ownership of the key centres of production, distribution and exchange – a minority part of 'the commanding heights of the economy' – meant that those capitalists who retained ownership of the other 80% dictated to the governments in ownership of the 20%.

Regardless of how many welcome legal regulations were introduced by Labour governments of old – strictly before the mania for deregulation of the capitalist markets under Thatcher, Blair and their successors – you still can't control or plan what you don't own. The capitalists dictated to past Labour governments, just as they did to the far more pliant Tory ones. At times they brutally blackmailed them, as with their threats to bring the economy crashing to its knees through a strike of investment when Harold Wilson's 1974 Labour government talked of quite modest taxation of the rich and big business.

But in a different sense too, the partial public ownership of the past only provided 'socialism for the rich'. Publicly-owned core industries and services – investment from the public purse, in turn filled by workers' taxes – provided cheap, subsidised sources of energy and infrastructure to big capitalist industries. For instance, a public network of roads and railways – including freight lines – for the transportation of goods, oiled the wheels of trade for the private profiteers still dominating the economy. Cheap, state-subsidised gas, electricity and coal gave a leg-up to the industrial capitalists.

* * * *

However, the insatiable greed for ever more wealth and power impelled the capitalists, their ideologues and puppet politicians to drive out the state sector, in the mighty, ideologically-driven wave of privatisations under Thatcher in the 1980s. This was added to by her son-and-heir in 'free market' capitalism, Tony Blair, in the 1990s. This variety of capitalism has been branded 'neo-liberalism'. But the only thing really 'liberal' about it is the enforced generosity of the millions of working-class (and lower-middle class) taxpayers, towards big business and its bloated overlords.

State subsidies to the citadels of capital take several forms. And contrary to the appearance created of a 'free market' – where everyone 'stands on their own two feet', and where those who succeed in becoming unimaginably rich are just good at what they do and very hard-working – contrary to these myths, there is an even greater dependency by the capitalist rich on public funding and state subsidies now than was the case before the wave of privatisations 30-odd years ago. Billions of pounds are donated to the coffers of big business annually in the form of regional development grants, training and skills development funding, Employment Allowances, return-to-work schemes, youth employment schemes, European Union subsidies – multiple state bribes to set up shop, hire workers and make a profit for the central owners and shareholders.

The government invests at least £10billion every year in Research and Development, which hugely, directly benefits private companies, who are notoriously poor at such innovative investment from their own profits. One of the causes of the current collapse in productivity in the UK compared to its capitalist competitors is the very low level of investment in modernising technology, which leaves British companies lagging lamely behind.

And far from such public investment into R&D being exclusively for the good of all, an obscene £890million a year is sunk in the devilish pursuit of the technology of death and devastation, the arms trade. That's £13,000 in public subsidy for every single arms export industry job! In fact, for every £1 invested in research on clean, green, sustainable forms of energy, the British state spends £34 of taxpayers' money on weapons research. That in turn is one of the biggest sources of profit for private corporations – the likes of BAe Systems.

American singer, songwriter, actor and holder of many weird and wonderful opinions, Frank Zappa, truly wasn't wrong when he quipped:

"Politics is the entertainment division of the military-industrial complex!"

Thirty years on from privatisation of the energy industry, public funds are poured down the throats of a handful of profiteering producers, with a massive bias in favour of the most environmentally destructive versions of energy, as opposed to planet-friendly options.

The nuclear power companies currently enjoy subsidies of £2.3billion a year. They are further relieved of liability in the event of a nuclear disaster, where they'd only have to fork out £140million, with the rest covered by the taxpayer. Even without a nuclear accident as such, the state (ultimately, workers' taxes) shoulders the vast bulk of the estimated £100billion current cost of decommissioning and cleaning up nuclear waste.

Fossil fuel industries have been mollycoddled by the state, with cuts to VAT on petrol, coal and gas from 20% to 5%, saving the oil magnates £billions, on top of various tax breaks granted to them.

The SNP led the chorus of politicians 'standing up for oil bosses' in early 2015, demanding business tax cuts to bail them out in the context of temporary falls in the price of oil on the world markets. They ignored the fact that if this industry had been taxed at the level applied by the Norwegian government over the last decade, an additional £118billion would have been available to the state Treasury for investment in clean, green energy and/or a range of frontline public services. Another example of 'socialism for the capitalist rich' – funded by pay cuts, job losses, tax increases and astronomical energy bills for the rest of us.

* * * *

Fundamental infrastructure provided by the state – for example, roads, rail and airports – make it possible for big business to function, and profit, on behalf of the handful of giant shareholders who own the core economy. In classic proof of the double standards of big business – or to be more accurate, the standards dictated by their own class interests, which are diametrically opposed to the class interests of the majority of the population – the Confederation of British Industry (CBI) relentlessly pushes for cuts to public services, alongside demands for even more cuts to Corporation Tax, whilst simultaneously lobbying the government for vastly increased expenditure on infrastructure projects that help their businesses, such as road networks.

In 2012, the Coalition of capitalist parties in office at Westminster duly obliged. They slashed the incomes of workers relying on in-work benefits to top up pitiful wages (routinely paid to them by CBI members!) and vulnerable sick and disabled people, but sunk £28billion in road networks; the biggest investment in roads since the 1970s. And just to be consistent in their defence of capitalist profiteering, at a terrible price to the rest of us, the CBI demanded a greater share of the costs of this infrastructure investment to be transferred to the individual car-user, through road tolls.

Roads are not the only route to heavily subsidised capitalist profiteering in the transport sector. When the railways were privatised in the 1990s, we were bombarded by messages of how this would eradicate 'the waste of taxpayers' money' under the old nationalised British Rail. Aye, right! State spending on the railways in 2013 was six times higher than at the point of privatisation! A TUC-commissioned Report stated:

"Privatisation meant risk and investment-averse private companies positioned themselves as value extractors, thanks to high public subsidies."

From 2001 onwards, the government made up for the abject failure of privatised companies to invest some of their profits in renewal of the rail infrastructure, investing heavily in new rolling stock and tracks. In just the four short years from 2007-11, the five largest privatised rail companies pocketed £3billion in state subsidies, helping them wallow in over £0.5billion in operating profits, which they promptly handed nearly all of to shareholders. Overall, the 15 private Train Operating Companies (TOCs) rely on state subsidies for up to 36% of their income.

So much for their much-vaunted 'free market' capitalism; the system that's supposed to benefit us all through the genius of 'supply and demand', unfettered by interfering government, strictly self-reliant, in no need of the attentions of 'the nanny state' – as the apologists of capitalism accuse the poorest and the working class in general of being. We live in 'a something for nothing society for the rich', more like!

Privatisation, in its many guises, has been an Aladdin's Cave of treasure for big business. One of the most disgusting forms of plunder of public resources for the profit of the privateers has been the alphabetti spaghetti of PFI, PPP and such like. Private Finance Initiative (PFI) was initiated by the Tory government of John Major, but continued by New Labour in office, along with its rebranded version, Public Private Partnership (PPP), accompanied by the mantra 'it's the only money in town'. We were told, repeatedly, that it was either this scheme – whereby the state paid an annual fee to private contractors to build and manage schools and hospitals, which these private consortia then leased back to the government – or nothing!

It never occurred to the capitalist fundamentalists of either the Tories or Labour that a progressive taxation of the rich and big business could not only provide the funding for new schools and hospitals – but also that the state could borrow on the world money markets far more cheaply, with far lower interest rates than forked out by the PFI or PPP consortia, because the state is deemed to be infinitely less likely to go bankrupt. The outcome? Taxpayers carry the burden of risk, while the private consortia carry away the cash piles to their bank accounts.

Over the last 20 years, £55billion worth of projects have been issued to private consortia by the state, usually in the form of 30-year contracts. By the time payments end, the public will have given the profiteers a predicted £310billion! So for every £1 invested in schools and hospitals, privately owned firms will have got back about £6. That's public subsidies to the profits of the stinking rich.

Subsidised profits for constructing school buildings vital to the education of the next generation of workers... who in turn will generate profits for capitalist employers. And subsidised profiteering for ensuring hospital buildings for the treatment of the health of workers (current and future)... in part so they're fit to work and generate profits.

So next time you hear some overpaid politician, or bloated boardroom boss, tell us we have to cut back on in-work benefits, or that business simply couldn't afford a decent living minimum wage of £10 in this day and age, bear these facts in mind. And don't forget they are only a sample of the swag bags of subsidies handed out to big business by the state from the taxes of working people. Capitalist subsidy junkies rule and ruin the lives of millions, whilst pleading poverty in the face of demands for a living wage for their workers.

16

TAX CUTS FOR THE RICH – TAX CREDIT CUTS FOR THE REST

One of the most frequent objections to £10 Now, in 2015, is that businesses would go to the wall, collapse, and create mass unemployment.

We have already sampled the sumptuous feast of subsidies meted out to private capitalism by an ever-willing state, which the latter fund by picking the pockets of workers. So not only do capitalists make their fortunes from the unpaid labour of the workers they hire, but also have their bounty subsidised from the public purse.

But the subsidies don't end there; not by a long chalk. Every time a business owner suppresses the wages of his workforce to below anything resembling a living income, he is aided and abetted by the government system of Working Tax Credit, Child Tax Credit, and Housing Benefit... and their new-born successor, Universal Credit.

This system means the taxes of middle-income and better-paid workers are used to prop up – and encourage – the low pay that turbo-charges the profits of gluttonous multinational and national corporations. The government's own HMRC has produced mind-boggling statistics on the fortunes thus devoured by parasitic capitalist companies every year; taxpayers' money used to slightly ease the pain of deprivation suffered by millions of workers who've been robbed of a decent living wage in the name of profit maximisation.

In just seven short years, from 2003-04 to 2010-11, a monumental sum of £175.636billion was spent on subsidising low pay through these two top-up systems alone. More recently, this public subsidy for the theft of wages by private profiteers has risen to £30billion a year. That's just about identical to the sum given to the Scottish Government annually in the block grant from Westminster. And those figures don't even include the additional cash mountains consumed in Housing Benefit – currently £26billion per annum – the child of a coupling between poverty pay and skyrocketing private landlords' rents.

In-work tax credits are a huge subsidy to low-paying profiteers. Rather than pass minimum wage legislation that forced the employers to pay a wage guaranteed to lift all workers above the breadline, successive Labour, Coalition and Tory governments have instead propped them up in their payment of pathetic hourly rates by topping up workers' pay a miserly bit above the buttons they get off their employer. The amounts by which workers' wages are topped up are certainly not generous. For example, the New Policy Institute calculated that in 2012-13, families in receipt of Working Tax Credit got an average of £48.80 a week; those with dependent children averaged £66.30 in WTC.

But the sums involved in encouraging continued cheapskate wages being paid by big business are certainly not trifling! In the years 2004 to 2011, tax credits added up to an average of over £7,000 for every employee in the UK. In 2009-10 alone, £27.3billion was used in tax credits to part-compensate for the failure of the profit-hungry to pay their workers a living wage. That's an average of over £1,100 per employee. It's no wonder the cost of tax credits is rising, rapidly. Behind the honeyed phrases about job creation in a Britain which – according to Tory Chancellor George Osborne – is 'the bounce-back kid', lurks the ugly truth. Since 2010, 1.1 million more jobs paid less than £20,000, whereas 800,000 fewer jobs paid above £20,000.

Housing Benefit is another version of state subsidy arising from failure by employers to pay adequate wages. The chronic shortage of cheaper social housing – depleted by the theft of social sector housing under the Right to Buy scheme, compounded by a conscious decision not to build houses for affordable rent – combines with poverty pay in an unstable cocktail that has led to an explosion of Housing Benefit bills.

It costs about £26billion a year right now. And increasingly these payments go to people in work, but poorly paid, rather than to the unwaged. For instance, the Building & Social Housing Foundation reported in 2012 that 90% of all new Housing Benefit claims in the first two years of the Tory/Lib Dem Coalition were from working households. The response to this rocketing bill – by both the 2010-15 Coalition and Her Majesty's Labour opposition – has been to cap benefits, but do nothing to cap the rip-roaring rents charged by landlords in the burgeoning private rented sector.

Likewise, their response to the cost of Working Tax Credits is not to legislate for a decent living wage that would lift all workers above the level that condemns them to dependency on top-up benefits. Instead, they pursue the mirror opposite: leave workers on the same appalling wage levels, but make it much harder to claim tax credits and other in-work benefits.

First, they amended the hours required to work in order to qualify for tax credits, with clauses stipulating a minimum of 24 hours a week for a couple, but with one of the couple having to work at least 16 hours (as opposed to two people on 12-hour contracts each, for instance). More punishing still, a 30-hours-a-week threshold for a single, childless person, and then only if they're over 25 years old. And they saved the state another few million quid by shrinking the period of back-dated payments from 90 days to 30.

In 2012 alone, they wiped £550million off the tax credit bill, slashing the list of low-paid people entitled to a top-up. The 2010-15 Coalition devalued Child and Working Tax Credits by freezing them for three years, then capping them at 1%.

My own union, Usdaw, calculated that this made Working Tax Credit worth £500-a-year less on average; that tax and benefit changes from 2010-15 cost families an average of £1,100 per annum; and Universal Credit will hit families by a further cut of £650 annually.

* * * *

Not content with those barriers to in-work benefits, the Westminster regime recently started limbering up to erect even higher hurdles, with plans to disqualify workers who don't prove they are trying hard enough to get more hours of work. That is one of the clauses they plan to include in the new-born Universal Credit system.

Hot on the heels of being elected in May 2015, Cameron's Tories unveiled plans in their July 2015 Emergency Budget to slash tax credits by £4.5billion this year alone. Of course, this is not by lifting guar-

anteed wages by that amount so workers are no longer dependent on
state top-ups. No, the Tories want to strangle the power of unions to
fight for such pay rises, with the most repressive Trade Union Bill in
decades, and simultaneously bury their well-heeled boots into part-
time workers, kicking and harassing them off tax credits unless they
prove they're seeking additional hours of work… and by slashing their
access to these top-ups.

For instance, up until now the threshold income – also called the
'earnings disregard' – at which tax credits start to be gradually withdrawn has been £6,420. That keeps in perspective any notion you
may have been moulded into thinking by the media about workers
living on the fat of the land with free state handouts on top of their
generous wages. Anyone earning over £6,420 a year – which works
out at 19-hours-a-week on the 'adult' £6.50 minimum wage – starts
to have tax credit clawed back off them. But since the July 2015 Tory
budget, it is set to get worse, far worse. The new threshold has been
slashed from £6,420 to £3,850.

What's more, the rate at which tax credits are withdrawn for workers
earning above the thresholds just described – what's called the 'taper'
– is set to shoot up from 41% to 48%. So instead of losing 41p for
every £1 earned above £6,420 a year, workers will now lose 48p for
every £1 in wages over £3,850. These punitive measures against the
low-paid – part-timers and women workers especially – led the Institute of Fiscal Studies to conclude, after the July Tory Budget, that:

> "Tax credit changes could hit three million families, who are likely to
> lose an average of £1,000. Even taking into account higher wages, peo-
> ple receiving tax credits would be significantly worse off."

In an age defined by the escalating number of jobs that are short-
hours contracts – not to even mention the super-exploited army on
zero hours contracts – this is an undisguised assault on workers' incomes, hitting the low-paid part-timers in order to reduce state
spending on in-work benefits. All this at the same time as they've
awarded every millionaire in the country at least £43,000 a year by

slashing the top tax rate from 50% to 45% since 2013, with further tax handouts to the 1% in the pipeline. Again, we witness the stomach-churning merry-go-round of low pay boosting profits for big business, which in addition is heavily subsidised by the state – the same state which in turn saves money on its expenditure on in-work benefits to workers unable to survive on the squalid levels of pay given to them by the same capitalist subsidy junkies!

* * * *

When you begin to break down the state subsidies on wages into their allocation to different sectors of the economy, a clear, devastating picture leaps out. The first attempt to measure where Working Tax Credit goes was conducted by the New Policy Institute in October 2014. They based their study on data from 2010-11 and 2011-12. The figures are devastating if you're an apologist for the misnamed 'free market'; for the claimed superiority of private ownership over public.

A massive 80% of all the workers in receipt of Working Tax Credits are employed in the private sector. A mere 1% of workers relying on state top-ups are employed by central government. A further 10% of workers getting these all-too-modest top-ups are employed by local government, and another 5% by the NHS.

In turn, the types of jobs in the private sector that are so pitifully paid as to merit Working Tax Credits is extremely revealing. It's precisely those sectors that are dominated by highly profitable giant companies, such as retail, which accounts for a whopping 20% of the entire Working Tax Credit bill. This is followed by health and social care – a privatised sector – which accounts for another 18% of all the Working Tax Credits meted out to workers relying on a few quid to eke out an existence.

These two categories of employment also near the top of the table for the percentage of their total workforces dependent on Working Tax Credit. An outrageous 14% of retail workers thus qualify – one in seven of the total – as do 12% of health care staff. What an appalling indictment of capitalist society; people caring for the elderly, sick, disabled or young children are forced to jump through the hoops of means-tested benefits to survive. Hospitality workers topped this league of abominable pay requiring state subsidies: 18% of them got Working Tax Credit due to rampant low pay.

Subsequent analysis of tax credits, by Citizens United in April 2015, exposes the same reliance of retail giants on state subsidies in the form of top-up benefits to their underpaid staff. Using figures from the unions and the government's Labour Force Survey, they calculated that Tesco last year (2014) gained a net subsidy of £364million for hiring its workforce. That's not the total tax credits paid out to supplement Tesco workers' pay, which are actually far higher than that. It's the net amount, after deducting the sums paid in Income Tax and National Insurance Contributions by the workers involved, plus the National Insurance Contributions paid by Tesco for the same workers.

In the same Citizens UK analysis, they broke down the figures to show individual examples of the levels of subsidy paid out from workers' taxes to other low-paid workers, and conversely what could be saved by forcing employers to pay a higher hourly rate of pay. First they looked at the case of a couple with two dependents, one of them working a 16-hour week at £7.20 an hour, the other a 35-hour week on £8.29 an hour. The net public subsidy caused by low pay rates amounts to £87.09 a week, or £4,528 a year. And of course many millions of workers are on substantially lower hourly rates than either of this couple.

The other case they examined looks at things through the other end of the telescope; what could be saved in public subsidies by a pay rise. In this case study, a single full-time worker with two kids, currently on the minimum wage of £6.50-an-hour, gets a pay rise to the so-called Living Wage of £7.85. Savings to the public purse, paid instead by this worker's boss? £43.39 a week, or £2,256 a year.

We need to expose the subsidy junkies, the capitalist parasites who live off the body of working-class taxpayers. But not so as to help them punish the victims of poverty pay, by sitting back and letting the Tories rob them of even more. Not by standing idly by whilst the Tories rob low-paid workers through the already-existing three-year freeze on Child and Working Tax Credits, plus their new, escalated theft of £4.5billion this year from these wage supplements to the low-est-paid families, or with sanctions on part-time workers for 'not getting enough hours of work'.

Instead, the trade union movement, community organisations and socialists should spearhead the battle to stop the Tories stealing 'out of the mouths of babes' (and children and adults) through their planned butchery of Child Tax Credits and Working Tax Credits. We should fiercely resist a single penny being lost in what are lifeline supplements to the 'working poor'.

But the same campaign needs to simultaneously advocate the one, central measure best suited to eradicate the need for state subsidies to wages: by mounting a serious struggle to force the vampires of profit to pay a minimum of £10-an-hour to all their staff – without exception, from the age of 16 upwards, male and female, indigenous or immigrant workers, apprentices, agency or temporary workers alike.

Why should we tolerate any longer the double mugging of workers for profit, through unpaid labour and public subsidy?

17

THIS TOPSY TURVY SYSTEM

Socialists are often accused of wanting to turn the world upside down. To that I would plead guilty and proud of it! When we suffer a system that is standing on its head, where nonsense has become sense, where chaos and criminal inequality are treated as the norm, we need to turn it upside down so society can stand on its feet.

We endure a system, capitalism, where vast public funding is devoured to prop up – and even encourage – large, highly profitable employers paying their workers peanuts – whilst small enterprises already suffer closure and bankruptcy. Last year alone, 849 companies in Scotland were declared insolvent, and that's as nothing compared with the legions of small shops and cafés that constantly open, shut down, change hands and then stop trading again, in a neighbourhood near you.

When we advocate a guaranteed £10 minimum wage, people routinely question whether that would be affordable to smaller businesses, or whether it would simply drive them under, shedding the handful of jobs they each currently offer. That's where we need to begin to turn things upside down, challenging the underlying assumptions used to reject a decent living wage for all workers, regardless of where, or by whom, they're employed.

Let us recap a few stern facts. A mighty 80% of all the workers who depend on tax credit top-ups to their paltry pay are hired in the private sector. Retail alone makes up 20% of all the workers dependent on these supplements, and the privatised health and social care sector another 18% of the grand total. So straight away we can see that these state subsidies are being forked out to sectors of employment dominated by big firms – not just a few family corner shops. For instance, it's the billionaire owners of retail empires – not the hard-pressed micro-businesses employing 0-9 workers, or the small enterprises with 10-49 staff – that are the main beneficiaries of taxpayers' money.

So when giant employers plead poverty in the face of the demand for a decent living wage, we should demand that the government applies to them the means test methods which are currently reserved for use against the very poorest in society. They should demand opening up of their secret business accounts to full public inspection. To a social audit, with involvement by the unions covering their workforces; the government; tax inspectors and other experts in the field. A social audit should be conducted into their profits – the real ones, not those they reluctantly admit to in front of HMRC – the salaries, shares and bonuses of their top bosses; the usefulness of what their business does; their profit margins; the state subsidies they've had, and how they were used – and the information gathered then used to call their bluff on their pleas of poverty. The government should then insist on payment of a decent living wage, legally enforced and inspected.

In those sectors where such large businesses are important to the national economy, but still refuse to pay a decent wage, the government should take over running of the business, guarantee all jobs and implementation of a £10 minimum wage, and where appropriate retrain and redeploy workers by agreement with their unions.

As part of 'turning things upside down', a clear distinction should then be made between these corporate Scrooges and the micro-businesses or small enterprises that are genuinely struggling to afford a £10 minimum to their tiny workforce. Again, it's only socially fair and reasonable that their accounts; the state of the premises in terms of health and safety; the social usefulness of their enterprise; any existing government aid they are in receipt of and how it's been used; and the incomes, perks and privileges of the owners, should all be subjected to thorough public scrutiny. A means test, not to mince words.

If such a social audit discovers a small business can easily afford to pay a decent living wage without state assistance, they should be legally obliged to do so, with the additional powers of planning permission used to enforce it, if necessary.

If they are running a sweatshop death-trap – an inexcusable form of exploitation that deserves to be shut down in the interests of the health, safety and wellbeing of the workforce and wider society – the government and local authorities should redeploy the workers, guaranteeing them safe, well-paid jobs, for instance by assisting other local small businesses, or through the formation of workers' cooperatives.

For those deserving cases identified – socially useful small businesses which genuinely can't afford to keep all existing jobs if they pay a £10 minimum – the government should assist them. They should stop stuffing cash in the mouths of big profiteering capitalists who rely on pitiful pay to fuel their profits, underpinned by state subsidies, and instead use the taxpayers' funds thus released to establish a Small Business Living Wage Fund. A scheme of repayable loans or grants to small businesses that merit at least temporary help in meeting their wages bill, based on paying nothing less than £10-an-hour, in 2015 figures.

This Small Business Living Wage Fund could easily be financed by a combination of the huge savings made on the £30billion annual cost of – mostly – propping up the low pay imposed by large chains and big businesses, and increased Corporation Tax on the same giants of capitalist ownership.

Aside from any other sources, it's an astonishing fact that just the top hundred companies in the UK – the FTSE 100 – are currently hoarding a total of £53.3billion in what is politely termed 'cash piles'. That's £53.3billion that they've made in profit, but refuse to invest, refuse to pass on in increased wages, and decline to even pay taxes on in most instances. If these 'high'-class hoarders were compelled to cough up their fair contribution to society, imagine the transformation in the fortunes of small businesses and their employees?

In a nutshell, society should stop subsidising totally undeserving big businesses, and start a scheme to assist any deserving small employers, based on full public inspection of their case for a loan or grant to sustain jobs with a decent living wage. That's turning things upside down compared to the present outrageous, involuntary generosity of working-class and middle-class taxpayers towards the millionaire and billionaire class of capitalist vampires – who suck blood out of workers' wages and taxes, to quench their insatiable thirst for profit.

A further simple truth should not be forgotten either: paying workers in small businesses a decent living wage boosts their spending power, and therefore enhances the chances of the same small businesses surviving through increased sales. It's a virtuous circle – not the vicious circle of widespread poverty pay slashing spending power, thus adding to the likelihood of small businesses being particularly prey to failure – especially as they can't compete with the 'economies of scale' and ability to survive a bad spell of business that the monopoly capitalists enjoy.

We need to turn this topsy-turvy system upside down, to bring some rational planning to jobs and decent wages for all, rather than allow the continuation of the irrational system of subsidised exploitation for the profit of the few.

18

PAY RISES AT A TERRIBLE PRICE

We've mentioned the retail sector as a prime example of low pay, and as the biggest single employer in the country, hiring workers who stand to gain more than most from a bare minimum of £10 Now. However, you could be forgiven for thinking this is an outdated assertion, given the wholesale media celebrations of retail pay hikes of late.

In mid-2015, sections of the retail sector announced a series of increased hourly pay rates that outwardly marked welcome progress. German-owned discount supermarket Lidl became the first to declare it would exceed the Living Wage, paying a minimum of £8.20 from the summer of 2015 (£9.35 in London) to their 9,000 staff. Next in the queue, IKEA announced in July it would match the Living Wage Foundation figure from April 2016 for its 8,000 workers in Britain and Ireland.

Sainsbury's – who employ 137,000 – raised their hourly rate by 4%, from £7.08 to £7.36 from October. In late September 2015, Morrison's offered a rise from £6.83 to £8.20-an-hour, in a package negotiated and recommended by Usdaw union officials to members amongst the 90,000-strong workforce. Then, to trump all its rivals, the other German-owned discounter, Aldi – who now boast that half of all UK households do at least some of their shopping in – declared a minimum rate of £8.40 (£9.45 in London), which means a pay rise for about 5,000 of the 28,000 they hire in their 600 stores across Britain and Ireland.

* * * *

Why this shift on wages, after the retail giants have doggedly refused – for decades – to improve on wage rates that makes it the single biggest concentration of low-paid workers? For instance, the October 2015 KPMG report on low pay identified 920,000 retail workers earning below £7.85 per hour – the Living Wage Foundation figure at the time of their research.

Several factors explain this trend on hourly pay – some of them encouraging, others downright dangerous. A limited campaign of pressure by the unions has had some impact. For instance, Usdaw targeted Lidl and Aldi for a unionisation drive this year, only to be ordered off their premises, with branch managers instructed by head office to call the police.

So in the immediate aftermath of this attempt to recruit to the union, the owners will have calculated an hourly pay rise as an affordable sweetener to avoid more radical demands in future by an organised workforce. As confirmation of this being part of their calculation, Lidl initially only declared their new £8.20 rate for England, Scotland and Wales. They excluded their stores across Northern Ireland. Usdaw union members there erupted in angry protests, and within two weeks Lidl beat a retreat, extending their pay rate to these workers. This action and outcome was a clear illustration of the value and consequences of workers being organised.

In IKEA, a prolonged lobbying for a genuine living wage by some shop stewards and members – but sadly not in the least by Usdaw nationally – made at least a modest contribution to the company's decision.

Another obvious factor is the pursuit of kudos, to look good, and avoid losing face by comparison with their competitors, where periodic price wars are now accompanied by a 'pay war'. This is the product of growing public awareness and anger at the cesspit of low pay that is retail. In a survey by *Retail Weekly*, they found that over 60% of shoppers "would not knowingly shop in a company which failed to pay a living wage to its staff".

So the campaigning by trade unionists and socialists has a lot of potential, even more so if it was coordinated and relentless. Retail is especially dependent on 'image' and 'reputation', especially in a period of cut-throat competition, where rival retail profiteers in many cases over-stretched themselves during the previous credit binge, when 'consumers' were coaxed and conned into spending far beyond their real means, store cards and credit cards in hand.

Now in the years of the post-binge spending hangover, shoppers hunting for a bargain in hard times don't always have the luxury of 'ethical shopping' – especially those on low incomes – but at least a section do, are increasingly aware of the Scrooge employers, and thereby add the threat of at least an informal boycott to retail bosses who fall to the bottom of the wages league. And a simple, central factor should not be forgotten: these retail giants, many of whom count their profits in £billions rather than £millions, can easily afford it!

* * * *

Trade union and public pressure in part explains a marked change in hourly pay rates in at least some retail giants. But the more sinister aspect to this new turn is hidden from the view of those who may be encouraged to drag their shopping trolleys into those establishments sporting a 'Living Wage Employer' logo. In a downright dangerous trend, these outwardly progressive pay rises are accompanied by savage attacks on other terms and conditions for the very same workers in at least several of the retail profiteers seeking public acclamation for their recent – very belated – pay rises.

Workers are losing with the left hand what they gain with the right. For instance, in the much-trumpeted pay package negotiated with Usdaw in September 2015, Morrison's are wiping out premium payments for those who work Sundays – scrapping the current time-and-a-half they've had. In flat contradiction to Usdaw's claim to be fighting off the deregulation of Sunday trading, Morrison's – in common with most other retail outlets – is converting Sunday into 'just another day at work'. They are also scrapping premium payments for overtime, late shifts and early shifts. Supplementary payments to café cooks and fork lift truck drivers are to vanish too. And paid breaks are set to disappear, which means that somebody working and paid for a 39-hour week would hereon only get paid for 36.5 hours.

In some of these oh-so-progressive companies, basking in the afterglow of their press releases on becoming Living Wage Employers, measures such as increased, compulsory weekend working and the monstrosity of obligatory 10-hour shifts at weekends are being pursued. Aldi has a swagger in its step right now, boasting the best hourly pay rates of any of the rival supermarkets – £8.40 an hour. But lurking behind the headlines is a seedier side to the outfit declared Supermarket of the Year 2015 by *Which?* magazine.

As revealed by Channel Four's *Dispatches* team, who sent undercover reporters in as workers in their stores in Scotland and the north west of England, Aldi sets mind-blowing time targets for various tasks. All workers are compelled to multi-task. They have impossible time targets to unload pallets, stack shelves or scan items at the till. This ends up with them chucking bread, damaging food items, and not having the time to check food on display being within its sell-by date. All this rushed labour resulted in the *Dispatches* reporters finding squashed, damaged, mouldy and rotting foodstuffs on sale on twelve out of the 20 days they worked there; in one case, finding bacon for sale three weeks after its sell-by date.

The health and safety of staff (and customers) is sacrificed on the altar of profit, with fire exits routinely blocked by trolleys and stock, and staff ordered to climb on shelves to save time whilst stacking them. The high-speed drive for productivity is hellish on Aldi's tills. Anyone who's shopped there will have witnessed the breakneck speed at which workers scan items, virtually ordering you to hurry up and get out of the place with your trolley. In fact, this is not some character flaw in people who work there! It's driven by Aldi policies, described in the staff handbook, and mercilessly enforced.

* * * *

In those companies gaining credit for a pay rise, the age-old method of exploitation is ever-present in efforts to compensate the owners: more and more work is heaped on fewer and fewer workers, as staffing levels fall, and 'multi-tasking' without equivalent pay supplements are demanded of those who remain in the jobs. Workers are being made to pay a heavy price – in losses of terms, conditions, actual wages, and their work/life balance – for a welcome rise in hourly pay, which is the only aspect of the package that the general public will ever know about.

A new additional demand needs to be added to the fighting policies of those trade unionists and socialists battling for an immediate, legally-enforced living minimum wage of £10 for all workers.

We need to also insist this is implemented "without loss of jobs, paid hours, premium payments, staffing levels, terms or conditions". Otherwise, just as the Tory theft of Working Tax Credits is more than cancelling out any wage rises millions of workers get, so too many employers will switch from suffering the opprobrium of being branded Scrooges for the hourly rates they pay, to robbing back at least as much off workers in other payments and conditions.

It's the very nature of the beast. Capitalist employers are not in business to make cars, or steel, or electronics, or build houses – or to distribute food, clothes, footwear or household goods. They are in business to make money – and distribute it amongst the obscenely rich. To cream off the unpaid labour of the working class, their source of profit. So what they concede in a higher wage, including the sanitised, semi-official 'Living Wage', they will claw back in reductions to the overall wages bill by slashing double-time or time-and-a-half for Sundays or public holidays; anti-social hours premiums; paid breaks; or by back-breaking shifts that avoids the need to employ extra staff.

The mechanisms may change in detail, but the system remains intact: profit is boosted at the expense of workers facing longer hours, cutbacks on staffing levels, lessened conditions, more intensive exploitation of their labour.

So long as we have capitalism, any gains on hourly wages will be temporary; a concession won from a system whose very life-blood depends on the exploitation of workers' labour for employers' profit.

This whole episode – headline-grabbing pay rises granted by some retail empires more noted for their miserly habits towards staff – illustrates the more general need to combine demands for a legally-enforced living minimum wage with the construction of powerful, democratic and fighting trade unions, engaged in collective bargaining on behalf of members.

Workers need legal protection from being super-exploited, which is why the floor of a decent living minimum, legally enforced, is critical. But not at the price of trading away hard-won terms and conditions – which in some cases means workers actually being worse off financially at the end of the working week, and certainly worse off in terms of daily working conditions.

19

JOBS: THE STRUGGLE
DETERMINES THE OUTCOME

"I sympathise with the idea of a £10 minimum, without discrimination against young people, women or black workers – who currently earn an appalling 48% less than white workers. But surely it would destroy jobs?"

How many times have you heard – or maybe even thought – that fear expressed, by perfectly decent people with no desire to accept the status quo? It's another example of our minds being chained and our visions narrowed by the ideology of the rich; by the straitjacket we're put in by those out to maximise their own class's wealth and privilege.

Why is that the case? For starters, the fight for higher wages is a battle for a bigger share of the nation's wealth to go to wages, as opposed to profits. To continue the metaphor of the economic cake, the bigger the slice allocated to workers' plates in the form of wages, benefits and social wages, the thinner the slice of cake that remains for the profits, privileges and perks of the owners and their Chief Executives. So there is no logical necessity whatsoever for the number of jobs to fall, or for the size of the cake to shrink, on the back of a £10 minimum wage. It's purely a question of the distribution of the cake. So the only threat to jobs comes from the greedy profit-seekers, who frankly would prefer if workers were content with a few crumbs, let alone a thin slice of the overall cake (production) they've created through their work.

* * * *

The demand for a decent living wage is a measure aimed at wealth redistribution. A device to challenge the mind-boggling wealth transfusion to the capitalist minority, especially over the past 30-40 years, as the wage share has plummeted by a cumulative total of £1.3trillion since 1975.

Even within the limitations, the straitjacket, of a capitalist system of production, higher wages do not have to mean job losses. On the contrary. In a study by the New Economics Foundation think-tank in September 2015, they demonstrated how in virtually every European country, the wage share had fallen in tandem with a decline in the numbers and influence wielded by trade unions. In turn, they proved, this led to a shrinkage in the market, and a drag on profits and growth of national output (GDP). In the case of the UK, the NEF research concluded:

> "For every 1% reduction in the GDP going to wages in the UK, GDP is cut by £2.2billion."

They added that the decline in trade union density (the percentage of workers in a union) has cut GDP by up to 1.6% – what they called "a significant permanent loss." Then in a devastatingly powerful answer to enemies of trade unions, and of decent wages, the NEF measured the following:

> "Restoration of trade union density to its early 1980s levels, through a rise in the wage share, would add £27.2billion to the UK's GDP."

That's an increase in wealth production very close to the annual Scottish government budget. Imagine the number of well-paid, secure jobs that sum alone could fund, even before looking at the wider measures described in this book, including a whole new green industry that could create at least 100,000 new jobs in Scotland alone?

To avoid any doubt about the implications of this scientific study: bigger and stronger unions lead to better pay, a bigger share of the cake to workers, which in turn actually increases the size of the cake! And that's all within the confines of the system that relies on the profit motive to get employers to hire workers, to work for wages that are never equivalent to the wealth these workers produce.

Increased wages creates increased spending power. All things being equal, that should also create the need for more workers, more jobs, to produce for the increased demand. A virtuous circle.

However, we're talking about capitalism here, not logic! Employers forced to pay at least £10-an-hour to their workers – instead of the present set-up where KPMG has just announced that six million UK workers are earning below £7.85, compared with 5.3 million last year – such employers will fight like fiends to save every penny that they're forced to grudgingly hand over in hourly rates of pay.

The same KPMG report was an in-depth assessment of the economic impact of a universal £7.85 Living Wage. No such research seems to have been done for a £10 figure, but their study is very illuminating. For the whole of the UK, they measured that a £7.85 Living Wage, applied universally, would add £11.1billion to the wages bill. It sounds a lot, but it's a tiny 1.3% increase in overall wages. However, the government would recoup 59% of that – £6.6billion – through higher income tax and National Insurance Contributions, and reduced benefits payments. That in turn, provided there was a socialist government, could vastly improve public services, the social wage.

KPMG then went on to paint four different scenarios for covering the cost of the £11.1billion enlargement of the slice of the cake going to wages. They looked at it being paid for either by increased prices; increased productivity; cuts to the numbers and/or pay of other better-paid workers; or cuts to profits.

Here's the kernel of the matter: the government's own economic model assumes any pay rise will be paid 70% through price rises, the other 30% through job losses. They never even consider the option of cuts to profits! Nor would they; they're a capitalist government that seeks to protect the engorged share of the cake going to the rent, interest and profit of the landowners, bankers and industrial capitalists of this class-divided nation.

* * * *

So the central answer to the genuine query, "Will it cost jobs", is that there's absolutely no excuse for it doing so, and in fact better wages should expand the number of jobs – but the outcome will be determined by the struggle. The struggle between workers and their organised unions – and the employers and their organised government. The battle over what size of slice from the cake goes to which class, labour or capital, worker or capitalist employer.

Just as we already witness attempts to make workers pay a terrible price in back-breaking workload, loss of premium payments, loss of paid hours and other worsened conditions for the sake of an improved hourly rate of pay that gives kudos to the employer, so too the corporate bosses will try to shed jobs to compensate themselves for any increased wages bill. The struggle will determine the outcome.

Workers, trade unions and socialists need to struggle collectively for the £10 Now, and not just passively wait for legislation to introduce it – with enough strings attached to strangle the working class. Critically, in doing so, we need to break out of the ideological straitjacket, the mental chains that make us assume capitalist ownership and the pursuit of profit from the unpaid labour of the working class is the natural order of things. It's not. It's only been around on the planet for a few hundred years; not even an eye-blink in recorded human history.

And whilst fighting for every penny extra in pay, we should never lose sight of the need to change, utterly, the actual system of political economy. That includes increased taxation of big business and the enormously rich, to fund better wages and job creation. It includes campaigning for the rational planning of production, distribution and exchange through democratic public ownership of the main centres of the economy.

To go back to the cake metaphor: we shouldn't be content with just perpetually battling for a slightly larger slice of a cake of a fixed size. We should demand control and ownership of not only the cake, but the bakery. So as to decide the ingredients and size of the cake. So as to plan the production of things and services that people actually need, in a fashion that protects people and planet, a sustainable economic plan. And to democratically determine what size of slice goes directly to wages, how much in modernisation and investment, how much in universal provision of life-enhancing public services like health, education, housing, transport and recreation.

20

IT'S GOOD FOR YOUR HEALTH

Sean O'Casey, the socialist Irish playwright, once wrote:

"Money doesn't make you happy but it quiets the nerves."

Elsewhere, he wrote of aspiring to a society where ordinary people could reach all-sided fulfillment:

"A loaf of bread under the worker's oxter, a bouquet of flowers in his hands."

The benefits of a decent living wage are many, massive, and proven. It would eliminate the current horror stories of people forced to hold down two or three low-paid jobs to try and make ends meet. Many of them have to choose between lunch and dinner; not just to reduce the food bills, but because they are running from one job to the next, with different employers, missing out on breaks. One of the many by-products of this lifestyle is eating 'on the run' – invariably an unhealthy option.

They miss out on family life too, merely existing to work, rather than working to live a fulfilled life. Unicef carries out an annual measure of what they term 'Children's Wellbeing in Rich Countries'. Six different categories of wellbeing are assessed: material; health and safety; education; peer and family relations; behaviours and risks; subjective sense of wellbeing. So this is a comprehensive measure of not only definable incomes and safety, but also children's social and emotional state, including their own sense of how they feel.

In the 2007 study of 21 nations in the industrialised world, the Scandinavian countries took the top four places... and the fifth-largest economy in the world, the self-proclaimed mother of democracy, Britain, managed to conquer an appalling, derisory 21st place out of

21 countries! Children with parents driven to distraction by financial pressures, or working anti-social, long hours, undoubtedly suffer reduced happiness.

The impact of a breadline existence goes far beyond the individual worker affected, to wider society – something Maggie Thatcher infamously denied exists, but which millions rely upon for the basic things that make for a civilised existence. As Rev Lucy Winkett, rector of St James's Piccadilly, London, and an advocate of the Living Wage, put it:

> "A healthy, active civil society is reliant on people volunteering their time and enthusiasm for the good of others. We risk losing that great tradition if our families are too troubled with tackling household expenditure. Hard working people should have enough to live, not simply survive."

Amin is a cleaner. His story could be told by hundreds of thousands of others:

> "Before, I had to work two jobs to put food on the table and pay the rent. I had no time for my family or my community. Since getting the Living Wage, I was able to prioritise the one job and that means I've been there for my family, and set up a youth group in my community. What I've been given, I'm now able to give back."

The Scottish Living Wage Campaign regularly reports findings from both the workers affected and employers who became Accredited Living Wage companies. The stark statistics of success in paying better wages include 25% reduction in absenteeism; 66% of employers reporting "a significant positive impact on recruitment and retention", with accountancy giant PwC reporting "turnover of contractors fell from 4% to 1% since they adopted the Living Wage"; a rise in staff motivation and psychological well-being; and 75% of workers reporting an increase in the quality of work.

A major study, published in December 2014, by the authoritative Scottish Public Health Observatory, drew this very definite conclusion:

"Introduction of a Living Wage and benefit increases made more difference to health than schemes to help lose weight or stop smoking."

Their comprehensive study into health and health inequalities
found that the health gap has widened since the 1970s, and is wider
in Scotland than most of Europe. The researchers found cycling to
work had only "a minimally positive effect on health"; and taxation
on tobacco was positive for health but made little impact on health
inequalities. The Report's Executive Summary stated:

"Introduction of a Living Wage generated the largest beneficial impact
on health, and led to a modest reduction in health inequalities."

It went on to calculate that whilst tobacco taxation would bring in
£17million over ten years, a 10% rise in Job Seekers Allowance would
save £41million over the same period, and paying a living wage an
impressive £138million – both of the latter two from savings for the
NHS through prevented hospitalisations.

* * * *

Raising the spending power of the working class would not just liberate individual workers from the stress and unhappiness of constantly
having to scrimp and save. It would also transform whole communities. In far too many town centres, villages, city districts and housing
schemes, small shops have been shut down, boarded up, or decorated
by one of those massive posters pretending to be a butcher's, green-
grocer's, bakery or hardware shop. This vain attempt to lift the spirits
of the locals only serves to remind us of the record levels of closures
and bankruptcies suffered by small businesses and family firms.

In part this is a result of being crushed between the hammer blows of
multinational supermarkets and other retail chains, and the anvil of profiteering banks robbing them with interest charges on loans. In part also
it's the consequence of widespread low pay, for instance as hard-pressed
families hunt for the cheapest food available, which is usually also the

unhealthiest. The latter is sold by big chains (and fast food multinationals), which drives small, independent shops to the wall, because they can't undercut the prices of giants enjoying the 'economies of scale'.

Recent reports confirm that the price of fresh food has risen by far more than average inflation, whereas that of processed, unhealthy food has fallen relative to inflation. So rather than fork out a bit extra on freshly baked bread, or fresh fish or meat, or organically grown fruit and veg, workers' families without two brass farthings to rub together will buy frozen food in Iceland or Farmfoods, or fill up with a 'treat' in McDonald's or Burger King, enlarging these chains' profits – and their own waistlines – in the process.

Working families are also driven to retail parks, supermarkets and often 'cheap and nasty' food shops by another factor in their working lives: this country combines some of the lowest pay with the longest hours of work in Europe.

We live in a system where millions are stressed out of their minds by too much work, other millions by having too little, or literally none. So when it comes to eating out or shopping, frequently it's an issue of time available, rather than having the luxury of 'shopping around' for the best, the healthiest – or indeed the cheapest.

If the millions trying to cope on poverty pay were instead awarded a decent living wage – at least £10-an-hour in current figures – they would spend it. Sometimes in the large retail chains, making all the more secure the jobs of the massed armies of workers in these big businesses. Other times in their local corner shops, cafés, pubs and restaurants, boosting the prospects of small family and independent businesses.

* * * *

Various other health-enhancing measures, all based on a society putting people before profit, could and should be combined with this enlargement of the slice of the economic cake on workers' plates. Measures such as systematic education and support on healthy eating, from nursery groups right through to adult education classes; extension of the ban on junk food and advertising in schools, colleges and public buildings; rigorous enforcement of healthy food and drink standards at all producers, distributors, shops and eating places; community cafés in every district with healthy, affordable food, supplied by local producers; and opening up of local markets in every community for the direct sale of local farm produce, at affordable, farm-gate prices.

Alongside these steps towards healthy social provision, higher pay could also lead to higher levels of health. Better financial choice could help counter the frightening trends towards junk food, obesity and related ailments. A living minimum wage isn't only good for your bank balance, but also for your health and work/life balance.

21

THERE IS AN ALTERNATIVE: STRUGGLE!

So having agreed a £10-an-hour minimum is the bare essential for a decent standard of living in Scotland 2015, how do we go about achieving such a guaranteed wage for all workers over 16?

As the genius socialist theoretician Karl Marx wrote back in 1845, in his *German Ideology*:

> "The ideas of the ruling class are in every epoch the ruling ideas. That is, the class which is the ruling material force in society is at the same time it's ruling intellectual force."

This idea was further developed in the 1920s by the Italian Marxist, Antonio Gramsci, who argued that the capitalist class don't hold onto their power and privileges purely by political and economic coercion – including use of violence, when they think it necessary – but also through ideology; what he termed 'cultural hegemony'. In essence, by use of all manner of modern communications and institutions that they control, the capitalist minority consciously seeks to dampen down the rebellious spirit of the working class majority by confusing them into accepting the values and norms of the capitalists as 'common sense'. The tiny handful with all the power use cultural influences to mould the mass of the population into thinking that what is good for capitalism is also good for the working class.

One of the 'ruling ideas' of the early 21st century is that 'there is no alternative'. The expression was much favoured by arch-free marketeer Maggie Thatcher in the 1980s. It was even condensed into the acronym 'TINA' and bandied about like a new, unchallenged religious truth. It sought to cow the working-class majority population into believing it was pointless struggling to improve their lot. It accompanied one of Thatcher's other openly avowed aims: to bury socialism under a triumphalist capitalism.

In the wake of defeating the heroic miners in 1985, and in the shadow of the collapse of the bureaucratic Stalinist regimes of Eastern Europe five years later, Thatcher, Reagan and a whole army of capitalist ideologues felt supremely confident that they and their system were indeed unchallenged; the class struggle dead and buried; socialism extinct. As one of their own, philosopher and economist Francis Fukuyama, declared in 1989:

"What we may be witnessing is not just the end of the Cold War, or the passing of a particular period of post-war history, but the end of history as such: the end point of mankind's ideological evolution and the universalisation of Western liberal democracy as the final form of human government."

There is no alternative, it is pointless seeking radical change, accept what's conceded to you by those in power – and be thankful for small mercies... though seldom expressed in such clear language, those were 'the ruling ideas' from the mid-1980s onwards.

* * * *

Labour leaders, from Neil Kinnock on through Tony Blair and Gordon Brown, echoed this philosophy and coined their own variation in the mid-1980s – 'New Realism', an acceptance of the capitalist status quo, on the utterly false premise that there was no alternative for the working class but to cosy up to the ruling powers and employers, accepting their right to rule, seeking a few crumbs of concessions through collaboration with them – dumping such outdated notions as 'class' and 'class struggle'. Having capitulated to the ruling ideas of the ruling class, Labour leaders (and all too many trade union leaders) abandoned any residual belief in collective action to enhance the standard of living of working people; any suggestion of uniting in struggle to win a bigger share of the national economic cake.

They instead morphed into a belief that the interests of workers and employers, labour and capital, are one and the same. Various labels were invented by New Labour spin doctors for this abandonment of 'old-fashioned' class struggle socialism: the Third Way, and Social Partnership, being prime examples of what is far more accurately described as class collaboration! Gordon Brown even had the intellectual audacity to declare 'boom and bust' a relic of the past. Something socialists always recognised as an inherent feature of capitalism, Brown claimed New Labour had removed through their ingenious balancing act between the interests of capitalists and workers, rich and poor.

This treacherous route took millions down the road to lowered expectations, lowered wages and lowered public services. It is no accident that the subsequent 30 years have been marked by a single, startling, shocking fact: the national wealth of Britain has doubled over those 30 years, but the number of people living in poverty in the same affluent Britain has also doubled over the same time-span.

* * * *

Rocketing levels of inequality have been a feature of both the post-2008 recession – the worst in 80 years – and the subsequent 'recovery'. So much for an end to capitalist 'boom and bust'. So much for 'social partnership'. And so much for the 'trickle down theory' espoused by Thatcher and her New Labour sons and heirs; the arrant nonsense that by allowing the millionaires to get even richer, some of their wealth would spill down to the plebs, the millions. The false image of a rising tide that lifts all the boats – as opposed to shipwrecking and sinking the smaller boats, drowning those on board, which would be a more accurate metaphor for modern capitalism.

Back in the 1920s and '30s, former Oklahoma real-life cowboy and vaudeville actor, Will Rogers, was an enormously popular film star and incisive political satirist. During the Great Depression of the '30s he quipped:

"Money was appropriated at the top in hopes that it would trickle down to the needy!"

Unfortunately, by the '80s, another American – the make-believe cowboy of the movies, Ronald Reagan – made out as if he took this 'trickle down theory' seriously – as did his mentor Margaret Thatcher. The atrocious consequences of Reagan and Thatcher's application of this 'theory', for millions of working class people the world over, brings to mind a further Will Rogers wisecrack:

"I don't make jokes. I just watch the government and report the facts."

Whilst treating us to claims of how beneficial her 'trickle down theory' was to us all, Thatcher was much more honest with her other shameless boast: "It is our job to glory in inequality." Something she and her class certainly did, while Labour stood back without as much as a whimper of opposition to the biggest wealth transfusion to the rich from the rest of us in history. Or at least the biggest redistribution of wealth upwards until that of the 25 years since Thatcher was driven out of Number 10 Downing Street, that is!

In 2014, we had on display the grotesque emblem of the profound class division created in post-Thatcher Britain, when a City of London company, Property Partners, installed metal spikes to prevent any of the homeless in the real and actual city of London from sleeping rough in the doorway entrance to their property development offices.

* * * *

So if we're serious about reversing this trend, this unprecedented transfer of wealth and power from the millions to the millionaires, from labour to capital, we need to first convince masses of people that the dictatorship of capital witnessed over the past 30-odd years has been an unmitigated disaster for most of the population – and that there IS an alternative. A thousand small actions help towards lifting the scales from the eyes of the millions of people cowed, conned and browbeaten into thinking 'there is no alternative', that it's pointless trying to change the world we live in.

Every time we issue a leaflet, or write an article, or make a speech, or simply talk to somebody, highlighting the disgusting contrast between the fabulous wealth of the few and the pitiful poverty of the many, we help to embolden people through the anger they feel at such injustice. Every time we use street stalls and street protests to paint the stark, contrasting picture of plentiful profits for a company that pays pitiful wages or uses zero hours contracts, we help lift people's eyes to a potential better future, because there's plenty of wealth around. Every time we expose the profits of big companies hiring workers on the legal minimum wage, we help chip away at the big lie that society can't afford a £10 living wage. Every time we organise a demonstration for a decent living wage, we strengthen the confidence of all who take part and thousands more who observe, by showing in action that workers sick of being paid poverty wages do not stand alone.

A vital component force in this struggle to transform the expectations of the working class, in order to go on to transform their actual living standards, is the organised trade union movement. When SSP members successfully fought for policy Motions at union conferences over the years – including the civil service PCS union and Scottish Trades Union Congress, amongst others – demanding a minimum wage based on two-thirds median male wages, we helped arm activists with arguments and ammunition in the war on poverty. When the Bakers' union, BFAWU, moved the Motion for "a £10-per-hour national minimum wage for all workers" at the British Trades Union Congress in September 2014, they made an invaluable contribution to mounting a battle by workers who for years had resigned themselves to working for peanuts.

One of the prime tasks of socialists is to hold the leaders of the trade union movement to account, demanding they take serious action in pursuit of their own unanimously agreed policy of a £10 minimum wage. Every time one of us moves a Motion to this effect at a workplace meeting or union branch we are helping to engage and mobilise fellow workers, and light bonfires beneath the backsides of those union leaders with absolutely no intention of transforming fine words at a TUC or other union conference into decisive deeds.

In battling to break the grip, the mental chains, of defeatism and downtrodden expectations on the minds of people who've been left leaderless for decades, we need to acquaint them with success stories from the past, but also from here and abroad in recent times. One such case is the successful battle by staff in the Ritzy cinema, in Brixton, London for implementation of the London Living Wage. Another, much broader in its sweep, the inspirational struggles of fast food and retail workers in the USA.

First, let's learn from the Brixton blockbuster. The Ritzy is an arthouse cinema now owned by one of the biggest cinema chains in Europe – Picturehouse – which in turn is owned by the multinational Cineworld. Picturehouse enjoyed a 31% boost to its profits in 2013, to £1.3m. In part they reeled in this hefty profit margin because they only paid their 252 staff an average of £14,554 each in 2013 – an epic 75p a week more than they were granted in 2012! In case you think this story is a classic 'weepy', control your emotions; the parent company, Cineworld, officially coined in £31million in profit in 2013.

The Ritzy is the only trade-unionised cinema in the whole Picturehouse chain – so far. For a full year, the staff and supporters conducted a campaign of leafleting, strikes and negotiations in pursuit of a pay rise to the London Living Wage. Eventually management conceded, but accompanied this concession with the announcement of redundancies for over 20% of the staff. There was a huge backlash, from a public which had been made aware of the issues over the previous year's actions and publicity by the workers, including when they courageously went on strike. In the face of this uproar, the owners hastily made a complete U-turn, announcing there'd be no redundancies after all. A substantial wage rise was won through the tenacious efforts of workers who stuck their necks out, striking as well as standing up for the principle of a living wage, setting an example to workers in the rest of this heavily exploited sector. A victory to emulate.

* * * *

Next, let's learn from the battles in Seattle. The US is the one advanced capitalist country that outstrips even the worst excesses of poverty pay, eye-watering inequality and repressive anti-trade union practices that are rampant in the UK. In this colossus of world power and capitalist global dominance, low pay is a way of life: pay has stagnated and fallen in the USA since the 1970s.

The US is of course the homeland of the fast food industry, ironically arising with the spread of car ownership amongst working families in the 1940s and '50s, where they developed the habit of driving off the highways to burger joints as a convenient way to feed their families. In the past 40-odd years, the capitalist US is also the homeland of what was nicknamed McJobs – cheap-labour, insecure, non-industrial jobs that replaced better-organised, better-paid, more secure jobs in the likes of the car industry and other manufacturing sectors with the onset of crises since the 1980s in the world's biggest capitalist power.

The whole concept behind the burgeoning fast food industry, from decades ago, was the mass production of pre-prepared food, all made to identical standards throughout the country, then made ready to eat in the restaurants by simplified mechanical procedures, rather than any pretence of applying the care and craft of a chef.

That lent itself to de-skilling the job, allowing McDonald's, Burger King et al to consciously hire young staff on dirt-cheap wages. In fact, in the initial years of its growth, the industry almost exclusively hired teenagers, whose life inexperience also made them easier prey to exploitation – and they also initially hired attractive young women to serve customers in their cars, before the sit-in meal became common. To be termed a 'burger flipper' became an insult, a mark of working in a low-status job, with accompanying low pay. Of course there's more, much more, to these jobs, and they involve not just drudgery but dangers, including constant burns, constant stress, and often coercion from a management unrestrained by union organisation.

Also, contrary to the common myth, these jobs are no longer just held down by teenagers keen on pocket money! The median age of a fast food worker in the US currently is 28 – and 32 for women, who make up two-thirds of the entire fast food workforce. These jobs are the only ones available after the decimation of millions of middle-income manufacturing jobs in the recessions of the early 1980s, early

1990s, and post-2008 – the one and only source of income for millions of employees. In fact two sets of fast food companies – the Yum! Brand (Pizza Hut, KFC, Taco Bell) and McDonald's – are the second and third biggest employers in the USA, after retail colossus Walmart (owners of 'our own' ASDA). In the face of brutally anti-union employers like McDonald's, these workers across the USA have begun to stand up for improved rights and rates in recent years.

* * * *

The Occupy movement of the early 2000s arose from growing disgust at the outrageous poverty amidst plenty. They coined the expression 'the 1%' to capture the horrendous concentration of wealth created by capitalism. The Occupy movement was varied and sometimes even confused in its own aims, but it jolted vast numbers of people into greater awareness of the inequality inherent in monopoly capitalism. Their actions, occupying city centre sites, including Wall Street itself, chimed with the fury at inequality that had grown in the workplaces and working class communities, as did their central slogan: "We are the 99%."

As the 20th century reached its dying days, a new anti-capitalist movement was born. One of the most spectacular displays of this uprising, largely spread through the internet, occurred in Seattle, where 100,000 demonstrated and revolted against 'globalisation' – the term coined in the 1960s to describe the growth of international monopoly capitalism, the system of global domination of people and planet by a tiny handful of big corporations, who robbed the working class and peasantry of the world of their labour, their land and their living standards in the ruthless pursuit of profit.

The target of the mass protests in Seattle was the World Trade Organisation, which alongside the World Bank and International Monetary Fund act as the intensely secretive but ruthlessly brutal enforcers of world capitalist demands for repayment of debts to the capitalist Masters of the Universe – through further cuts to wages, further privatisations of services, further environmental desecration of whole nations, further growth of cash crops at the expense of starvation for the populations growing them. In a phrase, through death and destruction for billions of people on our planet to boost the profits of billionaires.

It was poetically fitting that the most prominent tide of this modern-day revolt against globalised capitalist exploitation and inequality took place in Seattle. It's the birthplace of Microsoft's Bill Gates, the richest man in the world. Seattle is also the home base of Amazon.com, the notoriously anti-trade union, exploitative capitalist giant that has a habit of sacking whole workforces in Scotland in the middle of their nightshift, with no way of getting home, or by text message!

And it is more than sheer coincidence that Seattle is now to the fore in the battle for better wages for fast food workers. The battle of Seattle 15 years ago left its mark on people's thinking, encouraging the revolt of downtrodden workers that has forced massive concessions out of the grubby, money-grabbing fists of employers like McDonald's, Starbucks, Subway, Burger King, Macy's and their ilk.

* * * *

Back in November 2012, fast food workers started to defy the bullying and threats from bosses by walking off the job in their masses, across dozens of different fast food joints in New York City. They formed pickets outside their workplaces, demanding better pay, better hours and union rights. Their slogan "We can't survive on $7.25" captured the imagination of thousands, both in these fast food joints and their working class allies in local communities. Trade union locals (especially the Service Employees International Union – SEIU), community activist groups like New York Communities for Change and Black Lives Matter, formed the Fast Food Forward Campaign.

It built up workers' confidence to take action, which they did with phenomenal courage and determination. Their demand for $15 was a massive increase in militancy compared with previous struggles for pay rises, a challenge to decades of wage concessions and the downward spiral in living standards.

The same month, November 2012, witnessed equally courageous strike actions by Walmart workers in over 1,000 of their stores, on

Black Friday, the day of annual consumer frenzy orchestrated by big retailers to turbo-charge their profits. These workers defied threats, and actual sackings, in their demand for $13 minimum – from the Walmart owners, the Walton family, whose wealth is greater than the combined wealth of 42% of all families in the USA!

These workers' brave deeds did wonders for the fighting morale of others across the US. The most immediate victory was in the small city of Sea Tac, on the outskirts of Seattle, which includes Seattle and Tacoma's international airport. There, a coalition of left trade unions taking action helped win a $15 minimum wage from the city authorities.

In Seattle itself, this movement was both reflected in, and boosted by the election of Kshama Sawant, the first openly socialist councillor to be elected in the city in 100 years. She had put the demand '$15 NOW!' at the heart of her election campaign, winning nearly 100,000 votes. She proceeded to help spearhead the formation of grassroots Action Groups – called $15 NOW – of fast food workers and their allies in pursuit of legislation for this as the minimum wage through the city council. They held public meetings, pickets of McDonald's, street stalls to enlist public awareness and support, motions to the city council, mass signatories for legal changes, demonstrations on Martin Luther King Day and May Day with the '$15 NOW' banners and placards dominating... in essence, a massive campaign outside the city council aided by socialist agitation within the city council. Above all it was the decisive, fearless collective actions of thousands of workers – who'd had enough of being ripped off for fabulous profit whilst they couldn't afford to live – which won a breakthrough in 2014.

In June 2014 the Seattle city council agreed to phase in $15 for all these workers. Although the $15 minimum agreed by the city council tried to soften the blow – to profits – by staging the increase annually up until 2018, it nevertheless meant an immediate increase for 100,000 workers in Seattle. It meant a massive wage rise, from $7.25 to $11 on 1st April 2015, for 100,000 workers in Subway, Burger King, McDonald's, KFC, Macy's, etc. Economists have calculated that over the next decade this will transfer $3billion to low paid workers in the city. From profits to pay, that is. A $3billion wealth transfer from capitalists to workers over ten years, in a city the size of Glasgow. Imagine that in Scotland! And the momentum is gathering in other cities and states across the USA. For instance, San Francisco has granted a much better, faster version of the $15 minimum in the wake of the Seattle victory for workers' mass action. California state Senate passed a $13 minimum in June 2014, potentially to the benefit of 7.9 million workers in that state. New York City has agreed $15 by 2018, and Los Angeles by 2020.

Socialist contender for the Democrat Presidential candidacy, Bernie Sanders, has come out forcibly in favour of the $15 minimum, vastly enhancing the profile and impact of the drive started by a tiny minority of fast food workers three years ago. Strikes and other workers' actions for $15 have hit over 100 cities, including on the international day of action on 15 April 2015. The momentum of a militant movement of workers taking industrial action and staging high-profile protests has bludgeoned several city and state authorities into concessions on the minimum wage rates. The dam has been broken.

* * * *

All this is a rich and inspirational lesson for those of us in Scotland battling to break the chains of poverty pay that manacle masses of workers and their families. After decades of workers in the USA suffering wage cuts, the tide was turned by what initially was a tiny force of very brave women and men in the fast food sector in New York City – in part inspired by the previous political movement called Occupy, but mostly driven by the sheer necessity of a wage rise to survive.

These heroic fighters defied threats from capitalist employers with a vested class interest in keeping wages as low as possible: capitalism is driven by the hunt for profits, the unpaid labour of the working class. For decades the majority of trade union leaders (labor leaders, in the language of the US) had capitulated to the devastating claw-back of past gains, the decimation of workers' wages, with little or no struggle.

Cosy, overpaid labor leaders were remote from workers' daily struggles to survive, and all too often closer to the employing class in income, outlook and social circles. They also tried to tie labor – the unions – to the Democrats, one of the twin capitalist parties of the USA, rather than strike out with any independent political representation of the working class. They relied, for instance, on the promises of Barack Obama in 2008 that he would introduce a federal minimum wage of $9.50 by 2011 – a figure still far below a liveable wage, and a measure the US working class are still waiting in vain for Obama to implement, seven years later!

The sum total results of this approach? A massive collapse in workers' wages, accompanying falls in union membership (to a puny 7% of workers in the private sector), and burgeoning profits for Walmart, Yum! Brand, McDonald's and other giant corporations' profits margins. Sound familiar to a worker in Scotland or the UK? It should! Substitute the names of right-wing union leaders, change the unions' initials, change Democrat party to Labour Party, and sometimes (but only sometimes) change the names of the profiteering multinationals, and we have a perfect description of events and results in this country over the past 30 years.

* * * *

Now it's down to us to apply the rest of the story from the US. The courage to stand up to the billionaire bullies. The organisation of direct action and grassroots workers' struggles. The linkage of the best trade unions and trade unionists to low-paid workers who have not yet joined but need a union more than anyone to boost their incomes and rights. The combination of workers' and communities' struggle to that of socialists prepared to rage against the money machine and champion workers' rights and the redistribution of wealth from profits to pay. And simply to use the currency exchange rate to translate the fighting slogan of $15Now into £10 Now!

The breakthroughs by these workers in the US, previously bullied and bereft of leadership against rotten pay, should fuel our determination to pound the politicians – whether SNP or Labour – in control of Scotland's 32 councils, and the Scottish Government itself, with the demand they put their money where their mouths (sometimes) are. We need to mobilise workers and communities to cut through the excuses from those elected to represent us, as they whinge that "Westminster controls the minimum wage."

That's true, of course. But instead of lying down and accepting the status quo, organised workers, communities and socialists should demand the Scottish Government, Cosla and individual councils not only seek the kudos of being Accredited Living Wage employers, but that their version of a 'living wage' will be set at £10 – the level required to clear the hurdle of dependency on state subsidies.

The Scottish Government and Scotland's local authority employers should join forces with the 630,000-strong trade union movement and bombard Westminster with demands to transfer some of the £93billion handed out in subsidies to capitalist corporations, this year alone, to the Scottish block grant budget. Instead of HMRC topping up paltry pay – further subsidising profits that are already obscenely inflated – Holyrood and the local town halls could thereby fund a guaranteed 'Scottish Living Wage' of £10 to all their employees, apprentices included.

Furthermore, Scotland's elected politicians at national and local level should enforce contract compliance schemes – until such time as all work is brought back in-house, as part of the systematic reversal of privatisation – insisting that contract firms they hire pay at least the £10 minimum. If this requires defiance of EU regulations (and that is certainly not clearly proven to be the legal case), then so be it. Scotland's councillors and MSPs weren't elected to uphold the rule and ruination of people's lives and livelihoods by the Eurocrats, and the monopoly capitalists that dominate the EU. They were elected on the assumption they would represent the population that they rely upon for their paid jobs as politicians – the vast majority of whom are working class, and in dire need of enhanced incomes and public services.

This side of winning Scottish independence – and all the powers over minimum wage legislation that would accompany full self-government – those bold steps would get round the short-term obstacle of the legal minimum wage being a matter reserved to Westminster.

A £10 'Scottish Living Wage' – established by political choice, voluntarily, in contrast to the pathetically poor UK legal minimum wage – would set a shining example, which would enormously encourage Scotland's working class majority population to vote for full self-government; to seize power over the legal minimum wage in an independent Scotland.

22

SIGNPOSTS & WEATHERVANES

Anyone who doubts their ability to change the political climate, to drag it to the left in favour of a massive redistribution of wealth from profit to pay, need only scan the pre-General Election pronouncements of various parties in Scotland and Britain in early 2015.

Hanging concentrates the mind wonderfully, as the saying goes! And with their cushy livelihoods hanging on voters' verdicts once every five years, opportunist politicians are liable to make promises they spurn the rest of the five years – in far too many cases, with absolutely no intention of doing after the election what they say before the polling stations close.

Five years since the last British General Election, workers' real annual wages are over £1,600 lower than five years ago – the first time that has happened under any Westminster government since the 1920s. This is one factor in the recent onset of deflation – zero or even negative inflation – with price wars by rival retailers and others seeking to sustain their market share in a marketplace where low wages deprive millions of workers of the ability to buy their products, and with record levels of household debts. That partially explains the superficially incredible outburst by Tory leader and exponent of the virtues of the capitalist market, David Cameron. In early 2015, he told the assembled worthies of the British Chamber of Commerce that "Britain needs a pay rise."

* * * *

Perhaps the cruellest deceit deployed in the run-up to the 2015 General Election was that conducted by Labour. In a desperate lunge at winning back votes from the working class that had abandoned Labour in their droves, we had the unsettling spectacle of Scottish Labour leader Jim Murphy – arch-Blairite, voter for vicious Tory cuts, shameless warmonger and collaborator with the Tories and big business against Scotland's democratic right to self-determination – making cooing noises about working people needing a pay rise. Murphy and Miliband's Labour issued millions of pledge cards, leaflets and endless media statements promising "an £8 minimum wage."

To the casual reader, listener or viewer this would be a very attractive offer, especially to millions of workers living on or just above the miserly £6.50 legal minimum wage. Not to mention the further millions of young workers on even lower rates, victims of the legalised daylight robbery of their labour-power with youth development and apprentices' minimum wages of £3.79, £5.13 and £2.73-an-hour.

But those jumping with joy at promises of such a leap in their living standards would do well to sit down again, and study the fine print in Labour's false prospectus! If the offer was to raise the minimum wage from £6.50 to £8 here and now, in 2015, and if it was going to apply to every worker in the land, regardless of age, it would indeed have been cause for major celebration. Maybe not quite a recipe for unrestrained spending and settling down into the lap of luxury, but it would certainly pay many an urgent bill for hard-pressed workers.

But let's look at the cruel deceits in Labour's election pledge. Pitfall number one: they made it plain, but only under questioning at the likes of union meetings – or more particularly at meetings to reassure big business luminaries – that they actually didn't intend to introduce the £8 until 2020. So the millions hoping to escape poverty pay by putting their X beside the Labour candidate were expected to survive the next five years on a pittance – while the Labour MPs they elected pocketed their full basic salary as it rises from £67,000 to £74,000!

And with most economists predicting a rise in oil prices, interest rates and inflation on life's daily essentials by 2016 – and God knows what price rises in the subsequent four years – what difference would £8 be in 2020 compared with £6.50 in 2015? Even the leadership of Usdaw – amongst the most craven Labour leadership loyalists – published figures recommending this pledge as being worth a miserable 50p extra after predicted inflation.

Pitfall number two: Labour plans to continue the enforced poverty for workers who dare to be young! There was no promise of scrapping the lower youth rates. In fact, they've threatened all manner of punishments – including complete loss of benefits – for young people who decline Mickey Mouse jobs or training on peanut pay.

Pitfall number three: can we believe the promises of a Labour Party on what they'll do five years hence anyway? After all, they made promises to abolish zero hours contracts way back in 1995, including in Labour conference speeches by one Anthony Charles Lynton Blair. But the numbers chained to the poverty pay and poverty of workplace rights on these modern forms of serfdom have multiplied exponentially since that promise was made – including during the 13 years of Labour in government. So no, we can't trust a Labour Party that has long since married itself to capitalism in a shameless betrayal of the principles and aims of its founders. And they're not exactly promising a New Jerusalem, in 2020, in any case.

* * * *

In the aftermath of the majority 'No' vote in Scotland's September 2014 referendum, the Smith Commission was set up to examine what powers should be graciously granted to the Scottish Parliament under continued devolution. This was a cynical exercise in 'managing expectations'. A charade of appearing to listen to the Scottish people – to the millions who either voted for outright independence, or voted 'No' in the hope and expectation of large measures of 'Home Rule' – whilst keeping the power and purse-strings firmly in the grip of the political wing of British capitalism, at Westminster.

In that context, it's worth examining the contrasting stance of two, very different, pro-independence parties in Scotland, specifically on the minimum wage. Two parties which had combined forces in the broad-based, mass-membership Yes Scotland campaign. The Scottish Socialist Party (SSP) and the Scottish National Party (SNP). Throughout the final year of the referendum campaign, every Scottish Socialist Party branch in the west of Scotland held street stalls, mass leafleting and umpteen public meetings with the slogan "Vote Yes for a Decent Living Minimum Wage" – at the time advocating £9-an-hour, based on two-thirds male median wages. This class-based demand cut through a thicket of confusion whipped up by the Unionist media, reaching many working-class people with a very concrete, material argument in favour of full self-government. This helped, at least modestly, to raise the level of debate beyond issues of national identity, or Unionist falsehoods about independence threatening the end of workers' solidarity. It convinced countless numbers to vote Yes who were at best sceptical, at worst downright hostile, to the SNP.

On the Saturday morning after the No vote was cast, at the SSP national executive committee, I proposed we adjust to the post-referendum landscape by publicly and forcibly demanding the Scottish Parliament be conceded the power (amongst several others) to set a Scottish minimum wage of £10-an-hour – based on updated wage calculations, plus the fresh decision of the British TUC Congress to demand a £10 minimum. The proposal was unanimously agreed and acted upon, with the immediate launch of nationwide SSP street campaigning and actions within members' trade unions to demand this devolved power to vastly boost the livelihoods of hordes of workers chained in poverty pay.

The SSP demanded a place at the table of the Smith Commission, precisely to advocate such working-class priorities for the powers of an enhanced Holyrood parliament, whilst maintaining our unswerving commitment to the goal of an independent socialist Scotland. Unsurprisingly, but outrageously, Lord Smith of Kelvin denied access to his closed club to one – just one – out of the six political parties officially registered as campaigners during the referendum – the SSP.

Despite this denial of our democratic right to bring the voice of working people into the proceedings, we presented an official SSP submission to the unelected, ermined Lord's Commission – with the power to set a £10 Scottish minimum wage (and abolish all zero hours contracts, and repeal all anti-trade union laws) featuring prominently.

The other five parties from both the Yes and No sides of the referendum – Tories, Lib Dems, Scottish Labour, SNP and Greens – were all given full access to the Smith Commission. Here's the crunch. Up until the SSP's submission, not one of these parties had demanded devolved power over the minimum wage. In fact, it was only in the very dying days of its proceedings that the SNP raised this demand – only for Labour to block it, mercilessly.

* * * *

This sequence of events is instructive in many ways. It shows the profound differences between a genuine socialist party and Scottish Labour in their attitudes to workers' wages – particularly when Labour imagines their actions are well hidden from public scrutiny. It shows the difference between a pro-independence socialist party, and a nationalist party that seeks to tack and weave between winning a working-class base with social democratic reforms, and winning the approval of multinational capitalism with reassurances that their profits are safe under an SNP government. Above all, it shows such social democratic (but pro-capitalist) parties can be shoved substantially towards supporting reforms by even a relatively small socialist party that is rooted in the daily lives, needs, conditions, struggles and aspirations of the working class.

However, if a party only responds to pressure from below, to curry public favour, they can't be trusted to challenge the powers that be in the interests of the working-class majority population. It's another reminder that politics is populated by two contrasting types: signposts and weathervanes. People of firm guiding principles, and inconsistent opportunists. Socialists who steadfastly point the way forward towards equality of power and incomes, and forces that blow with the prevailing winds of public opinion.

23

A MAXIMUM WAGE

Picture the scene. A committee of workers from neighbouring workplaces meets annually to decide what wage increases, if any, should be awarded to each workforce represented. The people present stand to gain directly if they convince a majority of a pay rise for their own company or service. Likewise, they can seek to influence the vote by demonstrating their generosity towards the pay levels of their neighbours. "You scratch my back and I'll scratch yours", cynical critics might say. The only restraining factor is their social responsibility to wider society. A socialist dream? Let's park expressing an opinion on that for now. But a capitalist employer's worst nightmare, certainly.

Picture instead a different – but at least analogous – scenario. Committees of the biggest company executives meet annually to decide what pay package to award the chief executives of… well… each other's companies. They call themselves the Remuneration Committee. They decide the pay packages for each of the chief executives of the FTSE 100 companies.

Like any troop of monkeys, we have to assume these meetings include a carnival of mutual back-scratching. They each have a vested interest in pleasing the rest of the committee – to gain 'adequate remuneration' for themselves. As to restraints on their mutual generosity, well, there aren't any. 'Corporate social responsibility' to wider society is a great phrase for mission statements, but it doesn't seem to curtail these Remuneration Committees from lashing out largesse like there's no tomorrow, either for the economy or the planet.

Research shows that over one-third of the members of the Committee are themselves chief executives of other companies. The same research reveals that the members of these Remuneration Committees enjoyed average incomes of £441,383 (each!) in 2014 – which is 16 times last year's average worker's wage of £27,200. The highest-paid Committee member was awarded – by other Committee members – a cool £9.2million last year, which is a mind-swirling 339 times the average worker's wage the same year. A socialist's nightmare? A capitalist's Utopia? Both, actually. And reality in modern Britain.

* * * *

Over the past ten years, company chief executives' pay has risen nine times faster than that of the median wage-earner. Some bosses are now being paid 1,000 times as much as the national median worker's wage. Put another way, the average FTSE 100 chief executive is (by 2015) getting 183 times as much in his pay packet as the average employee in his company; and that's the average – some are on over 450 times as much annual pay as the workers they employ.

One or two big firms caught onto the fact there's a growing mood of outrage at this Grand Canyon separating the pay rates of bosses and 'their' workers, and tried to display 'social responsibility'. But their feeble, belated efforts only add to the outrage, when you look at the limitations of their 'corporate social responsibility', as the modern buzz phrase goes. For example, John Lewis has capped the pay of their executives at 'only' 75 times that of their lowest-paid staff. The TSB similarly has limited the chasm to a mere 65:1. And these are the good guys, in the world of capitalist inequality! As the High Pay Centre think-tank wrote:

"The typical FTSE 100 CEO's pay has risen from about £100-200,000 in the early 1980s, to just over £1million by the turn of the century, to £4.3million in 2012. This represented a leap from about 20 times the pay of the average UK worker in the 1980s to 60 times in 1998, to 160 times in 2012."

And as just mentioned, that ratio has now climbed higher still, to 183:1. Alarmed not at this obscene and growing gap, on a galactic scale, between the incomes of workers and capitalist bosses, but rather at the fact they were found out by growing numbers of an increasingly angry population, even the Tory-led Coalition of 2010-15 had to be seen to do something. They certainly had no intention of seriously curtailing the corrupt practices of top bosses who are robbing the rest of us blind. For instance, George Osborne denounced European Union moves to cap bankers' bonuses – not their salaries, just their bonuses – as 'illegal'. So instead of decisive action against daylight robbery by those in high places, the government declared a few meaningless measures and aims at 'transparency' and 'simplicity' – empty platitudes immediately and eagerly echoed by the Labour 'opposition'.

The nearest to anything concrete forthcoming was new powers for company shareholders to reject pay packages for their company chief executives. The reality shows that any voluntary system of 'pay restraint' – the concept that successive governments have lectured ordinary workers about the unacceptability of – is predictably futile amongst those wielding power over company shares, and in fact a complete con-trick. Not a single set of shareholders in a single one of the FTSE 100 companies has so far overturned the pay hikes handed out to the top dogs by the aforementioned Remuneration Committees. Probably the nearest we got to a shareholders' rebellion was in the advertising and marketing giant, WPP. There, a grandiose 22% of shareholders at the company AGM declined to endorse the £43million pay package given to CEO Sir Martin Sorrell – a man whose fortune even prior to this outrageous bounty was £300million, according to the *Sunday Times* Rich List. WPP employs over 100,000 people. Sorrell's salary leapt nearly 50% from a 'modest' £29million in 2013; those of his average employee actually fell from £39,900 to £38,500 the same year.

* * * *

The grossly inflated incomes of company executives is nothing short of institutionalised theft, arranged between the thieves, siphoning off a huge slice of the wealth created by their workforces, for a few at the top who have neither earned nor generated the wealth. All their self-justifying guff about being the 'risk-takers' is easily dismissed by a simple fact: it has been shown that the bosses of big companies are 13 times less likely to be sacked than the lowest-paid workers in their company! And unlike the stress, heartbreak and upheaval for entire families of workers made redundant or dismissed from their job, even if the top dogs lose their job and never work again, they'll have invested so much – and been gifted such enormous 'golden goodbye' packages of pension pots and shares – that they'll live a life of luxury for the rest of their days.

The real 'risk-takers' are the armies of workers who traipse into work for lowly wages, with no room to save for 'a rainy day', and who are mostly powerless to prevent summary dismissal or redundancy when the over-paid bosses and owners dictate that that's the price of protecting their bonuses, dividends and profits. And don't forget, company executives have a legal duty to look after the interests of the shareholders and owners. So they're not about to become soft on sackings if they think that sacrificing the livelihoods of a few (or many) workers will boost share values, profits and dividends.

Nor should we have any illusions in some shiny new phase of shareholders' democracy as a means to curb the stomach-churning obscenities of chief executives' pay packages. Back in the 1980s Maggie Thatcher trumpeted the case for wholesale privatisation with claims of a brand new society called a 'share-owning democracy'. In some sell-offs of state-enterprises, such as British Telecom, the workforce was offered a cheap sweetener of a few shares to try and buy off their opposition to the privatisation. But predictably enough, in the teeth of rising costs of living and stagnant wages, these workers took the very practical step of promptly selling their shares for a modest 'profit'. I believe the esoteric world of the Stock Exchange even has a term for those who indulge in this rapid sale of shares: Stags.

Contrary to the deceitful predictions and promises of a 'share-owning/property-owning democracy', we today live in a society more akin to a share-owning dictatorship. The proportion of stocks owned by individuals has plummeted from 47% in 1969 to a mere 10% by 2008. Furthermore, the percentage owned by overseas investors has rocketed from 7% to 47% over the same years. So forget any illusions of social justice being pursued through 'corporate social responsibility', or some mythical millions of egalitarian shareholders, some band of wee pensioners and average workers with a few shares and ISAs each, and a mission to curb the excesses of company bosses.

Profit-crazed overseas shareholders have scant regard for 'social justice' in Scotland or the UK – and in the case of oil sheikhs and oligarchical gangster-capitalists from the likes of Russia and Eastern Europe, they make damned sure there's no hints of 'social justice' or nonsense about 'equality' in their native countries either! Furthermore, regardless of where the giant shareholders who in real life own the vast bulk of capital in this country were born – whether America or Ayrshire, Petrograd or Perthshire – they usually move in and out of companies so rapidly, in pursuit of the fastest possible buck, that they're not around long enough to effect any reforms on pay differentials – even in the extremely improbable event of them wanting to.

* * * *

In certain specific or exceptional political circumstances, even some capitalist politicians have advocated mechanisms to curb the extreme differentials between low or median pay rates and those at the very top of the tree. For instance, as part of a drive to enlist mass public support for the war effort in 1942, US President Franklin D. Roosevelt proposed a maximum income of $25,000. As he put it:

> "While the number of individual Americans affected is small, discrepancies between low personal incomes and very high personal incomes should be lessened. In time of grave national danger, when all excess income should go to win the war, no American ought to have a net income, after he's paid his taxes, of more than $25,000."

He proposed a 100% marginal tax rate on incomes above $40,000 to achieve this. It was never implemented!

In the US, in 2000, Green Party presidential nominee Jello Biafra advocated a $100,000 maximum wage and zero taxation of all incomes below that threshold. Much more recently, forces much further to the left have advocated steep, progressive tax policies to cap top incomes and close the gap at least modestly. For instance the Left Front French presidential candidate in 2012, Jean-Luc Melenchon, argued for a 100% tax rate on incomes above €360,000... hardly a recipe for hardship at the top!

* * * *

Several organisations today advocate measures whereby the earnings of chief executives of a company are limited to a multiple of either the lowest or median earnings in that company: a relative earnings limit. But however well-meaning and progressive compared with the current free-for-all looting by chief executives, this proposal has severe limitations. Trying to measure the median income within a company could descend into a self-defeating rigmarole, over whether it would include the incomes of the chief executives in the calculations.

And the more transparent option of limiting a company chief executive's income to a fixed multiple of the lowest pay-rate in the company could – and doubtless would – be bypassed by companies contracting out the lowest-paid jobs to a third party. That's how many of them already avoid the public odium of hiring zero hours contract workers; they get a contractor to do it for them instead!

* * * *

A far more effective, straightforward and inescapable means of tackling the gaping and growing chasm between the incomes of the richest and the rest of us would be a national maximum wage, linked to the national minimum wage. In its early years, the SSP agreed to this policy, settling on a maximum differential of 10:1 between the minimum wage and the maximum allowable income. Some of us thought – and still think! – that that is an overly generous allowance for the richest, and that a powerful case could easily be made for a 5:1 or 4:1 maximum differential between the floor and ceiling on wages. But at least the generous nature of the 10:1 policy has one supreme merit; how in hell could any reasonable person argue against it? In current terms, in 2015, this policy means a legally enforced national minimum wage of £10-an-hour for all over 16, accompanied by a maximum hourly income of £100.

Now since we should also fight ferociously for a maximum working week of 35 hours – but without any loss of earnings for workers – let's apply those figures to show how liberal the policy is towards those at the top of the wages league. It would mean a maximum wage of £3,500 a week; yes, a week – and £182,000 a year! Maybe that's why I think it's a bit too bountiful in its ratio; but to repeat the point, who could dispute its modesty and moderation?!

Those on £100-an-hour wouldn't exactly be driven to swallowing their pride in pursuit of a Social Fund loan to tide them over, or a 3-days' supply of food from a food bank. They wouldn't even have to curtail their visits to the best eateries, or several luxury holidays a year. They could still live the life of Riley, with plenty to spare.

* * * *

In fact, less than 1% of the population in this country are on that kind of income right now, in 2015. The infamous '1%' are those people on roughly £140,000 and above, according to the High Pay Centre's figures. And the question needs to be posed point blank to anyone against such a ceiling on incomes: what on earth would anyone on more than £100-an-hour do with such an overdose of dosh? What could they possibly need in life that wouldn't be guaranteed beyond doubt on a maximum salary of £182,000?

A powerful piece of evidence backing up this case was produced by extensive research in 2010, by the Woodrow Wilson School in Princeton University. Through comprehensive studies, they identified what they called 'a happiness ceiling'. This is the income beyond which any further increase in wages does not in any way increase personal satisfaction. The 'happiness ceiling' they discovered was US$75,000, which is £48,930 annual salary. Even allowing for inflation, Princeton's findings imply that any wage over and above £50,000 does nothing to enhance happiness for the lucky minority on it in this country. So a 10:1

ratio between a £10 minimum wage and the maximum wage is far above what's required to earn the tag of being 'generous', or of offering healthy incentives. It frankly would still be pandering to a modern money-addiction, a financial drug which the uber-wealthy are hooked on. Those at the top end of such an income bracket would still be prone to moan, as the Rolling Stones sang in their classic swipe at commercialism and alienation, "I can't get no satisfaction."

It's indisputable that a 10:1 ratio between the highest and lowest wages would represent a revolutionary leap in the direction of wealth redistribution and greater equality, compared with the mind-boggling scissors opening up between workers' and bosses' incomes in today's capitalist jungle. The fact the average ratio was 160:1 by 2013 in the FTSE 100 companies, with chief executives averaging £1,200-an-hour, every hour, is a harsh reminder of the class-divided world we have to challenge and change. And now, two years later, it's 183:1 on average in the same top corporations.

So a maximum wage, applied across the country, set at ten times the minimum guaranteed wage, would be a mighty stride in the direction of a more equal society. And as time went on, with full democratic debate and decision-making, the differential could be gradually reduced, lifting millions into directly benefiting from the wealth created by workers' combined efforts. And the committees of workers imagined at the outset of this chapter could be augmented by representatives of government, and given the social responsibility of helping to decide adjustments to the minimum:maximum differential over time.

* * * *

Such a measure is not without precedent. Back in the infancy of the workers' and peasants' government that took power through the 1917 Russian revolution, Lenin, Trotsky and the Bolsheviks advocated a maximum differential of 4:1 in incomes, and passed a decree limiting the salary of all "high-ranking office employees and officials in all state, public and private institutions and enterprises" to 500 Roubles a month "where there are no children and 100 Roubles extra for each child."

It is no accident that this cap on top earnings was first undermined, and then officially, legally abolished in 1932, as the Stalinist bureaucratic nomenklatura seized power, wiping out the vestiges of working class democracy and egalitarian policies pursued in the first years of the revolution. Material privilege and growing inequality were hallmarks of a system that was a stinking, dictatorial negation of the socialist ideals of those who led the liberation of workers and peasants from 1,000 years of vicious Tsarist dictatorship in 1917.

Much more recently, in 2011, the popular Hugo Chavez government in Venezuela set strict limits on public salaries. The differentials varied according to different types of official positions. At the highest levels, officials were capped at salaries of no more than twelve times the minimum wage in the country. In other cases, such as State Governors, their public salary was limited to nine times the Venezuelan minimum wage.

* * * *

Fighting for a maximum wage tied by – at least initially – a 10:1 ratio with the guaranteed living minimum wage, would not only be a radical challenge to inequality here and now, but also a taste of a future socialist democracy. The SSP has the unique policy, embedded in its constitution, that no MSP, MP or other public representative should take any salary beyond the average skilled worker's wage in Scotland. That's a measure of accountability. It's a vital mechanism to combat careerism and corruption. And it's a bridge to a future, in a socialist Scotland, where all public representatives – whether in elected government, or elected to the management boards of publicly-owned services and enterprises – would have their incomes tied and limited to those of the working class they aspire to represent or manage.

It would help combat inequality and unequal power relations too. When the likes of the top management of a public enterprise – whether state-owned or a local cooperative, for example – were elected, subject to regular recall through elections, but also, critically, living on a skilled worker's wage, they would have an immediate incentive to improve the wages of all workers, as well as to treat them with dignity and respect. A system of working class control and management would unleash the talents of those with daily expertise in the system of production, distribution and exchange – to the mutual benefit of all, rather than for the exclusive profits of the 1% that capitalism inevitably grinds out of the reduced wage share of wealth right now.

24

BEYOND WAGES: TOWARDS SOCIALISM

It is the moral duty of trade unionists, community activists and socialists to forge weapons to cut through the cold, cruel chains of poverty, insecurity and exploitation that tie up millions of workers.

The sharp cutting tools of fighting for a living minimum wage – £10-an-hour in 2015 figures – is pivotal to a package of measures that could liberate a vast proportion of the population from the endless treadmill of deprivation, debt, stress and insecurity that blights those working to remain poor. Joined at the hip with campaigning for that legally guaranteed minimum, we need to popularise and pursue the policy of a maximum wage, starting with a 10:1 ratio of the minimum, as a vital instrument to confront inequality – the growing, ugly, conjoined twin of poverty. These two measures alone would transform lives.

To those living in academic aloofness from the daily grind of poverty pay, or the cosseted commentariat, these measures might seem 'old hat'. To hundreds of thousands of Scottish workers they are manna from heaven, an exciting escape route from the stunted lives they are condemned to by capitalist profiteering.

If you needed any proof of how critical such measures are to waging war on poverty and inequality, or the radicalism of these policies, you only need register the paroxysms of outrage and opposition to such demands from the rich and powerful. They know such measures fly at the heart of their economic system of exploitation like a well-aimed laser. We need to recognise the same.

Having said that, other policies and battles need to be pursued in tandem with the struggle for a decent minimum (and maximum) wage. The chains of poverty and exploitation can only be fully and permanently broken by a well-forged arsenal of interlinking measures to radically transform the balance of wealth and power in society.

This publication is not the place to comprehensively describe and justify every single socialist measure required to transform Scotland into an egalitarian socialist democracy. But it is right and proper to sketch out some key policies that should be pursued – to achieve a vastly increased wage-share of national wealth and drastically reduced levels of inequality, but also to bring about a society that breaks the endless cycle of struggle to defend what workers already have, and begin to build the Scotland that is both possible and urgently necessary.

To concentrate the energy, talents and organising skills of future generations on the construction of a new, egalitarian, humane form of society, based on collective effort and collective ownership – rather than consuming all our time on mere survival, protest, opposition and resistance to a system that destroys the lives of millions at home and billions abroad.

A Charter of Workers' Rights

One of the central links in the chains that imprison workers in poverty is the vicious package of anti-trade union laws – ushered in by Thatcher in the 1980s, kept intact by Blair's and Brown's thirteen years of Labour government, made worse by the Tory/Lib Dem Coalition, and being made infinitely more repressive by the current Tory regime. Time and again, in previous chapters, we've shown how shackling workers in legal chains – designed to stop us fighting back for a bigger share of wealth in wages and social wages – has been instrumental to the conscious, deliberate growth of inequality, as well as outright poverty.

The decimation of collective bargaining rights wasn't a meteor that accidentally landed from outer space; it was a consciously thought-out strategy by governments and big business to slaughter workers' collective power and shrink the share of the cake going to workers' plates. Likewise the sustained war on union organisation over the past 30-odd years.

As we've already written, it's no accident of nature that inequality was at its lowest levels in 1975 when 58% of workers in the UK were organised in unions, and 82% of all workers were covered by collective bargaining on wages and condition. Conversely, the wealth gap is at its worst ever, now, with only 26% union membership, and just 23% of workers having the protection of collective bargaining.

Even to pursue two of the central policies dealt with in this book – a living minimum wage of £10 now, in 2015, and abolition of all zero hours contracts – requires a fight to restore collective bargaining rights, across the board, and for repeal of all the anti-union laws that bedevil this state.

One fight is tied to the other. Free trade unions are critical and central to the conquest of well-paid, secure jobs. And the battle to win £10 Now is a golden opportunity to make the unions relevant to a whole new generation of workers – and older non-unionised workers – who stand to gain the most from such a policy being achieved.

* * * *

Immediately after being elected, Cameron's Tories launched savage class war on workers' rights, through the (anti-)Trade Union Bill 2015. It riveted new levels and measures of repression onto all the existing chains wrapped round workers and their unions during and since Thatcher's regime. The Bill virtually bans the legal right to strike in what they've maliciously termed 'important public services' and 'ancillary jobs'. Olympics-style high hurdles face any workforce seeking justice from victimisation, pay cuts, or job losses through industrial action. At least 50% of actual members have to vote (this applies to ALL sectors, not just 'important public services'). In addition, at least 40% of all members have to vote for the action to legalise it.

If those hurdles aren't high enough to block self-defence by workers, the wording on the ballots will be crawled all over by company lawyers to claim 'the wording is not sufficiently clear on the causes'; unions now have to give not seven, but 14 days' notice of the agreed action; pickets have to have a picket organiser, with ID, making them a target for victimisation; any more than six pickets constitute a criminal offence; unions are to be hamstrung financially and in functioning through removal of payment of union subs from wages ('check-off') and facility time for union reps; the government's Certification Officer is to be given dictatorial powers to interfere in union affairs, demanding membership lists, quizzing officers, intervening in internal union elections; and the 42-year-old ban on use of Agency workers to replace strikers is to be lifted, making these desperate, insecure workers a potential conscript army of strike-breakers. The only states to have similar restrictions on voting procedures for union collective action are Bulgaria and Romania – seldom regarded as models of democracy!

The trade union and socialist movement needs to mount a serious campaign to 'Kill the Bill'. The SSP shares the STUC's demands that councils and the Scottish Government should obstruct implementation of those aspects of the Bill they have control over, such as check-off, facility time and use of Agency workers against strikes. We also share the demand for employment law to be devolved to Holyrood – this side of Scottish independence.

It's right that unions demand repeal of the Bill, but this should never be separated from fighting for outright repeal of ALL anti-union legislation, which this Bill is only bolted onto. That demand for scrapping all anti-union legislation has never been enacted by Labour in government, and never once promised by the SNP leadership.

However, it would be foolish to await repeal by politicians. The best way to win repeal is to make the anti-worker laws inoperable, through mass defiance of them. That's what needs to be built against the 2015 Trade Union Bill. For instance, the first move towards criminalising pickets should be met by a mass mobilisation for mass picketing.

It's better to break bad laws than to allow them to break workers' backs. The vicious laws against so-called secondary action, and the rigmarole of ballot procedures, were gloriously ignored in the mass walkouts at oil refinery sites in 2009, which won outright (see chapter 14). Likewise postal workers and others have defied these measures over the years and won victories. The Glacier Metal workers of Polmadie, Glasgow, broke every law in the bosses' book in 1996 when they seized hold of the factory, staged a seven-week sit-in, and won a 100% victory in defence of union rights and conditions.

In fighting for repeal of all anti-union laws, we need to also put forward a positive alternative vision of workers' rights and workplace democracy.

The stain of having the most repressive anti-worker, anti-union, anti-strike laws in the western world needs to be wiped clean, with a

Charter of Workers' Rights implemented in its place. This Charter
would need to include guaranteed rights to join and be active in a
union, regardless of the size of workplace, without fear of victimisation or discrimination ; union recognition in all workplaces where
any workers join a union; full access to workers for unions to recruit
and organise; paid union facility time for elected union reps in workplaces, to organise and represent members; collective bargaining
rights on wages, conditions, staffing levels, health and safety, environmental policies, and company plans for all recognised unions; the
constitutional right to strike; the right to take solidarity strike action
and to strike against political decisions affecting the lives of workers;
freedom for unions to make all decisions, including those on industrial action, by a simple majority vote of the members, after full de-
bates at union meetings (supplemented by secure online voting) –
held during working hours, without media, employers' or state interference; and the rights to freedom of speech, to protest and to picket.

In order to begin to overcome the dictatorship of capital over labour
– of top management over the workers who produce society's wealth –
such a Charter would need to include concrete forms of workers' control over day-to-day decisions in the workplaces. Measures including
control of health and safety by elected union safety reps. And union
control over 'hiring-and-firing', including registers of unemployed
members for vacancies that arise, and places on interview panels, to
equality-proof appointments, and prevent victimisation, or the un-
dercutting of pay and conditions. Instead of the cruel deceit that is
fondly entitled 'Social Partnership' – whereby unelected 'employee
representatives', or a few token trade unionists, are absorbed into pursuing the profit-hunting class interests of the capitalist owners – we
need to fight for a system of democratic management.

Whilst 'social partnership' and a place for 'employee representatives'
sounds warm and seductive by comparison with the Arctic hostility
from employers and governments towards workers in today's capitalist Scotland, it is a road strewn with dangerous traps and pitfalls.

In many private capitalist enterprises, for instance in retail, senior
management enact a system of 'works councils' and 'workers' commit-

tees' that are nothing of the kind! Usually they consist of hand-picked individuals, accountable to nobody on the shop-floor in real life, subject to the pressures and flattery of top management – who almost always not only sit on these committees, but actually dominate them. Furthermore, senior management use them as a conduit to convey decisions they have already arrived at, with the pretence that these employees have had some say over them, thereby expecting them to advocate and implement the decisions amongst the workers they allegedly represent. In many cases these bodies are used to try and bypass the collectively-elected union representatives in the workplace or wider company.

* * * *

The broader idea of 'Worker Directors' has been advocated as a strand of the fabric known as 'social partnership' – for instance in the SNP government's White Paper during the Referendum campaign, *Scotland's Future*. This was proposed as Scotland catching up with 14 out of 28 European countries, where different versions of this are in place.

Of course, if elected union representatives, subject to accountability and recall by union members, thereby gained access to company plans, company accounts and any measures impacting on workers' job prospects or conditions of employment, that would be a huge advance from the way employers nowadays routinely ignore and exclude the unions from any such information. But there's the rub. In many instances, these 'Worker Directors' are not even elected, let alone accountable to that collective class formation known as a trade union. They are 'employee representatives'.

Furthermore, in most countries with such schemes, the 'Worker Director' either has no access to business secrets, or is sworn to confidentiality, unable to inform and thereby empower the very workers they are supposed to represent on the boards of management. In fact they frequently end up the mouthpieces of company directors' decisions – by dint of having to implement majority decisions on the board, even if they personally opposed them. That was the fate of such token 'Worker Directors' on the nationalised British Steel Corporation back in the '70s and '80s. Workers in the industry at the time often denounced them for transforming 'from tub-thumping shop stewards to mouthpieces for top management.'

More currently, the same condemnation applies to examples of 'Worker Directors' on Scotland's Health Authorities, and the case lauded in the SNP's White Paper as the paradigm of what should be applied more widely – First Group. As the SNP rightly explained in Scotland's Future, First Group has had a 'Worker Director' on its board of management since the Aberdeen-based company was founded in 1986. However, far from being a compelling case in favour of such a scheme being more widely applied, as the SNP claims, this example should act as a deafening warning in the ears of workers seduced by the idea of 'social partnership' and its pinnacle, 'worker directors' on the boards of capitalist enterprises.

Why? In 2010, the RMT union got wind of plans to impose Driver Only trains on the new Airdrie/Bathgate route operated by First ScotRail – the rail franchise held by the same First Group, in other words. They fought this proposal, tried to negotiate it away, but were forced to ballot members and take strike action. During the strikes they met with SNP Transport Secretary, Stewart Stevenson, who agreed their case for retaining guards was well-founded, and would only cost £300,000 in an overall £30million budget.

Here's the crunch: at no time did the 'Worker Director' on the company's board of management either distinguish himself by production of a Minority Report, opposing the Driver Only plans, nor denounce it in the media, nor even make a token appearance at one of the many picket lines staged by striking guards and conductors that he was supposedly representing. Nor did this tribune of workers' rights do anything to expose or resist the scandalous arrangement made between the SNP government of the day and First ScotRail bosses. This was a very revealing exposé of what social partnership is really about, behind the mood music and candlelit dinner-talk about 'the common interests between employees and employers'.

A full year in advance of the strikes, in February 2009, First ScotRail wrote to Alex Salmond's government, explaining their intention to introduce Driver Only trains, warning that the RMT was opposed and therefore strikes were likely. They moaned that with only four years remaining of their franchise, they could not recoup the losses this would incur, and therefore would be obliged to agree guards on the trains – unless the government was prepared to compensate them; subsidise them against strikes.

The SNP government's reply confirmed Driver Only Operations should go ahead, and gave extremely heavy hints they would underwrite First ScotRail out of public funds for any loss of income caused by strikes… against this assault on public safety.

In January 2010, ScotRail took their cue, asking the SNP government for £300,000 to 'train' and deploy staff – including ones drafted in from across England – to scab on the RMT members' democratically-agreed strike in defence of safety. As one ScotRail guard told me at the time:

> "The SNP tell us tough decisions have to be made about public spending, yet they are prepared to subsidise a company that made over £18million profits last year to break our strike. And to add insult to injury, the SNP Transport Secretary who has sneaked behind our backs to collaborate with big business is an RMT-sponsored MSP!"

And still not a word, nor a whimper, from the 'Worker Director'.

Social partnership is based on the utterly false premise that the interests of workers and employers who hire them, buying their labour-power, are one and the same. But the fundamental feature of capitalism as a system – private ownership and the profit motive at its core – means that the interests of workers and capitalist employers do not coincide, they clash. At root the conflict of interests is a struggle over who gets the bigger slice of the wealth produced: workers in their wages, conditions and 'social wage', or owners in profit and shareholders' dividends. It is not a partnership of equals, between two sets of people with common interests, but the partnership of the rider and the horse!

Rather than the tokenistic one or two 'Worker Directors' on boards of management that is advocated by the SNP and indeed many union leaders, the ultimate aim should be a working class majority on every board of industry or service – drawn from elected workers' union representatives within that company or government department; elected representatives of wider society, such as councillors and government reps; and representative consumer or user groups.

Cut Hours – Not Jobs or Pay

One of the craziest contradictions in capitalist society, in a system riddled with them, is the long hours worked by some and the nominal or zero hours worked by others.

Part-time (and low-paid, and insecure) jobs have grown enormously in recent times. Not as a measure of a healthier work/life balance for workers. Not as a means of sharing out the drudgery as well as the joys of working life. Not as a product of phenomenal technological innovation that renders human labour-time more productive and therefore allows for a rational, democratic reduction in the proportion of everyone's life that is spent working. No, none of those features are within the nature of the beast that is capitalism.

At least 1.4 million part-time workers in the UK want longer hours of work, but can't get them.

A Scottish Parliament survey in 2013 found a total of 143,000 workers ranked themselves as 'underemployed'. Subsequent research by professors David Bell and David Blanchflower found the proportion of Scottish workers underemployed had doubled since the 2008 recession, and that these people wanted extra hours equivalent to 50,000 more full-time jobs. Their desire for more work was not some epidemic eruption of workaholism; falling real wages, and actual cuts to hours by some firms during the recession, were the overwhelming reasons identified for the underemployed wishing for more work.

Even the burgeoning army of the self-employed include a growing proportion on part-time hours – which contributes to the startling statistic that 80% of the self-employed are officially in poverty – with an average income of £10,000 a year, down 28% on ten years ago. Alongside the underemployed we have the unemployed. And eight out of every nine of the unemployed, according to the DWP's own official reports, are either seeking work that they can't find, or feel blocked from getting by dint of their circumstances, such as disabilities that employers don't make sufficient allowances and adjustments for.

Cheek-by-jowl with this famine of jobs and hours of work for those in need of them resides a feast of long hours, overtime, unpaid overtime and rampant work-related stress, in part triggered by the burdensome levels of toil endured by millions of workers. Britain and Scotland are tainted by some of the longest working weeks and years of any advanced economy. The average hours worked each week in 2014 by full-time workers in this country were 42.7. In contrast, their equivalents in Denmark worked an average 38.3 hours a week.

This long hours culture – which Britain has in common with its big capitalist brother, the USA – is driven by governments and employers who seek to minimise the paid holidays and breaks workers get; minimise other overheads such as NIC contributions by minimising the hiring of additional staff to cover the hours required; and maximise the 'flexibility and availability' of every worker, whether part-time or full-time, by using overtime with no premium payments as a way of matching the fluctuations of 'business needs', rather than having 'surplus' staff for busier periods.

* * * *

However, the core cause of long and unhealthy hours of work in this rich country is the rotten levels of hourly pay that are spreading like a malignant tumour across the economy. Leaving aside the one greedy bandit that every workplace has – the one who grabs every hour of overtime on offer, as if it's a hyper-addictive drug – the harsh fact is that people sacrifice their family time, leisure hours and health to try and compensate for the pathetic wages they'd be saddled with if they only worked their contracted hours. For instance, a TUC survey on the long hours culture found 260,238 workers in Scotland (11.7% of the total workforce) doing more than a 48-hour week, and 53,847 of them exceeding 60 hours! But the same survey confirmed that 57% of those working PAID overtime wanted to cut their hours.

As wages have stagnated or actually fallen in the past five to seven years, many workers have become more desperately dependent on overtime to try and pay the mounting bills.

As more and more employers – both private and public sector – change contracts to make weekends, evenings and even nights part of the 'normal working week', abolishing premium payments for such anti-social hours, workers are under even greater pressure to make ends meet by putting in additional overtime.

In retail firms – where Sunday trading was only legalised in bigger shops as recently as 1993 – those few who had previously granted time-and-a-half for Sundays, or double-time for working on public holidays, have phased this out by changing contracts, obliging staff recruited in more recent years to put in these anti-social hours for straight, flat money – with no premiums for missing out on family life. In other cases, these companies are simply abolishing such premiums for all existing and future staff – including under cover of headline-grabbing pay rises in the middle months of 2015.

In all instances, this drives low-paid retail staff towards longer hours, full-timers included, in order to cope with life's bills. Amongst those hardest hit by the abolition of weekend or late-hours premium payments – a stark, massive pay cut – are part-time workers who do disproportionate numbers of weekends and evening shifts, including young workers and students, and women with care duties during weekdays.

In numerous councils and their arms-length offshoots -such as Glasgow Life – changes to contracts in recent years made any and all days and nights of the week – evenings and weekends included – part of 'normal working hours', provoking strikes to defend premium payments thereby abolished in a cost-cutting implementation of austerity at local government level. In the likes of Museums of Scotland, PCS union members went on strike this year against similar elimination of premium payments for weekend working, another cost-cutting exercise, presided over by the Scottish Government.

* * * *

Additional to that is the criminal level of unpaid overtime. Not even cheap labour for the enhancement of profits, but absolutely free labour. Working into their lunchtime breaks. Coming in early to catch up on the backlog. Staying after finishing time. Compensating for staff shortages and work overload by 'doing us a favour'. Desperately trying to please and appease senior management by putting in unpaid hours, often in fear of otherwise being targeted for planned or rumoured job losses. Working at home on paperwork or online tasks, unpaid.

Last year (2014) nearly 5.3 million workers in the UK – just over one in five of all employees – gifted their employers an average of 7.7 hours a week of unpaid labour. That's the equivalent of losing £6,050 in wages each over the year. A free gift from the working class to the employers to the total value of £32billion during 2014!

Scotland was no exception within these figures. 413,069 workers gifted their employers an average of 7.3 hours unpaid overtime every week, valued at £5,553 each over the year, totalling £2.294billion extra for profits.

That's the equivalent of the average worker starting back at the New Year but not being paid a single penny for their efforts until after 27 February. It's daylight robbery, on a systematic and monumental scale. And it comes on top of the inbuilt theft of workers' labour-power that is the very essence of the capitalist elite's source of rent, interest and profit in the first place.

* * * *

Alongside the fight for a decent living minimum wage, probably the other pivotal policy that should be pursued is a shorter working week – and shorter working year. An immediate maximum working week of 35 hours across the board would start to free people up for leisure, pleasure and participation in their communities and wider society. But with the technology available nowadays, which exceeds the sci-fi dreams of even a generation ago, it would be easy to rapidly move from a 35-hour maximum working week to a 4-day week, a 30-hour maximum working week, and beyond.

The galloping pace of technological development confronts us with two starkly different futures. Either a dystopian nightmare where robots and computer software programmes help to lay waste to millions of jobs and leave mass misery and deprivation in its wake. Or a society where technology frees humanity from long hours of drudgery, including dangerous work, slashing the working week without any reduction in incomes, with a vast enhancement of lifestyle and living standards.

Back in the '70s and '80s, a well-established fact that was popularised by socialists of the time, and by the likes of Jack Jones, leader of the Transport & General Workers Union, was that existing levels of technology meant it was possible to sustain (or even increase) then-existing levels of economic production with a maximum working week of 19 hours. Compared to the exponential blossoming of new technology in recent decades, the '70s and '80s look positively antediluvian.

Meet some of the new 'workforce' of the early 21st century. Baxter is a dexterous factory robot that can be programmed by grabbing its arms and guiding it through the motions involved in many types of work. Amelia is a virtual service desk employee, being trialled by oil giants like Shell, to help with employee training and inquiries. Watson is IBM's super-computer, which can assist in diagnosis of patients and suggested treatments. Blackstone Discovery has developed software to automate legal discovery, the task of gathering evidence for lawsuits, until now one of the key tasks of paralegals. Mining monopoly Rio Tinto currently 'hires' 53 autonomous trucks in its mines in Western Australia, dispensing with drivers.

Self-driving cars; software doing the job of office staff to update company records or research information from websites; computers that can recognise speech, visualise in 3D and make decisions; online education technology – these and many other developments are real, no longer the stuff of futuristic novels.

We've witnessed the growth of a Small to Medium Enterprise in books and studies on this issue of robotics and technological unemployment in recent years. In all the writings of experts in the field, a downright frightening scenario looms out at us – unless we fight for a whole new system of economy.

Of course, a central feature of capitalism as a system, based as it is on cut-throat competition for markets, efficiency in production and thereby maximum profit, is the relentless pursuit of the latest production techniques – where companies that invest in more productive techniques in general drive less-modernised competitors to the wall. Alongside that, new technologies can create new areas of production, new market niches. Therefore, new scientific methods don't have to automatically mean a net loss of jobs.

However, in one major survey in 2014, the 'futurist' American author Martin Ford asked the opinions of 2,000 experts in the field. Half of them believe that new technology will have displaced more jobs than it creates by the year 2025... a mere decade ahead.

An Oxford University report on the subject last year concluded that 35% of all UK jobs are at high risk of disappearing in the next 10-20 years through automation. An earlier study of the USA, where there is more manufacturing production, predicted that 47% of jobs there are at high risk.

Economists are divided on the issue. And it is indisputable that Britain and Scotland is cursed by too little investment in advanced technologies compared to world competitors, rather than too much. Technological unemployment, as it's termed, is NOT the primary cause of mass unemployment in recent decades in this country.

There is a further, very fundamental inbuilt contradiction in the capitalist system that means the glittering potential for new methods of production run slap bang into a barrier to progress. The source of profit is the unpaid labour of workers. The more a capitalist outfit invests in machinery and displaces workers, the less source it has of unpaid labour. That's one reason why many capitalists don't bother ploughing much of their piles of profit into new machinery, preferring to grab a fast buck. Indeed that was a generalised feature of the cosseted, protected economy of Britain in its past 'glory days' of being an empire – which actually helped lead to its economic downfall, as generalised failure to invest by the arrogant, lazy capitalist elite meant they were rapidly outstripped by more modernised industries in the likes of Germany, post-1945.

But the relentless march of new technique and super-technology poses point blank a choice of paths. We can either let fortune-hunting capitalists employ robots and Artificial Intelligence to displace workers – who have the inconvenient habit of organising and making demands on their profit margins – in order to outstrip rivals in the race for short-term profits… creating a massive army of unemployed and destitute people en route. Or we can fight to wield the potential inherent in these shiny new technologies to cut the hours of drudgery, slash the working week drastically, and create a society with vastly more time free for the mass of the population. Work-free time to develop their human potential, take part in the democratic running of all aspects of society, and lift humanity to new heights of development as a species, rather than being chained to work for endless hours like slaves to labour.

* * * *

Various experiments on the likes of a 30-hour week, and 6-hour days, in various companies and countries, have proven the benefits in health, happiness and indeed productivity levels. In the midst of the Great Depression, in 1930, breakfast cereal magnate W. K. Kellogg conducted an experiment in his Battle Creek plant, in Michigan. He replaced three 8-hour shifts with four 6-hour shifts… thereby shortening the working day for workers. The results were spectacular. Hundreds of new workers were hired. Production costs plummeted. Workers were more efficient. Stress at work fell and family life improved. Vestiges of the system lasted until 1985.

Fast forward to the winter of 1973-4 in this country. Tory Prime Minister Ted Heath sought revenge on behalf of his class for their defeat by the miners in the 1972 strike, provoking another showdown with the NUM membership. The miners' strike caused widespread power-cuts, with a whole generation of children – many of whom actively supported the even more cataclysmic battle between the miners and Thatcher's Tory regime a decade later – growing up with lasting memories of living by candlelight.

Ostensibly in response to the depletion of power supplies to industry – but actually more as a ploy to isolate and demonise the strikers amongst the wider population – Heath declared a 3-day working week. The results? Amongst others, productivity vastly improved amongst workers relieved of the tiring toil of their usual full 5-day week!

To take another contemporary instance: in Gothenburg, Sweden's second city, a year-long experiment in a 30-hour week, through cutting the working day to six hours, has just been conducted with a group of the city's care workers. When compared with their colleagues in the rest of the department, doing exactly the same jobs, but remaining on 8-hour days, the results were quite striking. The staff who had their working day reduced displayed higher motivation, less absenteeism or sick leave – and developed happier, closer, more caring relationships with the elderly people they care for than those care workers still working the longer hours.

This experiment by the Gothenburg city authorities followed that in the Toyota car plant in the same city, which has since 2002 operated 6-hour shifts... but on 8-hours' pay. The plant has thrived.

A shorter working week, plus greatly improved annual paid holidays – such as the 40 days guaranteed to all workers in Finland – would create tens of thousands of new jobs in Scotland for the unemployed or underemployed. But it must be without any loss of earnings for the workers involved.

Layoffs and short-time working imposed by employers during periods of downturn are all too common – punishing workers with pay cuts for crises not of their making. By definition, if we pursue the policy of 'cut hours, not pay or jobs' as a clarion call to action, that would mean an increase on hourly rates of pay.

Underpinned by a legally enforced minimum wage of £10-an-hour (2015 figure), this would boost spending power, helping to sustain local micro-businesses, co-ops and larger enterprises. It would be a major exercise in sharing out the work and wealth of society, instead of sharing out the misery – caused by profiteering – amongst working class people either stressed out by overwork or stressed out by too little or no work.

Just as critically, a shorter working week with no loss of earnings would free up workers' time to be part of participatory democracy, in their communities and the workplaces. Without economic democracy, political democracy becomes an empty phrase, a deceit, where the working class don't even have the time to be part of decision-making, and where we are subjected to the dictatorship of the rich, extreme minority rule, the dictatorship of capital.

It would be a substantial part of starting to build a society where the economy is made to work for people, instead of people being made to work for the economy – or for the profits of a tiny elite who dominate the economy, to be more exact.

For a Wealth Tax

Britain has the dubious distinction of being colonised by billionaires – a category of people whose numbers have doubled globally during the recent 2008 financial meltdown and subsequent recession. The UK houses 117 of them in 2015 – more than double the 53 billionaires in Britain when the Tories and Lib Dems seized office on their behalf in 2010. Their combined wealth has reached the dizzy heights of £325billion: far more than ten times the entire Scottish annual budget in the hands of 117 people! And London confirms its title as the playground of the rich, with 80 billionaires calling it home: more than in any other city on earth.

Above and beyond that ultra-exclusive club of the obscenely opulent we now have 10,400 with assets each of over £20million – variously described by statisticians and economists as 'core millionaires' or 'Ultra-High-Net-Worth-Individuals'.

Slumming it on the outskirts of this Paradise for Parasites lurk a further 840,000 British residents who are US dollar millionaires – i.e. 'worth' over £660,000 each. They carry the brand name 'High-Net-Worth-Individuals'. It's a term I find repulsive, as it measures worth by accumulated personal wealth, not by value to humanity, social usefulness – implicitly condemning those millions of us who work for a living as being 'low-net-worth-individuals'.

Nevertheless, these 840,000 British residents are certainly worthy of our attention, in pursuit of a more equal, happier society. Between them, they possess £2.3trillion in personal wealth. Put another way, they have grabbed hold of an incredible 38% of Britain's entire wealth! And contrary to what you'd be forgiven for thinking, some of them are in a district near you.

Given that Britain is the regionally most unequal state in the whole of Europe, it's entirely predictable that not far short of half of all the 'HNWIs' in the UK live in London – 376,600 of them. But don't get duped into thinking Scotland is bereft of dollar millionaires; of these expressions of the inconceivable wealth in the hands of a few, amidst the rampant poverty suffered by vast chunks of the population.

On the contrary; whilst 4.5% of the populations of both London and Manchester are these 'High-Net-Worth-Individuals', with over £660,000 in personal wealth each, the percentage of Edinburgh's residents wallowing in such wealth is substantially higher: 5.8%. That's nearly one in 17 of Edinburgh's population. It's a safe bet to say, though, you won't find any of them in the city's housing schemes! A tale of two cities, two classes, two worlds.

To tackle the gaping and growing chasm between rich and poor, and invest in social provision that would usher in a much happier society, a package of progressive taxes would help immensely. But only socialists are prepared to confront the obscenely rich with this prospect.

A wealth tax could in itself generate vast funds for the benefit of society as a whole. For instance, even a 10% wealth tax on the 840,000 dollar millionaires in Britain would raise £230billion. That's almost eight years' worth of the entire Scottish Government budget. Scotland clearly has more than its 'fair share' of this class of resident, but even a crude pro rata share based on overall population would mean a 10% wealth tax adding well over £20billion to Scotland's budget.

Imagine what could be done with that in improving housing, transport, schools, college education, our NHS, or in raising wages – including through a Small Business Living Wage Fund: repayable loans and grants to deserving cases of small firms, to help them pay their workers at least £10-an-hour (see chapter 17). And why should we stop at a 10% wealth tax? Would the dollar millionaires suffer deprivation if 20% or 30% was sliced off their pile?

Alongside a wealth tax, a whole new set of progressive income taxes could help tackle the inequality that curses modern Scotland. Back in 2012, the Westminster Coalition slimmed down 'top people's' tax from 50% to 45%. But that wasn't even half the tale of tax injustice. They'd offered this handout on earnings above £150,000 hot on the heels of a confidential report – which they chose to hide and ignore – showing how the UK's top earners use a series of aggressive tax avoidance schemes to pay a miserly 10% average income tax. So whilst the short-lived official 10% income tax for the pitifully low-paid was scrapped, society was robbed of £billions by the mind-blowingly rich, whose army of accountants and lawyers organised an unofficial 10% rate for them.

Is it beyond the wit of woman or man to restore top rates of income tax to the levels we had in this country before Thatcher dismantled them, followed by years of New Labour handouts to the rich? Back in 1979 the top rate was 83%. Even Maggie Thatcher, champion of the rich and 'small state' capitalism, didn't dare cut that rate to 60% for a full nine years, in 1988.

Tax reform in and of itself won't totally transform society, nor rid us of the underlying, systemic exploitation of the working class that is embedded in the very bone marrow of capitalism as a system of political economy. But it can certainly help. For instance, if the wage inequality in Scotland between 'the 1%' and the rest of us was reallocated the way it is in Denmark and Holland, 99% of us would be better off to the tune of £3,000 a year on average per household. (High Pay Centre figures.)

Axe the Council Tax – for the Scottish Service Tax

At an immediate, localised level, the Scottish Socialist Party has devised, costed and pioneered a brand new form of taxation for local government services and jobs, to replace the regressive Council Tax.

The Scottish Service Tax, based on income bands, on ability to pay, would mean at least 77% of Scots paying less than they do now, including zero taxation of the first £10,000 income. A series of tax bands and progressively rising rates of taxation on each makes this a redistributive measure. For instance, a 4.5% tax rate on the income band between £10,000 and £30,000; 15% tax on the band from £30-40,000; 18% on the £40-50,000 bracket; 21% taxation on £50-90,000; and a top rate of Scottish Service Tax of 23% on the element of incomes above £90,000.

Whilst the vast bulk of people would pay less, through its progressive ratings the Scottish Service Tax would literally double the money for council jobs, services and wages – from £2billion in 2015 from the Council Tax, to £4billion through this progressive alternative. Maybe not a device that would turn the whole world upside down, but certainly one which would transform the lives of many of the 250,000 council workers in Scotland, and the working class communities that depend on their provision of key public services.

Tax Big Business & Close Down the Tax Havens

Taxes on big corporations amount to a scheme of optional, voluntary donations – such is the level of systematic evasion, avoidance and non-payment. Many of the biggest corporations pay absolutely no tax on their profits, or rates so derisory that they would carry a jail sentence if workers tried to pay that level of income tax.

The National Audit of 2014 identified that one in five of all large British companies paid literally zero the previous year; and over 50% of the companies conceded less than £10million to the public purse.

It's not as if these industrial, financial and commercial behemoths are being driven to become corporate tax-dodgers because the tax on profits that they are asked to pay is punitive.

When Thatcher, the goddess of monetarism, took office in 1979, Corporation Tax was at 52%. Now it's set to plummet to 18%, the lowest rate in the entire western world, apart from Estonia and the South of Ireland.

By contrast, for instance, big businesses are taxed at the rates of 30% in Germany, 33.3% in France, and 40% in the US. Yet these countries enjoy substantially better rates of investment by big business than the UK, higher productivity rates and, at least in Germany and France, much better wages. And none of these states could be defined as a socialist Nirvana!

Several pieces of research, including one by Kimberley Clausing (2012) into all the OECD countries, have proven what might appear blindingly obvious to most of us: cuts to the rate of Corporation Tax mostly benefits Corporation profits.

Alongside that stark, simple truth – based on real experience – stands the startling statistic that just 100 companies in the UK are currently sitting on 'cash piles' of £53.3billion! That's money they refuse to invest. And don't forget, Corporation Tax only applies to profits exceeding £1.5million, so we're not targeting the minnows here, but the Great White Sharks.

So when the SNP outdo even Labour in their calls for reduced Corporation Tax, they are advocating a measure that is proven to just help send profits into outer space, and only really helping the big companies, not the SMEs that might be struggling.

Restoration of Corporation Tax to its pre-Thatcher level of 52% would harvest vast additional sums for the benefit of society's millions, as opposed to a militant minority of profiteers being given carte blanch to cream off profits with hooligan generosity to themselves.

* * * *

One of the many means by which hyper-rich individuals rob society of at least £120billion in lost tax revenue a year, every year, is through use of offshore tax havens. The sums sloshing about in these hideaways for the loot of the world's biggest thieves and exploiters are hair-raising. Oxfam is one of many organisations that estimate £21trillion is stashed away in tax havens. That's 38% of all global wealth!

Economists conservatively reckon that closing down the tax havens could yield an additional £118billion a year in tax – and that's before even thinking of the potential bonanza for society if we increased the rates of taxation on profits and the privileged rich. A vast sum that we are being deprived of for society's use, by the legalised theft of taxes by a minuscule minority of the population. And most of these tax havens are British territory.

Whilst a socialist government in Scotland couldn't eradicate this world system of robbery by the rich on its own, in isolation, it could certainly lead the way by mass exposure of this industrial-scale larceny, leading mobilisations of the Scottish people with demands for closure of all tax havens, reaching out to the people of other countries to pound their respective governments into action. More immediately, amongst the powers available to a socialist government in an independent Scotland, would be the levers to choke off the source of these stashes by the super-rich in the first place, here at home – through a combination of progressive income tax, a wealth tax and public ownership of the major economic centres of wealth production.

Universal public services

Whilst a legally enforced living wage for all would address a prime cause of both poverty and inequality, on its own it wouldn't wipe out all the ills of capitalist society. In tandem with a radical shift in the wage-share of national wealth, we need to pursue collective, universal provision of life's modern essentials; social provision that would not only transform the lives of individuals, but also act as an infinitely more cost-effective and safe means of running our part of the planet.

A Free, Public NHS

Profiteering from illness sums up the sickness of capitalism. Successive Tory and Labour governments have farmed out our treatment to the 'Big Pharma'. There was an entirely justified eruption of public fury at the fact the energy companies – the Big Six – doubled their profit rates in 2014... to an average margin of 8%. But the rate of rip-off that the energy companies subject us to is as nothing compared to the nauseating profiteering from sickness by the drugs companies. Another focus for public hatred is the banking system; and no wonder. But as the BBC wrote in November 2014:

"Imagine a company that generates higher profit margins than any other, is no stranger to multi-billion pound fines for malpractice, with widespread accusations of collusion and overcharging. Banking? No, Pharma."

This is a world where five multinational giants last year had average profit margins of 20%... and in the case of the big daddy of all drugs dealers, Pfizer, a stomach-churning 42%! They leech off the NHS. They dictate what medicines are available. They spend up to twice as much annually on marketing their drugs as they do on research and development. They hire armies of lawyers to prolong their exclusive patents and block generic versions of the medicines being supplied at a fraction of the price. They bombard GPs and hospitals with their products. In some parts of the world – including China – they routinely and literally bribe doctors. They are a form of parasite for which the only cure is the elimination of the profit motive, through democratic public ownership of the pharmaceutical industry.

Reverse PFI, PPP, Privatisation

Another form of leeching off the sick and general public has been Tory and Labour governments' use of PFI and PPP schemes to build hospitals. This scheme means the construction, upkeep and servicing of hospitals are stripped away from government control and government borrowing on the money markets, in favour of hiring the services of banks and construction consortia, paying them back over 30-35 years. UK taxpayers owe £305billion in PFI repayments across more than 700 projects for the next 30 years.

For 150 PFI hospitals signed off in December 2009 alone, the total capital raised to build was £12.8billion, but 'availability fees' will cost the public £42.8billion, and 'service fees' a further £30.1billion. That's like you borrowing £12.80 and paying back £72.90.

The annual payments to these profit-generating machines are inflation-proofed, regardless of the state of the economy, or the savage level of cutbacks to frontline public services by the government of the day. The exorbitant interest rates mean on average PFI costs this and future generations at least twice as much as traditional government borrowing and funding would. It's the supreme capitalist policy of 'get one hospital for the price of two'!

The SSP has already pioneered the abolition of NHS prescription charges in Scotland. But root-and-branch reforms will be necessary to rid society of the sick profiteering at the expense of our health treatment, and the vast health inequality that still bedevils Scotland. The NHS should be made universally free at the point of need, with this extended to dental care and eye-care. Such a comprehensive, free NHS should be funded and modernised through taxation of the rich and big business, instead of allowing PFI consortia to gorge themselves at public expense. And investment in prevention, treatment and care could be exponentially boosted by democratic nationalisation of Pharma; the integration of the sickeningly profitable pharmaceutical industry into an NHS owned and democratically controlled by the public.

Free Childcare

One of the central causes of workers being mangled up in 'the poverty trap' is the rip-roaring cost of childcare. Women in particular face the insoluble riddle of wanting to get a job, or of being browbeaten into seeking a job with the blunt instrument of benefit sanctions, but finding that the jobs on offer are overwhelmingly low-paid, utterly incapable of making childcare affordable.

During 2012/13, average childcare costs in this country rose three times as fast as wages. Alongside elderly care, this sector has become one of the most lucrative sources of profit for new businesses in recent years, due to the shortages of public sector provision in many areas. Many part-time workers just about literally go to work, to earn enough to pay the fees at private nurseries or after-school clubs, to be able to go to work!

Another model entirely is possible and necessary, and would greatly boost the struggle against poverty, inequality – and the gender pay gap. A comprehensive network of top-quality pre-school nurseries, playgroups and after-school centres – funded from general taxation and free at the point of use – with well-paid, qualified staff, would not only enhance the social and personal development of children in their formative years, but also give parents a genuine choice of working.

The jobs this would create – directly in the childcare sector, plus the vastly enhanced opportunities for parents to go to work – would boost spending power in the local economy, and cover much of the costs of such public sector provision through increased tax receipts.

Alongside that vision, imagine for a minute if workers in Scotland enjoyed even the already-existing rights to paid parental leave that workers in Sweden are entitled to. Parents there are guaranteed 480 days of parental leave for each child. And the state pays 80% of their salary throughout. So when the SSP campaigns for twelve months' maternity leave, and a month's paternity leave – both on full pay, with the right of parents to reallocate some of the paid parental leave between themselves – this is hardly cloud cuckoo land. It's merely advocating that Scotland starts to catch up with what is best in Europe.

Free Education

Education should be genuinely free – to people of all ages. From free, publicly-run pre-school nurseries to college and university, people should have equal and universal access, to boost education, training, the re-skilling of the workforce, and personal development. Instead of facing the harsh choice of getting a low-paid job on leaving school or being lumbered with the albatross of student debt, working class people should be provided a genuine choice of a well-paid, quality job; training on at least the living minimum wage; or a living student grant to remain at school, college or university after 16.

As well as vastly boosting the skills-set of the population, it would provide a vast expansion of jobs in the education sector, especially with a maximum class size policy of '20s plenty' for mainstream classes as a starting point, with expansion too of one-to-one tutoring on the model so successful in Finland.

Free Public Transport

Free public transport would be one of the most radical challenges not only to poverty amongst people, but also pollution of the planet. This policy has been uniquely pioneered and fought for by the SSP for several years.

Investment in an enlarged, publicly-owned, integrated, fare-free network of buses, trains, trams, Underground systems and foot-passenger ferries would slash car use and its attendant CO^2 emissions – where cars account for 80% of all the greenhouse gases attributed to transport.

As the mid-2015 scandal of Volkswagen being exposed for rigging the emission tests on their vehicles proved, so long as the transport industry exists for the amassment of capitalist profit, there will never be a serious, cast-iron means of combating pollution and its accompanying ill-health and climate chaos.

A comprehensive network of fare-free public transport would make over a million workers in Scotland £50-£100-a-month better off, and combat the isolation and social exclusion dictated by the increasingly unaffordable transport system of today, owned and run for the profit margins of those such as Brian Souter/Ann Gloag (who entered the hallowed circles of Scotland's billionaires in 2014), Richard Branson, Serco, or Dutch railway giant Abellio. Train fares have risen five times faster than wages in the five years from 2010-2015.

While such a nationwide scheme would cost (Scottish Government estimates) about £500million a year (in lieu of fares currently collected), plus the investment required in new buses, ferries and railway rolling stock, it would combat the annual £1.4billion cost of road accidents in Scotland, plus the CBI's estimate of £2.2billion lost to the Scottish economy every year through road congestion.

Tourism would expand, and rural jobs with it; the human and financial price of asthma and other respiratory illnesses plummet; and thousands of new jobs and apprenticeships would come on stream with the building, maintenance and staffing of this anti-poverty, anti-pollution measure of universal social provision.

Where it's been implemented in various European, USA and Latin American cities and conurbations it's been a roaring success. Scotland could become the first nation to transform the lives of its population, and help pressure governments abroad to travel the same radical road towards greater equality and healthier living.

100,000 Public Sector Houses in Four Years

Low-wage, high-profits market capitalism leaves legions of Scots in the lurch on the housing front. The housing bubble and speculative spree that helped fuel the 2008 financial meltdown has also bypassed millions in need of decent housing, including 157,000 families – not individuals, families – languishing on the housing waiting list in 2015 Scotland. Around 70% of those are officially classified as in 'acute housing need'. The pernicious strand of Thatcherite privatisation that was the 'Right to Buy' council houses, welded to a conscious demolition of public spending budgets at both national and local government levels over the past 30 years, has created a crisis-level social housing shortage, and left vast swathes of the population in dire need of new or refurbished housing – at affordable rent levels.

Public state subsidies – in the form of Housing Benefit – encourage the burgeoning high-rent, often low-quality private rental sector, with low-paid workers now the fastest-growing group of people dependent on this insecure source of housing, feeding the greedy guts of racketeering landlords and profiteering property sharks. Then, instead of capping the rip-off rents charged, the capped Local Housing Allowance system drives many working class tenants into the jaws of loan sharks to keep a roof over their heads.

Social housing has been demoted to the fringes by Westminster. New Tory laws were recently announced on the 'Right to Buy' council and housing association stock, alongside plans to charge the full market rent to tenants with total household incomes of £30,000 (bearing in mind last year's official average UK wage, for an individual, was £27,200).

A society that centres on 'Buy to Rent' grants for the richest minority, and woeful neglect of the housing needs of the low-paid, has further polarised wealth between those who parade their wallets round the property hotspots on our TV screens, in tow with Kirstie Allsopp and Phil Spencer, and the huddled masses who shiver through the winter months in sub-standard, damp or poorly-insulated homes.

A public project to build at least 100,000 new homes over the 4-year term of a Scottish Parliament, in the social housing sector, for affordable rent, could provide the foundations for a massive job creation programme. Including skilled jobs and apprenticeships giving dignity to a young generation, with an absolute minimum guaranteed wage of £10-an-hour. Built to the highest environmental standards in Europe, such houses could save tenants a fortune in domestic fuel bills, eradicating the crime of far more people in Scotland (in fact, one in three families) suffering the cruel indignity and deprivation of fuel poverty than is the case in far colder countries like Finland or Norway.

To achieve this massive, transformative house-building programme – accompanied by free insulation of all social sector housing, and renovation of older housing stock that doesn't deserve demolition – democratic public ownership of the construction industry and suppliers would be a necessary first step.

High-quality, affordable and environmentally-sound housing could then come on stream through councils, housing associations and housing cooperatives, with appropriate investment funds from the Scottish Government. We could at last achieve homes fit for humans, not a bonanza for the bankers and rip-off rents for racketeering landlords.

Nationalise Energy – for 100,000 Green Jobs

Tackling the close-related modern social crimes of fuel poverty and pollution requires one pivotal policy: public ownership and democratic control of all sources of energy, renewables included.

Capitalist enterprise – the allegedly all-knowing, all-seeing genius of the 'free' market – means six big energy companies are given a government license to print money; to rip the profit out of us, through the coordinated, exorbitant price rises this cartel of rip-off merchants impose on households every six months.

Taking the profit out of heating and eating requires, amongst other measures, the return of our energy supplies to public ownership, so as to run it as a public service, not a polluting paradise for the profiteers.

Compared with 20-30 years ago, there is widespread public awareness of the terrifying climate chaos and global warming caused by fossil fuels and industrial pollution in general (as well as the issues of CO^2 emissions already described in advocating alternative, socialist transport policies).

But for all their ever-so-green grandstanding and pious platitudes at climate summits, nothing meaningful will ever be done to combat this environmental desecration either by the energy giants driven by profit maximisation, or the landowners raking in a fortune in grants for sticking a few wind turbines on a corner of their vast estates. Or indeed any government of any party that puts profit before people and planet.

Wind turbines are 100% subsidised. On top of that, the landowners of unimaginable acreages who already get EU funding just for owning the land, are lapping up the profits from wind turbines. When they allow a few to perch on a patch of their ill-gotten landed estates, they are handed huge payouts, over a period of 25 years, paid for by higher electricity prices. Whilst a million Scottish households – not just individuals, households – are subjected to shivering through winter, cursed by fuel poverty, the bizarrely-named aristocrats whose ancestors robbed our land are gifted a total of £1billion to site turbines on what should in fact be public land. People like Sir Alastair Gordon-Cunningham (£10.87million), the Earl of Moray (£7.5million); and the Lib Dem Earl of Glasgow (£5.5million), to name but some of the more pronounceable beneficiaries of these risk-free rents.

Right now, as an illustration of their real-life priorities, for every £1 that is spent in Britain on research and development into clean, green sources of energy, a whopping £34 is spent on research and development into arms and weapons of mass annihilation.

A publicly owned and controlled Scottish green industry is the one sure route to simultaneously tackling pollution; diversifying away from fossil fuels, in a democratically planned fashion that protects the jobs of North Sea Oil workers; developing new eco-friendly forms of energy; creating 100,000 well-paid jobs and apprenticeships in engineering equipment, installation and operation of offshore and onshore energy methods – including wind, wave, tidal, solar and hydroelectric; and the construction of cheap, clean energy for all homes and workplaces. This could comprise a mix of nationalised sectors, local community cooperatives, and green energy-sources built into houses and public buildings.

Again, a virtuous circle of decent-paid jobs, increased spending power, eradication of fuel poverty, and a contribution to a genuine, international war on pollution and climate chaos.

Diversify Defence Jobs

During the Scottish Referendum, shipyard workers were held hostage by an unholy alliance of the Tory/Lib Dem Coalition, allegedly-left Labour MPs like Ian Davidson, and some anti-independence union officials. Hyper-profitable BAE Systems and Cameron's cabal declared outright closure of the Portsmouth shipbuilding yard, shedding 940 jobs. They tried to make a virtue out of not closing the yards on the Clyde and at Rosyth – whilst slashing 800 jobs.

Their decisions were a lethal cocktail of naked cash calculation – with BAE bosses and the military high command declaring the Clyde yards to be the more profitable option – and cynical political manoeuvres. They used this package to divide-and-conquer shipyard workers north and south of the border. They also used it to preach the alleged virtues of Scottish workers remaining part of the UK.

In a cynical division of tasks, the Labour wing of the anti-independence coalition demanded blackmailing 'break-clauses' to be written into the contracts to build a new fleet of Type 26 frigates, whereby the work would be removed from Scotland and given to (suspiciously unspecified) English yards if the Scots had the audacity to vote Yes to full self-government.

This appalling incident highlighted a core problem that needs to be confronted, as part of transforming working class lives and livelihoods. Why should workers and their families depend on war and destruction to hold onto a job and earn a crust? Why remain at the mercy of the military-industrial complex, which has meant decades of job insecurity, closures and chronic under-investment? Why not convert the shipyards into centres of production for peaceful, socially useful products?

For instance, industry experts have shown how existing workers' skills and technology in the Clyde shipyards could be deployed to instead build a fleet of new ferries. They demonstrated how the insane £3billion spent to build each aircraft carrier – which the crisis-ridden British economy can't even afford to put any actual fighter aircraft on – could instead fund the construction of 200 new ferries. The spectacular difference that they highlighted, however, is that such a project would generate ten times as many shipyard jobs as are being clung onto, with their fingernails, by workers relying on the Ministry of Defence (wars!) for a livelihood.

Scotland is in dire need of at least 100 new ferries to replace the ageing fleet and meet new EU regulations on clean fuel. So as a minimum, that alone could create five times the number of jobs that shipyard construction for destruction offers.

On top of that, the yards would be an obvious venue for developing and constructing marine engineering equipment and other technology for a massive new green industry. It would be a vital component in the re-industrialisation of Scotland; a plan to reverse the stampede towards low-paid, low-skilled, insecure jobs that came in the wake of the brutal elimination of better-paid manufacturing jobs since the 1980s.

Scrap Trident – for Peaceful Social Production

The same diversification of jobs to peaceful social production applies to those employed at the nuclear bases parked on the Clyde, housing our very own – well, America's very own! – very real weapons of mass destruction. Working in conjunction with the trade unions at these bases, a plan of alternative production could be devised, with the aid of scientists, guaranteeing not only jobs and conditions for all who work there, but as the STUC and Scottish CND have proven in studies, a substantial expansion of jobs.

Their studies of the post-Cold War closures of several military bases in the US shows how, with proper advance planning by government bodies and diversification authorities, the number of civilian jobs has actually increased. For example, at Grissom base, they expanded from 792 at the time of the base's closure, to 1,000 this year.

In the case of Trident, the Ministry of Defence admitted in 2012 that only 520 civilian jobs were "directly reliant on Trident." The STUC/SCND analysis concluded that:

> "Trident is not an efficient job creation scheme. More jobs would be created if the same amounts of money were invested in other areas of public spending."

They identified detailed options for socially useful civilian jobs in the area, backed up by other independent researchers. These included marine engineering; marine and other 'sustainable tourism'; offshore wind farms, including in the Clyde estuary; and other renewable energy projects. All types of employment matching the skills of the workforce at the Faslane and Coulport bases. All socially useful projects that are blocked from development by submarine and nuclear activity in the area. And all in contrast to the brutally simple fact that, contrary to all the claims by Trident apologists that it's good for the area, West Dunbartonshire suffers the worst levels of unemployment of any of Scotland's 32 local authority areas.

The SSP argues for Trident to be scrapped, ending the horrendous squandering of the recently-estimated £167billion on its renewal. But we simultaneously demand that all workers' jobs, wage levels and conditions are guaranteed, through a Scottish Diversification Agency embracing the workers' unions.

And there are plenty of precedents for a transfer of workers and their skills to peaceful, socially useful work. In 1977, union shop stewards at Lucas Aerospace's 13 factories combined their expertise with that of scientists to produce an alternative plan of production, proposing 150 different products that their skills, some retraining and existing technology could make, including medical equipment and renewable, green energy generation. That was in 1977! The working class have far more idea and far more commitment to people and planet than the corporate bosses and military top brass, who chose to ignore these proposals that are thoroughly modern in 2015, let alone 1977.

Likewise, in 1988, the unions representing 13,000 workers at BAe shipyard in Barrow produced detailed proposals for a switch to wind and marine engineering; ideas that would have put this country in the vanguard of green industry long before continental competitors led the way.

A new Scottish green industry could and should be invested in, publicly owned, harnessing workers' skills and know-how as well as harnessing the phenomenal potential wind, wave, tidal and hydro power that nature has provided Scotland.

Public Ownership of Banks, Industry, Construction, Energy...

Scotland's economy today is run and dominated by a tiny handful of giant companies, owned by a small elite of giant shareholders, run by faceless chief executives and directors on salaries that defeat the human imagination.

If anyone thinks the phrase I've often used – 'the dictatorship of capital' – is too harsh to be accurate, try to recall the events at Grangemouth refinery in 2013, at Scotland's biggest industrial site. The oil refinery and petrochemical plant is owned by INEOS, whose majority shareholder Jim Ratcliffe carefully planned how to provoke a dispute, in order to swing a wrecking ball at the unions and workers' conditions, as well as having the aim of wresting grants out of the government for his plans to invest, essentially, in the destructive process of fracking.

He was aided in his attack on the site union convener by the witch-hunt against him by the British Labour Party leadership, who were intent on halting Unite's attempts to win selection of their favoured candidate for the Falkirk by-election.

Workers were left with no choice but to strike in defence of their elected union convener. Ratcliffe locked them out, threatened to permanently close the entire, vast industrial complex, and thereby squeezed a total of £134million in grants and loan guarantees out of the public purse – including £9million in grants off Alex Salmond's SNP government. By holding the whole of Scotland hostage – and indeed Northern Ireland and the north of England, both dependent on Grangemouth for most of their energy supplies – this one-man capitalist dictatorship imposed brutal attacks on workers' livelihoods. He forced the workers and their union, Unite, to accept a 3-year pay freeze; 3-year no-strike agreement; £10-15,000 cuts to allowances and bonuses per worker; an end to Final Salary Pensions; and removal of all trade union facilities, including an end to full-time convenors.

So who is dictating to whom?! Here's an example of a capitalist dictator if you're in need of finding one; a man who not only rules the roost in a giant enterprise like INEOS, but also can dictate many of the actions of political parties like Labour and the SNP – precisely because neither of them are founded on the principles that reject capitalism.

The concentration of economic ownership and power into the hands of a shrinking minority removes real power and control from elected governments – let alone permitting any power over decision-making by the working people who provide these industrial, financial and commercial giants with their profits, privileges and therefore power in the first place.

Take a glance at the levels of concentrated wealth and might enjoyed by big corporations, multinationals and individuals.

We are dominated by the Big Six energy companies who dictate prices, impose fuel poverty in this energy-rich nation, and pollute the environment we live in.

North Sea oil and gas is primarily owned by a handful of transnational corporations – including ones which have a history of helping to overthrow elected governments, in the likes of 1950s Iran, when they successfully conspired to topple the elected radical government of Mohammad Mosaddegh, in 1953, in cahoots with the CIA, in response to his plans to renationalise Iran's vast oil wealth.

The likes of BAe systems and Lockheed Martin have a near-monopoly in the military-industrial complex, dictating job insecurity to shipyard workers and others.

Six or seven giant supermarkets dominate the market, set the prices of daily essentials, and dictate production and prices to farmers – as well as dominating the lives and livelihoods of their low-paid workforces and 'consumers'.

Half of all Scotland's land mass – one of our richest natural resources – is owned by 432 people.

Edinburgh is the second financial centre of Britain after London. But about half a dozen banks and finance companies bestride that sector like a colossus. Pension and insurance funds own a third of all shares in UK-registered companies: these institutional investors hold the deferred wages and life savings of working class people. But an incredible 49% of all UK pension funds are run by just five (yes, five) investment fund managers based in the City of London.

The Big Four accountancy and 'professional services' companies – PwC, Deloitte, Ernst Young and KPMG – were formerly the 'Big

Eight', before mergers and takeovers. They employ nearly a million staff between them. They dictate taxation policies to the government through the revolving doors between their boardrooms and government policy committees. In turn, they make themselves a fortune out of advising other giant companies and ultra-wealthy individuals how to dodge taxes – through the loopholes they devised in their role as government consultants!

The companies running the bulk of Scotland's transport networks could be counted on the fingers of one hand. Construction, manufacturing, food and drink are likewise monopolised.

Besides dictating much of public policy through their economic brawn, these large companies often impose wages below anything akin to a living income on the workers they hire, turbo-charging their profits in the process. A Scottish Government genuinely committed to guaranteeing a living wage to all and a rapid slashing of inequality levels would have to be prepared to confront these exploiters.

If large firms claim that they 'can't afford' to pay a £10 minimum wage here and now, the trade union movement and Scottish Government should immediately insist on public inspection of their secret company accounts. They should do a social audit of the enterprise, looking at the social usefulness of their activities, the wages, investment, state subsidies and profits involved. And if and when they are found to be lying about their ability to pay a decent wage, the government should insist on immediate introduction of the legal minimum, and call their bluff by retorting that 'we can't afford a system based on profiteering and exploitation' – and where necessary take over the running of the giant enterprises into democratic public ownership.

Not the old, bureaucratic nationalisation of Herbert Morrison and past Labour governments, which were saddled with exorbitant compensation to previous owners, the same old bosses and bureaucrats in charge, and in any case were used as sources of cheap energy, raw materials and infrastructure for the big capitalists who still owned 80% of the economy, even at the peak of nationalisation.

Instead, new, democratic models of genuine public ownership should be developed, which could embrace a mixture of national enterprises and services, council or community provision, and workers' cooperatives. The key common feature would need to be democratic control and management – with elected committees that gave workers' elected representatives, the wider local community, and the nationally elected government control of overall management and planning, and majority day-to-day control by elected workers' representatives. With the added proviso that any such decision-making bodies are not only elected, but have people on no more than an average skilled worker's wage – 'the wages of supervision', to use the golden phrase of Friedrich Engels 150 years ago.

That could not only help equalise incomes, but also equalise power relations within society. It could facilitate equality of gender and race, as well as the fundamental removal of the dictatorship of capital over labour, of the capitalist elite over the working class.

25

CARVE OUT THE FUTURE!

The battle to outlaw poverty pay and insecure jobs throws up a multitude of wider and deeper issues.

It highlights the inherently exploitative nature of the current economic system, capitalism. It spotlights the irreconcilable clash between the interests of pay and private profit, between workers and giant employers, between the main classes in capitalist society.

It exposes the cruel inequalities, and the crazy contradictions, of a system that we're told is all for the best, in the best of all possible worlds. It demonstrates the linkage between repression of workplace rights and the ruthless, relentless pursuit of maximum profit – the readiness of the ruling elite to trample on human rights if they impede their assumed right to be rich.

It underlines the need to marry immediate measures like a living level of legally enforced minimum wage with wider measures of universal public services and provision, in order to effectively banish poverty and inequality to the history books. It brings up fundamental questions of ownership and control, including the need for a vision based on democratic public ownership of the central services and major branches of production, distribution and exchange.

In publishing this thumbnail sketch of some aspects of the history of struggle for decent wages and secure jobs – and real-life examples of the conditions facing the modern working class of Scotland, Britain and beyond – we have hopefully added to the arsenal of those who want to take action against poverty, exploitation and environmental destruction. This book attempts to provide facts, figures, arguments and answers to some of the issues any genuine trade unionist or socialist will encounter in seeking to outlaw poverty, inequality and insecurity for the working class majority.

But words in isolation won't change the world. Words only become weapons of change, of progress, when they're on the lips of thousands, even millions, and used as guides to action, policies to mobilise around, slogans for struggle, visions to strive for.

Anyone serious about helping to break the chains of poverty pay, precarious jobs and exploitation will surely see the need to organise, to take collective action. To get active in their union and demand its leadership implement the espoused aims of union, TUC and STUC conferences on a living minimum wage for all workers, and wider, related policies. To play a positive part in campaigns to abolish zero hours contracts, and conquer secure jobs instead. To build a trade union movement ready and willing to defy and defeat the most dictatorial employment legislation suffered in any western nation. To help build bonds of struggle and solidarity between workplace unions and working class communities, including with people on benefits. To confront the vicious divide-and-rule tactics of employers and those politicians with an ideological and vested material interest in dividing working class people along lines of colour, creed, age, gender, sexuality or national origin.

Those who want to eradicate poverty and inequality need to square up to the conclusion that trying to do this on any lasting basis without also toppling the capitalist despots from their boardroom thrones is as futile as trying to rub out your own shadow on a sunlit day.

We need an entirely different kind of society than the one that dictates mass poverty amidst limitless existing and potential wealth. A society where the means of production and distribution of wealth in all its forms – goods, services, environmental protection and human happiness – is under the ownership and control of society as a whole, rather than being in the pockets of a few profit-crazed overlords who will gladly wreck people and planet alike in their hunt for a fast fortune.

We need not only organised unions as defence forces for working class people, but an organised socialist force to counter capitalist ideology, popularise a radically different vision for Scotland's future, and take decisive action to inspire masses of people into action to shape and conquer that future.

In the form of the Scottish Socialist Party, Scotland has a party skilled and experienced in the art of taking immediate burning issues that face the working class – such as poverty pay, job insecurity, inequality – to then elaborate a chain of fighting policies and demands that engage those same workers in the journey towards a socialist transformation of society.

Societies have only ever been fundamentally changed by the vision of pioneers who succeed in welding their ideas to active, determined movements of masses of people.

Words have to become deeds to effect change. Struggle without clear aims and alternatives is a futile waste of human dedication. Ideas without active struggle and engagement with broad masses, nowadays of the working class majority population, are a self-indulgent waste of talent.

A century ago, the great Edinburgh-born Irish trade unionist, socialist and internationalist James Connolly was tied in a chair and executed by the British ruling class, for daring to challenge their imperialist rule for power, plunder and profit. Connolly was a supreme example of what is needed a century later to change the face of Scotland: a man who married theory and practice, ideas and action, words and deeds. In one telling quotation from his writings, Connolly points to what anyone who has ideas of how to rid today's Scotland of poverty, inequality and exploitation needs to do:

"The only true prophets are those who carve out the future they announce."

If you're convinced of the fundamental ideas and policies argued for in this book, get organised; get active; carve out the future. Combine with others to strive for an independent, egalitarian, environmentally sustainable socialist future.

Cleanse the face of Scotland of the ugly scars of poverty, inequality and exploitation. Rise up in struggle, armed with a vision of what a socialist future could guarantee.

Break the chains of capitalism that manacle the millions for the profits and power of the millionaires. After all, we have nothing to lose but our chains.

Index

Because they occur so frequently or are the subject of entire chapters, words like Tories, Labour, capitalism, socialism, profit, Scottish Government, immigration, inequality and poverty are excluded from this index.